THE AI LEGAL HANDBOOK

A Guide to the Laws of Artificial Intelligence and the Future of Regulation

JUSTIN WALES

Electric Connected

Book Cover by Mai Sari.

Version 1 – June 2026

Contents

CHAPTER 1

Introduction

On November 30, 2022, a San Francisco startup called OpenAI released an experimental chatbot named ChatGPT. It allowed users to ask questions in plain language and receive coherent, useful responses in real time. For the first time, AI felt immediate and personal. The public went wild for it. One million people signed up in its first five days. Its user base reached 100 million only two months later. ChatGPT became the fastest-growing consumer application in history and, in the public consciousness, kicked off the modern artificial intelligence revolution.

If you're reading this book, you probably remember where you were when you first used it.

I do. It was early December 2022, just days after the launch. I was leading the legal team at Crypto.com, and by that point I'd spent over a decade watching the law struggle to keep up with advancing technologies. The pattern was always the same: a new technology would emerge, lawyers would scramble to apply old frameworks to new facts, regulators would oscillate between paralysis and overreaction, and by the time the dust settled, the technology had already evolved beyond the confines of the last debate.

When ChatGPT appeared, I approached it the way I approach any new tool: with a healthy dose of skepticism. I decided to test it on familiar ground. Years earlier, I had written a law review article on the First Amendment implications of Bitcoin[1]. The research had taken six months. Hundreds of hours of reading, writing, and

---

1 Justin S. Wales & Richard J. Ovelmen, *Bitcoin is Speech: Notes Toward Developing the Conceptual Contours of Its Protection Under the First Amendment*, 74 U. Miami L. Rev. 204 (2019), repository.law.miami.edu/umlr/vol74/iss1/6.

revision. Countless drafts. Endless citations.

I typed a prompt: *Write a memo analyzing the First Amendment implications of Bitcoin.*

Within seconds (not hours, not days, seconds) it produced a perfectly argued legal memo. The structure was sound. The analysis tracked the same constitutional principles I had spent months wrestling with. The prose was clear and confident.

But then I looked at the citations.

Every single one was fabricated. Case names that didn't exist. Law review articles with real-sounding authors and journals, none of which had ever been published. The memo cited *United States v. Zimmermann* for a proposition about encryption as protected speech, a reasonable-sounding case that was entirely made up.

In that moment, I saw both the promise and the limitation of AI. This technology was going to change everything. It could synthesize complex legal arguments in seconds, identify relevant frameworks, and communicate with remarkable fluency. But it was also confidently wrong in ways that could destroy a lawyer's career if they weren't paying attention.

It was going to change everything. And boy, was it going to be sloppy.

Something Big Happened

The weeks and months that followed ChatGPT's release felt less like a product launch and more like a before-and-after moment in history. Seemingly overnight, artificial intelligence went from something discussed in academic papers and science fiction to something my mother was asking me about at Christmas dinner.

But the thing about transformative technologies is they rarely emerge from nowhere. ChatGPT was built on decades of research in machine learning, neural networks, and natural language processing. The intellectual foundations behind ChatGPT itself had been developing since the 1950s, when researchers at the Dartmouth Summer

Research Project first proposed that "every aspect of learning or any other feature of intelligence can in principle be so precisely described that a machine can be made to simulate it."[2]

What made November 2022 different wasn't the underlying technology; it was the packaging. For the first time, cutting-edge AI was placed directly into the hands of the public through a simple chat interface that anyone could use. The result was a collective awakening. Suddenly, millions of people were experiencing firsthand what AI could do: draft emails, debug code, explain complex topics, write bad poetry, pass standardized exams.

They were also experiencing what it couldn't do: reliably tell the truth, cite real sources, write good poetry, or resist generating confident-sounding nonsense.

That tension, between AI's remarkable capabilities and its fundamental limitations, sits at the heart of nearly every legal question this book will explore.

In the years since that December evening, the technology has advanced at a pace that makes my hallucinated-citation story seem quaint. AI systems now generate photorealistic images, produce synthetic video indistinguishable from reality, write code that passes technical interviews, and make consequential decisions about hiring, lending, medical diagnosis, and criminal sentencing. Text, image, video, audio, decision-making: AI has become part of our daily lives and has impacted just about every industry imaginable.

The law has started to develop in response. But nowhere close to the speed of the technology's advancement.

Why This Book Exists

Let me be direct about what this book is and what it isn't.

This is not an academic treatise. It won't give you a comprehensive

---

2 John McCarthy et al., *A Proposal for the Dartmouth Summer Research Project on Artificial Intelligence* (Aug. 31, 1955), jmc.stanford.edu/articles/dartmouth/dartmouth.pdf.

survey of every AI-related statute, regulation, or case across all fifty states and the federal government. That would be outdated before it reached your hands, and frankly, it would be insufferably boring for me to write. Nor is this a technical manual. We'll deal with the technology as needed, and reading this book will give you a better understanding of how AI works, but it is written for non-technical people who need to understand high-tech legal issues.

This is a practical guide for lawyers, law students, legal professionals, and anyone else who wants to understand how the law is grappling with artificial intelligence. It's written with the assumption that your time is valuable and that you need to get up to speed without wading through hundreds of pages of dense legal scholarship.

If you're practicing law today, in virtually any field, artificial intelligence is going to affect your work. It's already affecting how contracts are drafted, how disputes are litigated, how due diligence is conducted, how compliance is monitored, and how legal research is performed. The question isn't whether you'll encounter AI-related legal issues in your practice. It's whether you'll be prepared when you do.

This book is a snapshot. A snapshot of where the law is now, how it is developing, and how it may continue to develop. It is technical where it needs to be, and philosophical at points. Some chapters will walk you through specific statutory frameworks and case holdings. Others will grapple with questions that don't have answers yet: questions about consciousness, personhood, accountability, and what it means for a machine to "decide" anything at all.

If you are reading this, you are here at the beginning of a new technological revolution. And that means something important: the way the law (both generally and within the profession) adapts to it can still be influenced.

The frameworks aren't set. The precedents aren't established. The regulations are still being written. I hope this book gives you the tools needed to guide that development in the right direction. Whatever that may be.

Who Should Read This Book

This book is written for several overlapping audiences.

Law students and lawyers looking to develop expertise in AI law. The honest truth is that "AI law" isn't really a distinct practice area in the way that securities or employment law is. It's more like internet law in the 1990s: a horizontal field that cuts across virtually every traditional legal discipline. An AI lawyer needs working knowledge of intellectual property, data privacy, product liability, contract law, administrative law, constitutional law, and more. This book won't make you an expert in any of those fields, but it will show you how they intersect with artificial intelligence and point you toward the resources you'll need to go deeper.

Practitioners who need to understand AI's impact on their existing practice. Whether you're a corporate lawyer advising on AI vendor contracts, a litigator handling a case involving algorithmic decision-making, or a transactional attorney navigating IP issues in AI-generated content, this book will give you the foundational knowledge to serve your clients competently.

Entrepreneurs, executives, and technologists building in the AI space. I've spent enough time representing technology companies to know that the people building these tools often have only a hazy understanding of the legal constraints they're operating under. That's not a criticism; they're busy building products. But understanding the legal landscape isn't just about avoiding liability. It's about building better, more responsible products that can withstand regulatory scrutiny and earn public trust.

Anyone trying to make sense of what's happening. Artificial intelligence is going to reshape our economy, our politics, our culture, and our daily lives. The legal frameworks we build around it will play a significant role in determining whether that transformation is beneficial or harmful.

You don't need to be a lawyer to care about these questions, and this book tries to make them accessible to a general audience while still providing the depth that legal professionals require.

We Really Have No Idea

If there's one thing I want you to take away from this introduction, it's this: anyone who tells you they know how AI law will develop is either lying or delusional.

We are at the beginning of something unprecedented. The technologies we're discussing are evolving faster than the legal system can respond. Courts are issuing rulings that will shape the industry for decades based on factual records that may not reflect how these systems actually work. Regulators are attempting to write rules for technologies whose capabilities change dramatically between the time a proposed regulation is drafted and when it takes effect. Legislators are debating bills that often reveal a fundamental misunderstanding of what AI is and what it can do.

I have opinions about how many of these issues should be resolved. You'll encounter some throughout this book. But I try to hold them loosely, and I encourage you to do the same. The people who got the internet wrong in 1998, including the Nobel Prize-winning economist who predicted its impact would be "no greater than the fax machine,"[3] weren't all stupid. They just couldn't see around corners that hadn't been built yet.

We can't see around those corners either. What we can do is understand the legal frameworks we have, think clearly about how they might apply to new technologies, and remain humble about our ability to predict the future.

How This Book Is Organized

The book flows chapter by chapter, beginning with the history and basic technology behind what we now call artificial intelligence. That context matters. You can't understand where AI law is going without understanding where AI came from: the decades of research, the cycles of hype and disappointment, the breakthroughs that made the

---

3 Paul Krugman, *Why Most Economists' Predictions Are Wrong*, Red Herring, June 1998, web.archive.org/web/19980610100009/www.redherring.com/mag/issue55/economics.html

current moment possible. From there, we move through the legal areas that form the first round of flashpoints as law and technology collide: intellectual property, employment, healthcare, criminal justice, national security, privacy, and the transformation of the legal practice itself.

This is not a comprehensive treatise. But by the end, you will have a solid understanding of where we are, how we got here, and where the people who spend a lot of time thinking about these things believe we may be headed.

This book is fairly US-centric. That's a deliberate choice: the American legal system is what I know best, and it's where most readers of this book will practice. But AI knows no boundaries. The technology is developed globally, deployed globally, and regulated (or not) by governments with vastly different values and priorities. The geopolitical dimensions of AI development and semiconductor manufacturing are addressed throughout, and where helpful I've included information about the approaches of other countries. A dedicated chapter on global AI policy demonstrates just how different the approaches to this field are and can be. The European Union's risk-based regulatory framework looks nothing like China's state-directed model, which looks nothing like the largely permissive American approach. Understanding those differences matters, even if your practice never leaves US shores.

Each chapter ends with a curated list of supplemental resources: articles, podcasts, videos, and other materials that you can use to explore topics in greater depth. I've tried to favor accessible resources over academic esoterica. The goal is to help you learn, not to impress you with how many law review articles or technical papers I've read.

The Clock Is Ticking

The obvious problem with writing a book about a fast-moving field is that it will be outdated the moment it's published. I've tried to focus on frameworks, principles, and analytical approaches that will remain relevant even as specific laws and cases evolve. But I also recognize that some of what's written here will be superseded by developments that occur between when I finish writing and when you read these words. So it goes.

For that reason, I encourage you to treat this book as a starting point rather than a definitive reference. Check the dates on any statutes or cases before relying on them. Verify that the regulations described here still reflects current reality. I intend to update this book periodically as the law develops. But if it's been more than a year or two since publication, assume that significant changes have occurred.

Let's Begin

In the fall of 2022, a little chatbot appeared and everything changed.

Whether that change will ultimately be beneficial (for society, for the legal profession, for you personally) remains to be seen. But one thing is certain: artificial intelligence is here, it's not going away, and the rules we build around it will shape how this technology develops and who benefits from it.

This book is about understanding those rules. Let's get started.

CHAPTER 2

What Is Artificial Intelligence?

"Any sufficiently advanced technology is indistinguishable from magic."
- Arthur C. Clarke

In the summer of 1956, a small group of researchers gathered at Dartmouth College for a workshop that would change the world. The organizers had secured funding from the Rockefeller Foundation to explore a radical idea: "Every aspect of learning or any other feature of intelligence can be so precisely described that a machine can be made to simulate it."[4]

They called this new field "artificial intelligence."

The Dartmouth workshop participants were wildly optimistic. They believed that building a machine as intelligent as a human would take about a generation, maybe less. In 1967, Dartmouth organizer Marvin Minsky wrote: "Within a generation, I am convinced, few compartments of intellect will remain outside the machine's realm; the problem of creating 'artificial intelligence' will substantially be solved."[5]

Nearly seventy years later we're still working on it.

That's not to say nothing has happened. The AI systems we have today would have seemed like science fiction to those Dartmouth researchers. But the history of AI is one of boom and bust, of extravagant promises and sobering limitations. Understanding that history, and the basic vocabulary that comes with it, is essential for anyone who wants to think clearly about the legal questions that follow.

---

4 John McCarthy et al., *A Proposal for the Dartmouth Summer Research Project on Artificial Intelligence* (Aug. 31, 1955), jmc.stanford.edu/articles/dartmouth/dartmouth.pdf.
5 Marvin L. Minsky, Computation: Finite and Infinite Machines 2 (Prentice-Hall 1967), cba.mit.edu/events/03.11.ASE/docs/Minsky.pdf.

So What Is Artificial Intelligence?

The frustrating truth is that nobody agrees on what artificial intelligence actually means.

The term has been defined, redefined, and fought over for decades. Some definitions are so broad they'd include a thermostat. Others are so narrow they'd exclude most of what we currently call AI. The definitional chaos isn't just academic; it has real legal consequences. When legislators write laws regulating "artificial intelligence" or courts adjudicate cases involving "AI systems," the lack of precision becomes a serious problem.

Let me offer a working definition that will serve us throughout this book:

> Artificial intelligence is technology that enables computers to perform tasks that would typically require human intelligence, such as learning from experience, recognizing patterns, making decisions, or understanding language.

This definition is deliberately practical rather than philosophically precise. It captures the systems we actually care about regulating, including the chatbots, recommendation algorithms, image generators, and autonomous vehicles that are already reshaping society, without getting tangled in debates about machine consciousness or whether a Roomba qualifies as intelligent.

But even this definition raises questions. What counts as "human intelligence"? Is a spam filter intelligent because it learns to recognize patterns? What about autocorrect? The calculator on your phone?

The candid answer is that the boundaries are fuzzy, and they're likely to stay that way. For legal purposes, what matters less is whether something is "truly" intelligent and more whether it behaves in ways that create novel legal questions. A system that makes consequential decisions about people's lives (whether to approve their loan, show them certain job listings, or recommend medical treatment) raises legal concerns regardless of how sophisticated its underlying technology might be.

The AI Family Tree

To understand what people usually mean when they talk about AI, it helps to visualize it as a set of nested concepts, like Russian dolls. Each category fits inside the one above it and understanding the relationships between them is essential for understanding AI-related legal issues.

Artificial Intelligence is the broadest category. It encompasses any system designed to mimic human cognitive functions. This includes everything from simple rule-based programs (think of the "if-then" logic in an old-fashioned thermostat: if temperature drops below 68, then turn on heat) to the most sophisticated neural networks.

Machine Learning is a subset of AI. Rather than following explicit instructions programmed by humans, machine learning systems learn patterns from data. Feed a machine learning system enough examples of spam emails, and it will learn to identify spam on its own, without anyone writing specific rules about what makes an email spammy. The system figures out the patterns itself.

Deep Learning is a subset of machine learning. It uses artificial neural networks, computational structures loosely inspired by the human brain, with many layers of processing. (The "deep" in deep learning refers to these multiple layers.) These networks can learn incredibly complex patterns from vast amounts of data. Deep learning powers most of the AI applications that have captured public attention in recent years.

Generative AI is a category of deep learning systems that can create new content (text, images, audio, video, or code) that resembles the data they were trained on. If you've used ChatGPT to write an email, asked DALL-E to create an image, or had Claude help you draft a document, you've used generative AI.

Think of it this way: all generative AI is deep learning. All deep learning is machine learning. All machine learning is AI. But the reverse isn't true. Not all AI involves machine learning (some systems still use explicit rules), and not all machine learning uses deep neural networks.

Why does this matter for lawyers? Because the legal implications differ depending on what type of AI we're discussing. A simple rules-based system might raise different liability questions than a neural network whose decision-making process is essentially a black box. A generative AI that creates content raises copyright questions that wouldn't apply to a system that merely classifies images.

Narrow AI vs. General Intelligence

Here's the most important distinction you need to understand: nearly all AI in existence today is what researchers call "narrow AI" (sometimes called "weak AI"). These systems are designed for specific tasks. A chess program can beat the world champion at chess but can't play checkers. A language model can write essays but can't fold laundry. A car's autopilot can navigate highways but would be useless at diagnosing diseases.

Narrow AI systems can be extraordinarily capable within their domains, often surpassing human performance, but they lack the flexibility that characterizes human intelligence. They can't generalize their skills to new situations they weren't trained for. They don't have common sense. They don't "understand" what they're doing in any meaningful way.

Artificial General Intelligence (AGI) is the hypothetical future technology that would match or exceed human-level intelligence across all domains. An AGI system could do anything a human could do intellectually, and presumably learn to do anything a human could learn. This is the AI of science fiction: HAL 9000 from *2001: A Space Odyssey*, Skynet from *The Terminator*, Ava from *Ex Machina*.

AGI doesn't exist yet. Despite occasional headlines to the contrary, no current AI system even comes close.

But the timeline is shortening, or at least, estimates of when AGI might arrive have been plummeting. In a 2024 survey of nearly 2,800 AI researchers, the median estimate for achieving "high-level machine intelligence" (defined as AI that can accomplish every task better and more cheaply than humans) moved from 2060 to 2047, a 13-year shift in expectations in just one year.[6] The prediction platform Metaculus, which aggregates hundreds of forecasts, showed even more dramatic shifts: from a median estimate of about 50 years away in 2020 to roughly five years as of late 2024.[7]

These predictions should be taken with many grains of salt. AI researchers have been wrong about timelines before, catastrophically so. The Dartmouth researchers thought they were a generation away from solving AI. Repeated predictions of imminent breakthroughs gave way to "AI winters" when funding dried up after the technology failed to deliver.

Still, something has clearly changed. When Anthropic's CEO Dario Amodei talks about potentially having "a country of geniuses in a datacenter" within a few years, these aren't random cranks.[8] These are people building the systems in question.

For lawyers, the narrow AI versus AGI distinction matters enormously. The legal frameworks we need for narrow AI (systems that are powerful but limited, that operate in defined contexts, that can be audited and understood with effort) may look nothing like what we'd need for AGI. A system that genuinely thinks, that can pursue goals across open-ended domains, that might have something like preferences or autonomy is a different category of problem entirely.

This book focuses primarily on narrow AI, because that's what exists and what current law must grapple with. But we'll return to AGI in Chapter 16 when we consider what the future might hold.

How Modern AI Actually Works

Let me give you just enough technical understanding to follow the discussions that come later. Modern AI systems, particularly the large language models and generative tools that have dominated

---

6 Katja Grace et al., *Thousands of AI Authors on the Future of AI*, arXiv:2401.02843 (Jan. 5, 2024), arxiv.org/abs/2401.02843.

7 Benjamin Todd, *Shrinking AGI Timelines: A Review of Expert Forecasts, 80,000 Hours* (Mar. 2025), 80000hours.org/2025/03/when-do-experts-expect-agi-to-arrive.

8 Dario Amodei, *Machines of Loving Grace* (Oct. 2024), darioamodei.com/essay/machines-of-loving-grace.

recent headlines, are built on a few key ideas. Each of these concepts is explored in greater depth in the supplements, and I encourage you to spend some time with those resources before moving on.

Training data. An AI system learns from examples. A language model learns from text: billions of pages of books, articles, websites, and other written content. An image generator learns from millions of images paired with descriptions. The quality, quantity, and characteristics of training data profoundly affect what the resulting system can do, and what biases it might inherit.

Neural networks. The dominant architecture in modern AI uses artificial neural networks: layers of mathematical operations loosely inspired by how neurons in the brain communicate. Each "neuron" in the network performs a simple calculation and passes the result to connected neurons in the next layer. Through training, the network learns which connections to strengthen and which to weaken.

Transformers. The breakthrough architecture behind most modern language models is called the "transformer," introduced in a 2017 paper by Google researchers.[9] Transformers use a mechanism called "attention" that allows the model to weigh the relevance of different parts of its input when producing output. If you've used ChatGPT (the "T" stands for Transformer), Claude, or similar tools, you've interacted with a transformer-based system.

Parameters. Neural networks have "parameters," numerical values that are adjusted during training. More parameters generally means more capacity to learn complex patterns. Early language models had millions of parameters. GPT-3, released in 2020, had 175 billion. Current frontier models have parameters numbering in the hundreds of billions or more. Notably, as the technology has advanced, smaller models have become capable of matching the performance of much larger predecessors. In 2022, the smallest model scoring above 60% on a standard language benchmark had 540 billion parameters; by

2024, a model with just 3.8 billion parameters could achieve the

9 Ashish Vaswani et al., *Attention Is All You Need, 31 Advances in Neural Info. Processing Sys.* (2017), arxiv.org/abs/1706.03762.

same score.[10]

Inference. Once trained, an AI model can be used to process new inputs, which is called "inference." When you ask ChatGPT a question, you're triggering inference: the model uses its trained parameters to generate a response. For legal purposes, several aspects of this architecture matter:

First, training data creates legal exposure. If a model trains on copyrighted material, that raises intellectual property questions. If training data contains personal information, that raises privacy concerns. If training data reflects historical biases, the resulting system may perpetuate or amplify those biases.

Second, these systems are fundamentally statistical. A language model doesn't "know" things in the way a human does. It generates outputs based on patterns in training data. It can produce confident-sounding nonsense because it does not always have a mechanism for checking whether its outputs are true. This tendency toward "hallucination" has serious implications for liability and professional responsibility.[11]

Third, modern AI systems are often opaque. We can examine a neural network's parameters, but we frequently can't explain why it produces a particular output in human-understandable terms. This "black box" quality creates challenges for transparency, accountability, and due process.

The Current State of Play

While AI has advanced significantly in recent years, not every technology now marketed as "AI" actually qualifies as such. Part of the confusion stems from what is known as the "AI effect," discussed in the next chapter, where technologies once labeled artificial intelligence come to be seen as ordinary software once they

10 Stanford Inst. for Human-Centered AI, *AI Index Report 2025 27* (2025), hai.stanford.edu/ai-index/2025-ai-index-report [hereinafter AI Index 2025].

11 The legal implications of AI hallucination for professional responsibility are examined in *Chapter 15: AI and Legal Practice.*

become widespread. But the problem also reflects market incentives. In recent years, companies have been rewarded for describing themselves as "AI companies," regardless of whether meaningful artificial intelligence is actually involved.

A 2019 study by the investment firm MMC Ventures found that 40 percent of European startups calling themselves AI companies used little or no artificial intelligence at all. The label was often applied for marketing purposes, because "AI" attracts attention and capital in ways that conventional software does not. This practice, commonly referred to as "AI washing," has real consequences. Investors may value companies based on capabilities that do not exist, a risk the SEC has already addressed through enforcement actions against firms that overstated their AI use. For consumers, the result is a loss of clarity and trust. When everything claims to be "AI-powered," from household devices to basic software tools, the term loses meaning and genuine innovation becomes harder to identify.

For policymakers and lawyers, AI washing creates a deeper problem: definitional drift. Regulation depends on clear categories, yet "AI" is now used to describe systems ranging from advanced neural networks to simple if-then rules. That confusion is especially dangerous given how quickly the field is actually advancing.

According to Stanford's 2025 AI Index Report, AI performance on complex reasoning and coding benchmarks has improved dramatically in just a year, while corporate investment reached more than $250 billion and the cost of running capable models collapsed by orders of magnitude.[12] The United States remains the leading developer of major models, though China has rapidly narrowed the gap and leads in publications and patents. Most strikingly, AI systems are increasingly being used to build better AI, accelerating progress in ways that consistently outpace expert predictions.

In this environment, grounding legal analysis in what systems actually do, rather than what companies call them, is not a matter of

---

12 The cost of running AI models has plummeted: querying a model at GPT-3.5's performance level dropped from $20 per million tokens in late 2022 to just seven cents by late 2024, a 280-fold reduction. AI Index 2025, *supra* note 10 at 27.

semantics. Regulatory obligations, liability exposure, and compliance costs must turn on real capabilities and real risks. Clear definitions are the starting point for effective rules, credible enforcement, and informed decision-making in a field moving faster than the language used to describe it.

Why Definitions Matter for Law

Everything in this chapter (the technical foundations, the distinction between narrow AI and AGI, the problem of AI washing) connects to the legal questions that occupy the rest of this book.

When Colorado's AI Act regulates "high-risk AI systems," what exactly counts? When courts adjudicate copyright claims over AI training data, does it matter that these systems don't "understand" their training data the way humans understand books? When liability frameworks address "autonomous" systems, how do we define autonomy in a world where even sophisticated AI operates within parameters set by humans?

These definitional questions will recur throughout the chapters ahead. The goal here is to give you the vocabulary and conceptual framework to engage with them intelligently.

Technology has a way of making yesterday's clear distinctions obsolete. The line between narrow AI and general intelligence may prove less stable than it appears. The definitions we develop today may need revision as capabilities evolve. That's not a reason to abandon precision; it's a reason to hold our definitions loosely, to build legal frameworks that can adapt, and to remain humble about our ability to predict where this technology is headed.

Arthur C. Clarke was right, sufficiently advanced technology looks like magic. But part of the lawyer's job is to look past the magic and make sense of the machinery.

Supplemental Resources

- **IBM Technology** (youtube.com/@IBMTechnology): Comprehensive video explanations of AI fundamentals, machine learning, deep learning, and neural networks. IBM's technology explainer series offers accessible introductions ideal for readers new to the field.
- **3Blue1Brown Neural Networks Series** (youtube.com/@3blue1brown): Award-winning YouTube series using elegant visualizations to explain neural networks and deep learning. Recommended for visual learners seeking mathematical intuitions without getting lost in equations.
- **Stanford HAI AI Index Report 2025** (hai.stanford.edu/ai-index/2025-ai-index-report): The most comprehensive annual survey of AI trends, capabilities, and impact. Essential reading with rigorous data on investment, research output, benchmark performance, and policy developments.
- **Two Minute Papers** (youtube.com/@TwoMinutePapers): Concise summaries of cutting-edge AI research papers in accessible two-minute videos. Excellent for staying current with AI developments without reading dense academic papers.
- **StatQuest with Josh Starmer** (youtube.com/@statquest): Clear explanations of statistics and machine learning concepts with memorable songs and visual aids. Particularly valuable for understanding the statistical foundations underlying AI systems.

CHAPTER 3

A Brief History of Artificial Intelligence

Long before any computer convincingly acted "intelligent," the dream of artificial minds existed vividly in human imagination. Philosophers speculated for centuries about mechanical thinkers. Science fiction writers envisioned robots that could speak, reason, and even feel. Until the mid-twentieth century, these visions remained firmly in the realm of fantasy.

Understanding how we got from those fantasies to the AI systems transforming our world today is more than an academic exercise. The history of artificial intelligence reveals patterns that repeat: cycles of excitement and disappointment, breakthroughs followed by sobering realizations, and a constant redefinition of what "intelligence" even means. These patterns have direct implications for how we should think about regulating AI, investing in it, and integrating it into our legal systems.

It is also a history that helps demystify the technology. To many observers, modern AI can seem almost magical, as if computers have suddenly learned to think on their own. In reality, AI's development has been incremental, marked by a pattern of setbacks and breakthroughs. Keeping that perspective is useful as we navigate today's intense period of AI enthusiasm.

The Dream Takes Shape (1940s-1950s)

The earliest research into thinking machines emerged from a confluence of ideas in the 1940s and early 1950s. Advances in neurology had revealed that the brain was an electrical network of neurons firing in all-or-nothing pulses. In 1943, Warren McCulloch and Walter Pitts published a groundbreaking paper demonstrating that networks of simple artificial neurons could, in principle, compute anything that could be calculated.[13] Their work laid the theoretical foundation for what would become neural networks, the architecture underlying most modern AI systems.

Meanwhile, Norbert Wiener's cybernetics described control and stability in electrical networks. Claude Shannon's information theory explained how digital signals could carry information. And Alan Turing's theory of computation showed that any form of calculation could be described digitally. The close relationship between these ideas suggested something tantalizing: it might be possible to construct an "electronic brain."

In 1950, the British mathematician Alan Turing introduced another radical idea that shifted the conversation. Rather than debating whether machines could truly think or possess genuine consciousness, Turing suggested focusing on observable behavior. His insight was elegantly simple: if a machine could carry on a conversation so convincingly that a human judge could not reliably distinguish it from a real person, that machine could reasonably be considered intelligent.[14]

This concept, now known as the Turing Test, changed everything. Intelligence was no longer an elusive internal quality but something practical and measurable based on interaction. Turing's approach immediately captured researchers' imaginations, prompting a new question: could human intelligence itself (including reasoning, learning, and problem-solving) be precisely understood and mechanically replicated?

In 1956, a small group of ambitious scientists gathered at Dartmouth College in New Hampshire to explore this question. Led by John McCarthy of Dartmouth, Marvin Minsky of Harvard, Nathaniel Rochester from IBM, and Claude Shannon from Bell Labs, they

---

13 Warren S. McCulloch & Walter Pitts, *A Logical Calculus of the Ideas Immanent in Nervous Activity, 5 Bull. Mathematical Biophysics 115* (1943), cs.cmu.edu/~epxing/Class/10715/reading/McCulloch.and.Pitts.pdf.

14 A.M. Turing, *Computing Machinery and Intelligence*, 59 Mind 433, 434 (1950), http://courses.cs.umbc.edu/471/papers/turing.pdf; For an accessible explanation of the Turing Test, *see* The Turing Test: Can a Computer Pass for a Human?, TED-Ed (Apr. 25, 2016), youtube.com/watch?v=3wLqsRLvV-c.

convened what became known as the Dartmouth Summer Research Project on Artificial Intelligence.[15] This gathering officially marked AI's birth as a scientific field.

McCarthy insisted on the phrase "artificial intelligence" to distance the work from related fields like cybernetics and automata theory. The name stuck, providing a conceptual umbrella broad enough to unite researchers interested in logic, learning, language, and neural networks under one banner.

The workshop's proposal stated, in bold terms, that it's goal was to test the assertion that "every aspect of learning or any other feature of intelligence can be so precisely described that a machine can be made to simulate it."[16] Given that the computers of the 1950s filled entire rooms and stored only kilobytes of data, this was nothing short of visionary.

The atmosphere at Dartmouth was euphoric. Participants genuinely believed human-level machine intelligence might be achievable within a few short years. This confidence came from early successes showing that computers could perform tasks previously thought exclusively human. At the workshop itself, Allen Newell and Herbert Simon debuted the Logic Theorist, a program that could prove mathematical theorems from scratch.[17] Here was a concrete demonstration of the symbolic AI approach that used logical rules to enable computers to reason.

This initial era laid important conceptual foundations. Early successes created the impression that machine intelligence was almost within reach. But beneath this enthusiasm lay a pattern that would repeat throughout AI's history: promising bursts of progress followed by sober realizations that human intelligence was far deeper, subtler, and more complex than initially imagined.

---

15 John McCarthy et al., *A Proposal for the Dartmouth Summer Research Project on Artificial Intelligence 1* (Aug. 31, 1955), jmc.stanford.edu/articles/dartmouth/dartmouth.pdf.

16 *Id.* at 2.

17 Allen Newell & Herbert A. Simon, *The Logic Theory Machine: A Complex Information Processing System*, 2 IRE Transactions on Info. Theory 61 (1956), rand.org/content/dam/rand/pubs/papers/2024/P868.pdf.

The First Wave: Symbolic AI and Early Breakthroughs (1960s)

In the years following Dartmouth, excitement around artificial intelligence grew rapidly. Researchers embarked on ambitious experiments, each aiming to demonstrate that computers could replicate human thought. The spirit of the age was captured by a simple, optimistic assumption: if a task required intelligence and humans could do it, there must be a way for a machine to do it as well.

This early optimism centered largely on an approach called symbolic AI. Think of it like following a cookbook: you clearly define the ingredients (symbols), provide step-by-step instructions (rules), and if the recipe is detailed enough, the computer can logically solve even complicated problems. With the correct instructions, researchers believed, computers could reason through almost anything.

The Logic Theorist exemplified this approach. Using logical rules, it systematically explored possible solutions to mathematical problems, validating or discarding them based on correctness. When it succeeded in proving complex theorems previously solved only by trained mathematicians, the program created a stir. Here was a computer performing intellectual tasks that seemed uniquely human.

Around the same time, another significant development emerged from IBM labs. Arthur Samuel created a program that could play checkers at an increasingly sophisticated level.[18] The revolutionary part was how it learned. Samuel's program did not merely follow preset rules. Instead, it used an innovative method now known as machine learning. The program repeatedly played against itself, analyzing moves that led to victories and gradually improving its strategy.

This concept represented a fundamental shift. A machine could improve through its own experience rather than relying entirely on explicit programming. Machine learning would later become the

---

18 Arthur L. Samuel, *Some Studies in Machine Learning Using the Game of Checkers,* 3 IBM J. Res. & Dev. 210 (1959). For a visual explanation of Samuel's approach, *see* Computerphile, Machine Learning: Living in the Age of AI, youtube.com/watch?v=ZJixNvx9BAc.

dominant approach in AI, but in the 1960s it was just one promising avenue among many.

Amidst this enthusiasm came a particularly fascinating experiment: a conversational program named ELIZA, created by MIT researcher Joseph Weizenbaum.[19] ELIZA mimicked a human therapist through a simple but clever trick. It looked for keywords in user input and responded by rearranging those words into reflective questions. If someone typed "I'm worried about my job," ELIZA might respond "Why are you worried about your job?"

Although ELIZA's conversations were simple and scripted, users often reported feeling genuinely heard or understood. Weizenbaum himself was startled by how readily people attributed intelligence and empathy to his creation.[20] This phenomenon became known as the ELIZA effect: the human tendency to perceive understanding or empathy in basic AI systems. It revealed something profound that remains relevant today. Even primitive systems can exert powerful psychological influence. Humans are surprisingly willing to attribute emotional depth to machines, even when none exists.

These early achievements captivated the public imagination and prompted bold predictions. If machines could already reason logically and learn through practice, full human-level intelligence seemed within easy reach. Some researchers confidently predicted that computers would become indistinguishable from the human mind within a decade or two.

But symbolic AI had fundamental limitations that would soon become apparent. It thrived in neatly defined, structured environments: solving puzzles, proving theorems, playing board games. When researchers ventured beyond these clear boundaries, complexity overwhelmed their methods.

---

19 Joseph Weizenbaum, ELIZA: *A Computer Program for the Study of Natural Language Communication Between Man and Machine*, 9 Commc'ns ACM 36 (1966). An interactive version of ELIZA is available at masswerk.at/elizabot.

20 *Id.* at 42. For a thoughtful discussion of the ELIZA effect and its continuing relevance, see 99% Invisible, *The ELIZA Effect* (July 2021), 99percentinvisible.org/episode/the-eliza-effect.

Human language, for instance, is full of ambiguity, context, and nuance that symbolic rules struggled to handle. Recognizing objects in images, interpreting the physical world, or reasoning through everyday common sense required enormous amounts of implicit knowledge that humans possess effortlessly but that proved extraordinarily difficult to encode in a machine.

At the time, these limitations were not widely appreciated. The prevailing optimism masked the challenges ahead. True artificial intelligence, it seemed, was inevitable. But the road there would prove bumpier than anyone anticipated.

High Hopes Meet Reality: The First AI Winter (1970s)

As the 1970s began, the optimistic predictions of early AI researchers collided with the complexities of human intelligence. The achievements of the 1960s had mostly occurred in simplified scenarios. When researchers attempted to apply these successes to broader, real-world tasks, they encountered unforeseen difficulties.

Natural language understanding proved especially frustrating. Programs like ELIZA could simulate simple conversations by responding to keywords, but they had no genuine understanding of meaning or context. In the United States, substantial government funding had supported ambitious machine translation projects, aiming to automate diplomatic and military communication. After years of minimal progress, the ALPAC Report of 1966 concluded that machine translation was far more difficult than anticipated and recommended drastic budget cuts.[21]

Computer vision presented similar challenges. Many researchers had believed teaching computers to recognize objects visually would be relatively straightforward. This optimism quickly faded. Interpreting even basic visual scenes required understanding subtle details, context, and implicit assumptions that humans handle effortlessly. Effective solutions remained elusive.

---

21 Nat'l Research Council, *Automatic Language Processing Advisory Committee Report* (1966), mt-archive.net/50/ALPAC-1966.pdf [hereinafter ALPAC Report].

In the United Kingdom, Sir James Lighthill's 1973 report to the British Science Research Council delivered a devastating assessment of the field. He concluded that AI had failed to achieve its ambitious goals and was unlikely to produce the promised breakthroughs.[22] The report triggered significant funding cuts and contributed to what researchers later called the "first AI winter."

A casualty of this period was neural networks. These computational models, inspired by the structure of the human brain, had initially sparked great excitement. Imagine a neural network as a web of interconnected switches, similar to lights connected by wires. Each switch represents an artificial neuron. When the network receives input, these switches activate depending on whether they detect particular features. By repeatedly adjusting connections based on experience, the network gradually learns to recognize patterns.

Early neural network models, particularly a simple version known as the perceptron, could identify basic patterns. But perceptrons faced significant limitations. In 1969, Marvin Minsky and Seymour Papert published a mathematical analysis demonstrating that perceptrons could not learn certain kinds of patterns, specifically those involving the relationship between multiple features considered together.[23] Their book was widely interpreted as proving that neural networks were a dead end.

Funding for neural network research rapidly declined. In retrospect, these early setbacks underscored a critical insight: significant AI breakthroughs often require not just software innovations but also hardware advances. Early neural networks struggled partly because the computational power and data storage needed for more advanced tasks simply did not exist yet. Far from being a dead end, perceptrons provided foundational insights that later researchers would build

---

22 Sir James Lighthill, *Artificial Intelligence: A General Survey, in Artificial Intelligence: A Paper Symposium* (Science Research Council 1973), rodsmith.nz/wp-content/uploads/Lighthill_1973_Report.pdf.

23 Marvin Minsky & Seymour *Papert, Perceptrons: An Introduction to Computational Geometry* (MIT Press 1969), direct.mit.edu/books/monograph/3132/PerceptronsAn-Introduction-to-Computational. For an accessible visual explanation of perceptrons and their limitations, see 3Blue1Brown, *But What Is a Neural Network?*, youtube.com/watch?v=aircAruvnKk.

upon extensively.

With neural networks temporarily sidelined, the AI community returned its focus to symbolic approaches. But symbolic AI faced its own difficulties. Capturing all the rules required to replicate even basic human reasoning and common-sense knowledge proved overwhelming. Human intelligence involves vast amounts of implicit, contextual information that cannot be easily reduced to logical rules.

By the late 1970s, progress had slowed considerably. But these setbacks offered critical lessons. Researchers recognized that intelligence was more than following clearly defined rules. It required new methods capable of learning, adapting, and interpreting complexity independently. Though AI lost much of its initial excitement, this period of apparent stagnation was quietly productive. New ideas and interdisciplinary approaches began taking shape beneath the surface, laying groundwork for the resurgence to come.

Knowledge Is Power: The Expert Systems Boom (1980s)

Every winter eventually gives way to spring. In the early 1980s, artificial intelligence experienced a revival thanks to expert systems. These were not designed to create machines that broadly mimicked human intelligence. Their goal was far more targeted: capturing the knowledge of human specialists and embedding that expertise into computer programs.

The idea was elegantly simple. Consider a skilled doctor who has spent years diagnosing rare illnesses, or a geologist who can pinpoint underground resources from subtle clues. If you could carefully distill their hard-earned insights into precise rules, you could program a computer to provide anyone with immediate access to expert-level decision-making.

Expert systems accomplished this through large collections of logical rules structured as "if-then" statements. Each rule captured a small but meaningful slice of human judgment. In medicine, a rule might say: "If a patient has a fever and a specific rash and a certain blood test result, then they probably have disease X." These rules were not generated automatically. They were created by meticulously

interviewing experts and translating their insights into logical conditions, a process called knowledge engineering.
Once established, these rules were processed by an inference engine, essentially the system's "brain" that applied logical reasoning to arrive at conclusions. Think of it as a detective following clues step by step until reaching the logical solution to a mystery.

One celebrated example was MYCIN, developed at Stanford University.[24] MYCIN specialized in diagnosing bacterial infections and recommending antibiotic treatments. In tests, it performed at or above the level of junior medical professionals for specific diagnostic tasks. Another influential system, DENDRAL, helped chemists identify the structure of unknown organic molecules.[25]

These successes demonstrated that even if fully human-like AI remained distant, expert systems could deliver immense practical value. Businesses took note. By the mid-1980s, corporations across industries invested heavily in expert systems for everything from mineral exploration to financial decision-making to configuring complicated product orders.

By 1985, the global market for expert system software and specialized hardware exceeded a billion dollars.[26] Japan launched the ambitious Fifth Generation Computer Project, aiming to create computers that could reason and communicate in natural language.[27] Concerned about falling behind, the United States and United Kingdom boosted their own AI investments significantly. For a moment, expert systems seemed to have found AI's niche.

---

24 Edward H. Shortliffe, *Computer-Based Medical Consultations: MYCIN* (Elsevier 1976), www.shortliffe.net/Shortliffe-1976/MYCIN%20thesis%20Book.htm.

25 Robert K. Lindsay et al., *DENDRAL: A Case Study of the First Expert System for Scientific Hypothesis Formation*, 61 Artificial Intelligence 209 (1993), web.mit.edu/6.034/www/6.s966/dendral-history.pdf.

26 Pamela McCorduck, *Machines Who Think 421* (2d ed. 2004), www.academia.edu/41375562/Machines_Who_Think.

27 Edward A. Feigenbaum & Pamela McCorduck, *The Fifth Generation: Artificial Intelligence and Japan's Computer Challenge to the World* (Addison-Wesley 1983), archive.org/details/fifthgenerationa0000feig.

Yet the expert system era eventually revealed significant weaknesses. The biggest challenge was keeping systems up-to-date. Knowledge is not static; experts regularly revise their views and adapt to new research. Each change had to be manually programmed, a cumbersome and expensive process.

Moreover, expert systems were notoriously brittle. They performed impressively within their narrow domains but failed abruptly when confronted with situations outside their carefully coded rules. They could not learn or adapt beyond their explicitly programmed knowledge.

By the late 1980s, these limitations became impossible to ignore. In 1987, many prominent AI companies folded, investment dried up, and public enthusiasm gave way to skepticism.[28] Researchers called this downturn the "second AI winter."

But expert systems left an enduring legacy. They proved that computers could deliver substantial value by capturing human expertise in structured rules. They also exposed a critical bottleneck: the difficulty of manually coding all the knowledge required for sophisticated decision-making. This insight pushed researchers toward a fundamentally different approach, one that would enable computers to learn directly from data rather than relying solely on hand-crafted rules.

The Learning Machines Strike Back (1990s)

After the collapse of expert systems, the AI community regrouped around a simpler, more pragmatic approach. The buzzword of this era was machine learning.

Machine learning represented a fundamental shift in perspective. Instead of painstakingly programming every possible rule and scenario, researchers aimed to build algorithms that could discover patterns on their own by analyzing data. Imagine teaching someone to distinguish cats from dogs not by explaining every detail but

---

28 Daniel Crevier, *AI: The Tumultuous History of the Search for Artificial Intelligence 203-09* (Basic Books 1993) (chronicling the collapse of the AI industry in the late 1980s).

by showing thousands of examples until they intuitively grasped the difference. Machine learning allowed computers to develop understanding through experience, gradually refining their ability to recognize patterns without explicit instructions.

One promising form of machine learning that regained popularity was neural networks. In earlier decades, single-layer networks called perceptrons had disappointed because they could only solve simple problems. But breakthroughs in the 1980s and 1990s in how multi-layer networks could be trained reignited enthusiasm.

The key innovation was "backpropagation," short for backward propagation of errors. In simple terms, backpropagation allowed networks to learn from their mistakes. If a neural network guessed wrong, the errors flowed back through its layers, adjusting connections so future guesses would be more accurate. It was as if a student, after answering incorrectly, could review precisely where the mistake happened and learn exactly how to avoid repeating it.

In 1986, Geoffrey Hinton and colleagues David Rumelhart and Ronald Williams published a landmark paper demonstrating the effectiveness of backpropagation for training multi-layer neural networks.[29] This work revived interest in neural networks and laid the foundation for the deep learning revolution that would transform AI decades later. Hinton's contributions were a significant factor in his receiving the 2024 Nobel Prize in Physics for his foundational work in machine learning.[30]

One impactful demonstration came in 1989 from researcher Yann LeCun, who developed a specialized neural network called a convolutional neural network (CNN).[31] CNNs are designed

---

29 David E. Rumelhart, Geoffrey E. Hinton & Ronald J. Williams, *Learning Representations by Back-Propagating Errors, 323 Nature 533* (1986). For an explanation of backpropagation, *see* 3Blue1Brown, *Backpropagation Calculus*, youtube.com/watch?v=tIeHLnjs5U8.

30 Press Release, Royal Swedish Acad. of Scis., The Nobel Prize in Physics 2024 (Oct. 8, 2024), nobelprize.org/prizes/physics/2024/press-release.

31 Yann LeCun et al., *Backpropagation Applied to Handwritten Zip Code Recognition, 1 Neural Computation 541* (1989), galileo-unbound.blog/wp-content/uploads/2025/02/lecun.neco_.1989.1.4.541.pdf;

specifically for visual tasks, analyzing images by identifying patterns like edges, curves, and textures. LeCun used his CNN to recognize handwritten digits on checks, something previously done only by human bank tellers. Banks enthusiastically adopted this technology, marking one of the first widespread commercial applications of modern neural networks.[32]

But neural networks were just one piece of the broader machine learning landscape. Throughout the 1990s, other methods also flourished. Decision trees became popular for their simplicity, operating like flowcharts that asked yes-or-no questions until arriving at an answer.[33] Bayesian networks tackled problems involving uncertainty, mapping how different factors influenced each other.[34] Support vector machines emerged as powerful tools for classifying data in complex scenarios.[35]

What these methods shared was their core strength: the ability to learn directly from examples rather than relying on human-defined rules. This was the key distinction from expert systems: instead of knowledge engineers spending years encoding rules, machine learning systems could discover patterns automatically.

As computers grew faster and digital storage expanded, machine learning algorithms thrived. Systems trained on huge volumes of data could perform tasks like recognizing speech, detecting fraudulent transactions, or recommending products with accuracy previously unimaginable.

Interestingly, despite these achievements, the term "artificial intelligence" became somewhat unpopular during this period. Past disappointments had tarnished AI's reputation. Researchers

---

32 *See* IBM, *What are Convolutional Neural Networks (CNNs)*, youtube.com/watch?v=QzY57FaENXg.

33 Normilized Nerd, *Decision Tree Classification Clearly Explained*, youtube.com/watch?v=ZVR2Way4nwQ.

34 For an introduction to Bayesian networks, see *LiquidBrain Bioinformatics, Bayesian Network | Introduction and Workshop*, youtube.com/watch?v=mebXoVrfchg

35 Visually Explained, *Support Vector Machine (SVM) in 2 minutes*, youtube.com/watch?v=_YPScrckx28.

preferred terms like "machine learning," "pattern recognition," or "data analytics."

Ironically, while public awareness of AI faded, the technology quietly embedded itself into daily life. Tasks that once epitomized advanced AI, like reading handwritten text or understanding spoken commands, became so commonplace that people thought of them as standard computing rather than artificial intelligence. This shift exemplified what researchers call the AI effect: tasks lose their mystique once they become routine. As AI pioneer John McCarthy quipped, "As soon as it works, no one calls it AI anymore."

By the decade's end, machine learning had firmly established itself as a practical, effective approach. AI had begun infiltrating numerous aspects of daily life, gradually and without fanfare. Yet the public was about to witness something spectacular that would thrust AI back onto the global stage.

Landmark Competitions: Machines vs. Humans

Nothing captures the public imagination quite like a head-to-head competition between humans and machines.

For decades, chess was viewed as the quintessential measure of human intellect. Mastering the game required strategic thinking, creativity, memory, and intuition. Many doubted any computer could defeat a top human champion. That belief came crashing down on May 11, 1997, when IBM's chess-playing computer Deep Blue defeated Garry Kasparov, the reigning world champion.

Deep Blue's victory represented a watershed moment, not just in AI research but in popular consciousness. Yet the way it won was surprisingly straightforward. Deep Blue did not learn like a human brain or simulate how a human approaches chess. It relied on brute-force computation, evaluating approximately 200 million positions per second and systematically calculating potential moves several steps ahead.[36]

---

36 Murray Campbell, A. Joseph Hoane Jr. & Feng-hsiung Hsu, *Deep Blue*, 134 Artificial Intelligence 57, 58 (2002). For footage of the historic match, *see Game Over: Kasparov and*

Some observers argued Deep Blue had not demonstrated true intelligence, just raw number-crunching. But undeniably, chess was no longer a uniquely human territory.

If chess showed computers could handle complex strategic calculations, the next major landmark pushed AI into an even more distinctly human domain: language. In February 2011, IBM's Watson competed on the trivia game show Jeopardy! against two of its most celebrated champions, Ken Jennings and Brad Rutter.

Unlike chess, Jeopardy! required far more than computational power. Questions were filled with wordplay, subtle hints, puns, and cultural references. Watson approached this challenge using natural language processing and massive knowledge databases.[37] It was not truly understanding questions in a human sense but rather analyzing them statistically, rapidly searching its vast store of knowledge to predict the most probable correct answers.

Watson won decisively, proving AI could operate effectively in linguistic and knowledge-based domains traditionally seen as exclusively human.

However, chess and Jeopardy! were structured, well-defined challenges. Researchers still viewed certain games as nearly insurmountable for machines, especially the ancient board game Go. With more possible positions than atoms in the observable universe, Go mastery requires intuition and pattern recognition developed through years of experience. Many experts thought AI would not conquer Go for decades. They were wrong.

In March 2016, Google DeepMind's AlphaGo defeated Lee Sedol, one of the world's greatest Go players, four games to one.[38] Even more remarkable was AlphaGo's style of play. At key moments, it made moves that baffled experts, moves considered bizarre by conventional

---

the Machine (Vikram Jayanti dir., 2003).

37 Jeopardy!, *Watson and the Jeopardy! Challenge*, youtube.com/watch?v=P18EdAKuC1U.

38 A documentary about the match is available at DeepMind, *AlphaGo*, youtube.com/watch?v=WXuK6gekU1Y.

wisdom, yet which ultimately revealed innovative winning strategies. AlphaGo's victory was groundbreaking because it combined two approaches: deep learning and reinforcement learning. Deep learning uses multi-layer neural networks to recognize complex patterns, while reinforcement learning lets a system improve through trial and error by playing millions of simulated games. AlphaGo learned not just by studying human games but by playing against itself, continuously refining its strategies.

Unlike Deep Blue's brute-force approach, AlphaGo displayed adaptive, strategic creativity that suggested something closer to genuine intuition. Machines were not merely matching human performance; they were redefining what optimal performance looked like.

This trend continued with AlphaGo's successor, AlphaZero, which mastered chess, Go, and the Japanese game shogi entirely through self-play, reaching superhuman levels within hours.[39] Other systems conquered poker, real-time strategy video games, and environments requiring complex teamwork and nuanced strategy.

Each competition forced society to reconsider what artificial intelligence meant and acknowledge the rapidly closing gap between human and machine capabilities. Deep Blue showed extraordinary calculation power. Watson displayed impressive linguistic processing. AlphaGo introduced AI that seemed to possess genuine creativity and strategic innovation.

Together, these competitions highlighted AI's evolution from brute-force number-crunching to flexible, adaptive systems capable of originality. Each breakthrough forced a new reckoning with what intelligence itself might mean, and how closely it could be replicated, or exceeded, by machines.

---

39 David Silver et al., *A General Reinforcement Learning Algorithm That Masters Chess, Shogi, and Go Through Self-Play*, 362 Science 1140 (2018), turing.iimas.unam.mx/~luis/cursos/IA2025-2/lecturas/AlphaZero.pdf.

Supplemental Resources

- **The History of Artificial Intelligence** (youtube.com/watch?v=R3YFxF0n8n8): An amateur documentary compiling historical footage of early AI projects, including researchers and demonstrations from the field's formative decades. Valuable for seeing the people and machines that shaped AI history.

- **AlphaGo** (youtube.com/watch?v=WXuK6gekU1Y): DeepMind's 2017 documentary covering AlphaGo's historic match against Lee Sedol. Essential viewing for understanding how AI can develop strategies that surprise even world-class experts.

- **Game Over: Kasparov and the Machine** (Vikram Jayanti dir., 2003): Documentary examining the 1997 Deep Blue versus Kasparov match, including the psychological aspects of competing against a machine. Features interviews with Kasparov and the IBM team.

- **A Brief History of Artificial Intelligence: What It Is, Where We Are, and Where We Are Going** (Michael Wooldridge, Flatiron Books 2021): A comprehensive and accessible history by Oxford's Head of Computer Science, who has spent 25 years in AI research. Traces the field from its origins through modern developments with insider perspective on the key debates and personalities.

- **Stanford AI100 Report** (ai100.stanford.edu): The "One Hundred Year Study on Artificial Intelligence" offers assessments of AI's progress and societal impact. Provides a long-term perspective on how AI capabilities and concerns have evolved.

CHAPTER 4

The Deep Learning Revolution

While the public marveled at victories like AlphaGo, an equally significant transformation was unfolding behind the scenes: the rise of deep learning. This technology rapidly became the dominant form of AI throughout the 2010s, fundamentally changing what computers could do and setting the stage for the generative AI systems that now dominate headlines.

Understanding deep learning is essential for lawyers grappling with AI-related questions, because virtually every AI system creating novel legal challenges today (from large language models to image generators to autonomous vehicles) is built on deep learning foundations.

AlexNet: The Big Bang Moment (2012)

Deep learning is essentially a modern, more powerful evolution of neural networks. Unlike the single-layer perceptrons that disappointed researchers in the 1970s, deep learning systems have many layers of interconnected neurons, hence the term "deep." This additional depth allows them to handle far more complex tasks.

But deep neural networks had been theoretically possible for decades. What changed in the early 2010s was a combination of three factors: dramatically increased computational power (particularly from graphics processing units, or GPUs, originally designed for video games), an unprecedented explosion of data from the internet, and algorithmic improvements in how to train very deep networks effectively.

A defining moment occurred in 2012 at a competition called the ImageNet challenge, where researchers tested their systems' ability to recognize and categorize objects in millions of images. That year, a deep neural network known as AlexNet, developed by Alex Krizhevsky working with Geoffrey Hinton at the University of Toronto, entered the contest and blew away the competition.[40]

AlexNet recognized everyday objects like cats, cars, and bicycles with stunning accuracy, dramatically outperforming all other approaches. Its success was so profound that within just a few years, virtually every researcher working on computer vision abandoned traditional methods in favor of deep learning. The field was permanently reshaped.

Around the same time, deep learning revolutionized speech recognition. Companies like Google and Microsoft achieved dramatic improvements in voice recognition software, significantly reducing errors in transcribing spoken words.[41] These advances directly improved voice assistants like Siri and Google Assistant, transforming them from novelty apps into indispensable everyday tools.

By the middle of the decade, deep learning had transitioned from promising research into technology embedded in products used by billions of people. Facebook automatically tagged friends in photos. Netflix suggested shows you might like. Your email sorted spam from wanted messages with remarkable accuracy. All of this was powered by deep learning.

How Deep Learning Works

Traditional AI methods required engineers to manually create and refine detailed features for recognizing things like faces or voices. Think of these features as carefully written instructions telling the computer exactly what to look for: edges, curves, colors, shapes. This

---

40 Alex Krizhevsky, Ilya Sutskever & Geoffrey E. Hinton, *ImageNet Classification with Deep Convolutional Neural Networks*, 25 Advances in Neural Info. Processing Sys. 1097 (2012). For an explanation of AlexNet's architecture, *see* Yannic Kilcher, *AlexNet Paper Explained*, youtube.com/watch?v=Nq3auVtvd9Q.

41 *See* Geoffrey Hinton, Li Deng & Dong Yu et al., *Deep Neural Networks for Acoustic Modeling in Speech Recognition*, IEEE Signal Processing Mag., Nov. 2012, at 82.

process was labor-intensive, required significant expertise, and often produced systems that were brittle when encountering anything outside their carefully defined parameters.

Deep learning eliminated much of this manual work. Instead, it allowed neural networks to figure out the important features directly from vast amounts of raw data.[42] To recognize faces, a deep learning model would first learn to detect simple features like edges and shadows, then combine these into eyes, noses, and mouths, and finally recognize entire faces. This process is known as representation learning, where the system discovers the most useful way to interpret its inputs without explicit programming.

This approach proved remarkably effective across domains. The same basic architecture could be trained on images, speech, text, or other data types. With enough examples and computing power, deep learning systems could match or exceed human performance on specific tasks that had long resisted automation.

Between 2012 and 2019, deep learning continued its relentless progress. It was not limited to images or speech; it also reshaped natural language processing, a field focused on understanding and generating human language. Around 2016, Google Translate switched to deep learning algorithms, resulting in a noticeable leap in translation quality almost overnight.[43]

The Transformer Revolution (2017)

A crucial turning point arrived in 2017 with the invention of a new neural network architecture called the "transformer."[44] Though this innovation is highly technical, it shaped the AI landscape in ways everyone would soon experience.

---

42 *See* 3Blue1Brown, *But What Is a Neural Network?* (video), youtube.com/watch?v=air-cAruvnKk.

43 Yonghui Wu et al., *Google's Neural Machine Translation System: Bridging the Gap Between Human and Machine Translation* (Sept. 26, 2016), arxiv.org/abs/1609.08144.

44 Ashish Vaswani et al., *Attention Is All You Need*, 30 Advances in Neural Info. Processing Sys. 5998 (2017). For an interactive explanation of transformers, *see* Jay Alammar, *The Illustrated Transformer*, jalammar.github.io/illustrated-transformer.

Transformers introduced a mechanism known as attention, allowing neural networks to focus selectively on the most relevant parts of data rather than processing everything equally.[45] Imagine reading a long text but instantly highlighting only the most relevant words. This selective focus made transformers far more effective at interpreting context and nuance in language.[46]

The introduction of transformers paved the way for large language models like GPT and Claude. By enabling the training of much bigger, more complex AI systems, Transformers allowed models to maintain context over longer stretches of text and produce responses with surprising coherence. The "T" in GPT stands for Transformer, and this architecture underlies virtually all modern generative AI systems for text.

AI Enters Everyday Life

By the end of the 2010s, AI had broken out of research labs and niche applications to become embedded in a wide array of industries and consumer experiences. Self-driving cars, or at least vehicles with advanced AI-driven assistance features, became commonplace. Medical AI systems using deep learning received regulatory approval to help doctors diagnose serious illnesses like cancer and diabetic eye disease. AI improved logistics and supply chains, detected credit card fraud in real-time, and helped farmers monitor crops.

If you are reading this and thinking "this is interesting, but how does it relate to me?", the truth is that even before AlphaGo made headlines or ChatGPT started writing essays, AI had quietly slipped into the fabric of everyday life.

The autocorrect on your phone is powered by AI language models. Your email spam filter uses AI trained on millions of examples. When your bank asks for extra verification after an unusual login, that is an AI security system detecting anomalies. When Netflix recommends a show or Spotify suggests a playlist, AI is analyzing your preferences

---

45 *Id.* at 5999-6000.

46 *See* 3Blue1Brown, *Attention in Transformers, Visually Explained* (video), youtube.com/watch?v=eMlx5fFNoYc (providing a visual walkthrough of the attention mechanism).

and those of similar users. Facial recognition to unlock your phone uses a deep neural network. Voice assistants like Alexa, Siri, and Google Assistant use AI for both speech recognition and dialogue generation.

In short, narrow AI systems proliferated in the 2010s to make services smarter and more personalized. They often do not feel like "AI" because we get used to them quickly. As soon as the machine does something well, we stop marveling at it and just see it as a feature. This is the AI effect in action.

One significant area is personalization and recommendation. Companies learned that AI algorithms could sift through enormous data and find patterns to tailor suggestions for each person. The result is a user experience that feels almost magically attuned to individual preferences. Of course, this raises new challenges around filter bubbles and privacy, but from a capability standpoint, it represents a remarkable achievement.

Healthcare embraced AI as well, albeit cautiously. AI pattern-recognition in medical images means algorithms can flag suspicious areas in X-rays or help measure tumors in CT scans, acting as tireless assistants to doctors. In some cases, AI systems reached performance comparable to medical specialists for specific diagnostic tasks.

Even agriculture saw AI deployment, with drones and cameras using deep learning to detect crop diseases or recommend optimal harvest times. Finance has long used AI models to predict market trends or assess loan risks.

The Rise of Generative AI

By the 2020s, one branch of AI took center stage: large language models, or LLMs. These systems are trained on massive amounts of text with the goal of predicting the next word in a sentence. At first glance, predicting the next word sounds trivial. But with enough data and a large enough model (billions of adjustable parameters), this next-word prediction task produces AI with surprising breadth of knowledge and linguistic ability.

One breakthrough was GPT-3, introduced by OpenAI in 2020.[47] With 175 billion parameters trained on an enormous dataset, GPT-3 could generate coherent, often insightful paragraphs on almost any prompt. Ask it to write an essay about renewable energy, and it would produce several paragraphs that looked as if a human wrote them. Give it a programming task in plain English, and it might produce working code. It could answer questions, summarize articles, translate languages, and write bad poetry.

GPT-3 demonstrated emergent intelligence with capabilities that arose from the scale of the model and data rather than being directly programmed in.[48]

Then, at the end of 2022, OpenAI launched ChatGPT, a user-friendly chatbot interface powered by an improved version of GPT.[49] ChatGPT made that powerful language model accessible through a simple dialogue format. Within two months, it had over 100 million users, making it one of the fastest-adopted consumer applications in history.[50]

The experiences people had ranged from delight to disbelief to concern. You could ask ChatGPT to explain complex topics, brainstorm ideas, compose emails, write poems in Shakespearean style, or role-play historical figures. But it could also generate misinformation or be manipulated into saying problematic things.

The emergence of large language models marked what many called AI's breakout into public consciousness. Previous milestones were impressive but often specialized. Now AI was in the hands of the public, performing a multitude of tasks. It felt as if a line had been crossed: AI was no longer just solving well-defined games or specific classification problems. It was engaging in open-ended dialogue and

---

47 Tom B. Brown et al., *Language Models Are Few-Shot Learners*, 33 Advances in Neural Info. Processing Sys. 1877 (2020), arxiv.org/abs/2005.14165.

48 *Id.* at 1878-79.

49 Introducing ChatGPT, OpenAI (Nov. 30, 2022), openai.com/index/chatgpt.

50 Krystal Hu, *ChatGPT Sets Record for Fastest-Growing User Base*, Reuters (Feb. 2, 2023), reuters.com/technology/chatgpt-sets-record-fastest-growing-user-base-analyst-note-2023-02-01.

creation.

In parallel with language models, other generative AI blossomed. Systems like DALL-E and Midjourney could create artwork from text descriptions.[51] Voice synthesis became so sophisticated that given a few samples, AI could speak in anyone's voice. At the same time, generative video moved from novelty to credibility. Early efforts produced uncanny, physics-defying clips, but rapid improvements in temporal consistency, lighting, and motion coherence soon made AI-generated videos look plausibly real.[52]

AI was showing it could not only analyze and classify information but also generate content that previously only humans could produce.

The Black Box Problem and Emerging Concerns

All these advancements highlighted limitations that have significant legal implications. AI systems powered by deep learning can be incredibly powerful but also opaque. It is often not clear why they make particular decisions.

Unlike the expert systems of the 1980s, which followed explicit rules that could be examined and explained, deep learning models make decisions based on patterns learned from data in ways that resist easy interpretation. This "black box" quality creates challenges for transparency, accountability, and due process that will recur throughout this book.

Deep learning systems can also fail in strange ways. An image recognition AI might identify a turtle as a rifle if the turtle has a certain oddly patterned sticker on its shell.[53] This is nonsensical to

---

51 *See* Aditya Ramesh et al., *Hierarchical Text-Conditional Image Generation with CLIP Latents* (Apr. 13, 2022), arxiv.org/abs/2204.06125 (describing DALL-E 2).

52 A commonly cited early benchmark was the viral "spaghetti test," in which an AI attempted to generate a video of Will Smith eating spaghetti. The surreal result became a shorthand for how far generative video still had to go, and how quickly it was improving once that bar was set. See Dani Di Placido, Google's AI Passed the 'Will Smith Eating Spaghetti' Test, Capable of Creating Convincing AI Video, Forbes (May 22, 2025), forbes.com/sites/danidiplacido/2025/05/22/google-passed-the-will-smith-eating-spaghetti-test.

53 Anish Athalye, Logan Engstrom & Andrew Ilyas, *Synthesizing Robust Adversarial*

a human but reveals that these systems do not "see" the world as we do; they pick up on statistical patterns that can sometimes be fooled or exploited.

There have been documented cases of AI systems exhibiting bias. Facial recognition systems have performed worse on darker-skinned faces because training data contained fewer such examples.[54] Criminal sentencing algorithms have shown racial disparities.[55] These issues began entering public conversation in the late 2010s, and people realized that while AI is powerful, it is not infallible or inherently fair. It reflects the data and design it was given.

By the late 2010s, AI was not only a technological phenomenon but also a deeply important social and political issue. These concerns have only intensified as AI capabilities have expanded.

The Living Definition Problem

Looking back at AI's history, from the dreamers at Dartmouth to the marvels of deep learning and today's chatbots, what definition of "artificial intelligence" emerges?

If there is one lesson history teaches, it is that AI is an evolving, living concept. In the 1950s, AI meant a machine that could do something ordinarily requiring human intelligence. That broad notion still holds, but what specific abilities count as AI has shifted with each generation.

In the 1960s, a program doing algebra was AI. Today, that is a trivial calculator function. Conversely, no one in the 1960s imagined AI making art or chatting in natural language. If they had, they would have called it science fiction.

Examples, 35 Proc. Int'l Conf. on Machine Learning 284 (2018) (demonstrating that 3D-printed turtle with adversarial texture was classified as rifle).

54 Joy Buolamwini & Timnit Gebru, *Gender Shades: Intersectional Accuracy Disparities in Commercial Gender Classification*, 81 Proc. Machine Learning Res. 77 (2018). The study's project page with interactive demonstrations is available at gendershades.org.

55 Julia Angwin et al., *Machine Bias*, ProPublica (May 23, 2016), propublica.org/article/machine-bias-risk-assessments-in-criminal-sentencing.

This is why regulating AI is so challenging. The frontier keeps moving. When a once-impossible task becomes possible and routine, we often stop marveling at it as "AI" and instead see it as ordinary software. This living definition means AI is not just defined by technical capabilities but by human perception. When a computer does something clever, we label it AI until it becomes ordinary. AI is just whatever hasn't been done yet.

For legal purposes, this creates significant difficulties. When legislators write statutes regulating "artificial intelligence" or courts adjudicate cases involving "AI systems," the lack of stable definitions becomes a serious problem. What counts as AI today may be ordinary software tomorrow. What seems like routine automation today may be reclassified as AI as our understanding evolves.

The story of AI is still being written, and we are all part of it as users, stakeholders, and citizens of a world increasingly shaped by intelligent machines. In the chapters ahead, we will examine how the law is grappling with this technology, from the regulatory frameworks emerging across states and nations to the fundamental questions of liability, intellectual property, and professional responsibility that AI raises.

Supplemental Resources

- **Neural Networks: Zero to Hero** (karpathy.ai/zero-to-hero.html): Andrej Karpathy's acclaimed video course builds neural networks from scratch, progressing from basic backpropagation to modern GPT architectures. Assumes only basic Python and high school calculus. The best hands-on introduction to deep learning available.

- **Transformer Explainer** (poloclub.github.io/transformer-explainer): An interactive visualization tool that runs GPT-2 in your browser. Experiment with your own text and watch in real time how the internal components process language. No installation required.

- **How Transformer LLMs Work** (deeplearning.ai/short-courses/how-transformer-llms-work): A free short course from DeepLearning.AI explaining how the transformer architecture powers modern language models, with code examples illustrating key components.

- **On the Opportunities and Risks of Foundation Models** (crfm.stanford.edu/report.html): Stanford's comprehensive 2021 report examining the technical, legal, and social implications of large pre-trained AI models. Provides a useful framework for thinking about policy challenges these systems create.

CHAPTER 5

AI Today: Capabilities and Limitations

We have traced the arc of artificial intelligence from the optimistic dreamers at Dartmouth through the cycles of boom and bust, from expert systems to deep learning, from academic curiosity to mainstream technology. Now it is time to take stock of where we actually stand.

This chapter serves as a bridge between history and law. Before we can meaningfully discuss how AI should be regulated, we need a clear-eyed assessment of what AI can and cannot do today. The capabilities are genuinely impressive and continuing to expand at a pace that surprises even researchers in the field. But the limitations are equally real and understanding them is essential for anyone who needs to make legal, policy, or business decisions about AI.

Recall our working definition: artificial intelligence is technology that enables computers to perform tasks that would typically require human intelligence, such as learning from experience, recognizing patterns, making decisions, or understanding language. With that definition in mind, let us examine the current landscape.

The Current State of AI: A Rapidly Moving Target

As of early 2026, the AI landscape is dominated by a handful of large technology companies and research labs developing what are called "frontier models," the most capable AI systems available. The major players include OpenAI (GPT-5 and its variants), Anthropic (Claude), Google DeepMind (Gemini), Meta (Llama), and several Chinese companies including DeepSeek, Alibaba (Qwen), and others.[56]

---

56 The major consumer-facing AI assistants can be accessed at: ChatGPT (chatgpt.com),

The pace of development has been remarkable. In late 2025 alone, within a span of just 25 days, four major AI companies released new flagship models: xAI's Grok 4.1 (November 17), Google's Gemini 3 (November 18), Anthropic's Claude Opus 4.5 (November 24), and OpenAI's GPT-5.2 (December 11).[57] This compression of innovation cycles means that any specific performance claims in this chapter may be outdated by the time you read it. That rapid evolution is itself a crucial fact for regulators and lawyers to understand.

What can these systems do? The answer depends heavily on the specific task, but frontier models now demonstrate remarkable capabilities across multiple domains.

In coding and software development, the leading models can now complete tasks that would take human developers hours. One benchmark (METR's software task evaluation) estimated that Claude Opus 4.5 could complete, with at least 50% reliability, software tasks that take humans nearly five hours.[58] These systems write code, debug programs, and even help maintain complex software projects.

In reasoning and problem-solving, models now achieve near-perfect scores on standardized tests that once seemed impossibly difficult for machines. Gemini 3 Pro achieved 100% accuracy on the AIME 2025 math competition when allowed to use code execution tools. GPT-5.2 scored highest on the FrontierScience benchmark covering Olympiad-level physics, chemistry, and biology problems, though it still falls short of expert-level reasoning on truly novel questions.

In language and communication, these systems produce text that is often indistinguishable from human writing. They can draft legal documents, write marketing copy, translate between languages, and engage in nuanced conversation across virtually any topic. According to a 2025 McKinsey survey, 88% of organizations now report using

---

Claude (claude.ai), Gemini (gemini.google.com), and Perplexity (perplexity.ai).

57 Stanford Inst. for Human-Centered AI, *Artificial Intelligence Index Report 2025* 6 (2025), hai.stanford.edu/ai-index/2025-ai-index-report [hereinafter Stanford HAI AI Index 2025].

58 METR, *Evaluating AI R&D Capabilities (2025)*, metr.org/blog/2025-01-10-evaluating-ai-rd-capabilities.

AI regularly in at least one business function.[59]

The economic implications are substantial. Corporate investment in AI reached $252.3 billion in 2024, with private investment alone up 44.5% from the previous year.[60] Enterprise spending on large language model APIs more than doubled from $3.5 billion to $8.4 billion in just six months during 2025.[61] ChatGPT has approximately 800 million users globally.[62]

Perhaps most striking is the dramatic reduction in costs. Performance that cost $20 per million tokens[63] when GPT-3.5 launched in November 2022 dropped to roughly $0.07 per million tokens by late 2024, a 280-fold reduction. This democratization of access means that capabilities once available only to well-funded research labs are now accessible to startups, small businesses, and individuals.

What AI Actually Does: A Technical Primer for Legal Purposes

To understand AI's capabilities and limitations, it helps to have a basic grasp of how modern systems work. You do not need to become a machine learning engineer, but some technical literacy is essential for anyone working with AI-related legal questions.

Modern AI systems, particularly large language models (LLMs), are fundamentally prediction machines. They are trained on enormous datasets of text (essentially much of the internet, plus books, articles, and other content) and learn statistical patterns about how words and concepts relate to each other. When you ask an AI system a question, it is not "looking up" the answer in a database. Instead, it is generating a response word by word, predicting which word is most

---

59 McKinsey & Co., *The State of AI: How Organizations Are Rewiring to Capture Value* (May 2025), mckinsey.com/capabilities/quantumblack/our-insights/the-state-of-ai.

60 Stanford HAI AI Index 2025, *supra* note 57, at 12.

61 Menlo Ventures, *The State of Generative AI in the Enterprise* (2025), menlovc.com/perspective/the-state-of-generative-ai-in-the-enterprise-2025.

62 *Id.*

63 A token is the basic unit of text that AI models process. Tokens are typically words or parts of words; for English text, one token roughly equals three-quarters of a word. The phrase "artificial intelligence" would be about three tokens.

likely to come next given everything that came before.

This is a crucial point that bears emphasis. These systems do not "know" things in the way humans know things. They have learned statistical associations between concepts, which often produces responses that appear knowledgeable but can also produce confident nonsense.

The key technical components worth understanding include:

Training data is the raw material from which AI learns. The quality, quantity, and biases present in training data directly affect what the system can do and how it behaves. Training data for frontier models includes hundreds of billions of pages of text, images, and other content. This creates both capability and liability. The system has been exposed to vast knowledge, but it has also absorbed every bias, error, and problematic content present in that data.

Parameters are the numerical values inside a neural network that get adjusted during training. Think of them as the settings that determine how the system responds to any given input. Frontier models now have hundreds of billions of parameters. GPT-3 had 175 billion; current leading models have significantly more. More parameters generally means more capability, but also more cost and complexity.[64]

Inference is what happens when you actually use a trained model. You provide input (a question, a document, an image), and the model processes it through its learned parameters to generate output. Each time you interact with ChatGPT or Claude, you are running inference. Think of it like a musician who has spent years practicing: training is the years of practice, while inference is the actual performance.[65]

Context windows determine how much information the model can

---

64 AI & SAP Basis Wizard, *AI Explained: What Does the Number of Parameters in an LLM Mean*? youtube.com/watch?v=dPalBLlA5yQ.

65 IBM, *AI Inference: The Secret to AI's Superpowers*, youtube.com/watch?v=XtT5i0ZeH-HE.

consider at once. Early models could only process a few thousand tokens at a time. Current frontier models can handle hundreds of thousands of tokens, meaning they can read and consider entire books or codebases in a single interaction.[66]

Fine-tuning and alignment are processes used to adjust a trained model's behavior. A base model trained on internet text might produce responses that are unhelpful, offensive, or dangerous. Through techniques like reinforcement learning from human feedback (RLHF), developers train models to be more helpful, honest, and harmless. This is an imperfect process, and the tensions between capability and safety remain an active area of research and concern.[67]

The Hallucination Problem

Perhaps no limitation of current AI systems is more legally significant than the phenomenon known as hallucination: the tendency of AI systems to generate confident-sounding statements that are factually false.

Hallucinations are not bugs that will be fixed with a software update. They are a structural feature of how these systems work. Because AI models predict likely text rather than retrieve verified facts, they can generate plausible-sounding nonsense with the same fluency and confidence as accurate information.

The legal profession has already experienced this directly. In the now-infamous case of *Mata v. Avianca*, a New York attorney used ChatGPT for legal research and submitted a brief citing multiple cases that did not exist. The AI had invented case names, citations, and even quotes from fictional judicial opinions. When the court discovered the fabrications, the attorney faced sanctions and public embarrassment.[68] Similar incidents have occurred across jurisdictions.

---

66 IBM, *What is a Context Window? Unlocking LLM Secrets*, youtube.com/watch?v=-QVoIxEpFkM.

67 IBM, *Fine Tuning Large Language Models with InstructLab*, youtube.com/watch?v=pu3-PeBG0YU

68 *Mata v. Avianca, Inc.*, 678 F. Supp. 3d 443, 448 (S.D.N.Y. 2023).

In October 2025, Deloitte submitted a report to the Australian government containing hallucinated academic sources and a fabricated quote from a federal court judgment. The company had to issue a revised report and partial refund.[69] The following month, another Deloitte report for the government of Newfoundland and Labrador was found to contain at least four citations to research papers that do not exist.[70]

How common are hallucinations? The rates vary significantly depending on the model, task, and domain. For well-optimized frontier models on straightforward factual tasks, hallucination rates can be below 1%. Google's Gemini-2.0-Flash-001 and certain OpenAI models report rates as low as 0.7% to 0.9% on factual consistency benchmarks.[71] But for complex tasks, specialized domains, or less optimized models, rates can climb to 5% to 10% or higher. Some analyses suggest professional services applications see hallucination rates around 37%.

A September 2025 research paper from OpenAI offered a revealing explanation: hallucinations occur in part because standard training and evaluation procedures reward guessing over acknowledging uncertainty. When AI systems are trained and tested in ways that penalize saying "I don't know," they learn to produce confident answers even when confidence is unwarranted.[72]

This has direct legal implications. Any professional relying on AI-generated content, whether for legal briefs, medical advice, financial analysis, or journalistic reporting, must verify the output independently. The confident, authoritative tone of AI responses can

---

69 Josh Taylor, *Deloitte Revises Report for Australian Government After Fake AI-Generated Sources Found*, The Guardian (Oct. 24, 2025), theguardian.com/australia-news/2025/oct/24/deloitte-revises-report-for-australian-government-after-fake-ai-generated-sources-found.

70 Elizabeth Whitten, *N.L. Asks Deloitte to Carry Out Review After 'Incorrect' Citations Found in $1.6M Provincial Health Plan*, CBC News (Nov. 24, 2025), cbc.ca/news/canada/newfoundland-labrador/nl-deloitte-citations-9.6990216.

71 Vectara, *Hallucination Evaluation Model Leaderboard* (2025), huggingface.co/spaces/vectara/Hallucination-evaluation-leaderboard.

72 OpenAI, *Prover-Verifier Games Improve Legibility of LLM Outputs* (Sept. 2025), cdn.openai.com/prover-verifier-games-improve-legibility-of-llm-outputs/legibility.pdf.

be deeply misleading about the reliability of the underlying content.

The Black Box Problem

A second significant limitation involves explainability, or more accurately, the lack of it. Modern AI systems, particularly deep learning models, make decisions based on patterns learned from data in ways that resist easy interpretation.

Unlike the expert systems of the 1980s, which followed explicit rules that could be examined and explained, deep learning models operate as "black boxes." We know the inputs (training data and architecture), and we can observe the outputs (model responses), but the process connecting them involves billions of mathematical operations that do not translate into human-readable explanations.

This creates challenges across multiple legal contexts. In employment decisions, if an AI system recommends against hiring a candidate, can the employer explain why? Fair housing regulations may require explanations for credit denials or adverse rental decisions. Due process concerns arise when AI systems influence criminal sentencing, parole decisions, or government benefits determinations.

Some jurisdictions are beginning to require "explainability audits" for AI systems used in consequential decisions like hiring and lending. The EU AI Act, which we will examine in detail in later chapters, imposes transparency requirements for certain high-risk AI applications. But the technology itself often cannot provide the kind of explanations these requirements contemplate.

Research into AI interpretability is advancing. Anthropic's 2025 work on "Tracing the Thoughts of a Large Language Model" identified internal circuits that influence when Claude declines to answer questions versus when it generates responses.[73] This research found that hallucinations can occur when internal mechanisms that should prevent responses are incorrectly inhibited. But such interpretability work remains largely a research endeavor rather than a practical tool

---

73 Anthropic, *Tracing the Thoughts of a Large Language Model* (Mar. 2025), anthropic.com/research/tracing-thoughts-language-model.

for everyday use.

Bias and Fairness

AI systems can perpetuate and amplify biases present in their training data. This is not speculation; it has been documented repeatedly across different types of AI applications.

Facial recognition systems have been shown to perform worse on darker-skinned faces, a finding documented in the landmark "Gender Shades" study by Joy Buolamwini and Timnit Gebru.[74] Criminal risk assessment algorithms have exhibited racial disparities, as revealed by ProPublica's 2016 investigation into the COMPAS system.[75] Hiring algorithms trained on historical data can learn to discriminate against women if past hiring patterns were discriminatory.

The problem is not that AI developers intentionally build biased systems. The problem is that AI systems learn from data that reflects existing societal biases, and they can encode those biases in ways that are difficult to detect and correct.

Training data for large language models includes content from across the internet, which encompasses everything from scientific papers to social media posts to historical documents. If the training data contains more positive associations with certain demographic groups and negative associations with others, the model may learn those associations. If the training data underrepresents certain populations, the model may perform worse when dealing with topics or questions relevant to those populations.

By the late 2010s, AI bias had become a topic of significant public concern. Conferences that once focused solely on technical research began hosting workshops on algorithmic fairness and social responsibility. The field of "AI ethics" emerged as a recognized

---

74 Joy Buolamwini & Timnit Gebru, *Gender Shades: Intersectional Accuracy Disparities in Commercial Gender Classification*, 81 Proc. Machine Learning Res. 77 (2018), gender-shades.org.

75 Julia Angwin et al., *Machine Bias, ProPublica* (May 23, 2016), propublica.org/article/machine-bias-risk-assessments-in-criminal-sentencing.

discipline. But translating ethical concerns into technical solutions and legal requirements remains challenging.

Agentic AI: The Next Frontier

As capable as current AI systems are, they have traditionally been reactive: you ask a question, they provide an answer. You give a task, they complete it. But a significant shift is underway toward what is called "agentic AI," systems designed to act autonomously over multiple steps to accomplish complex goals.

According to McKinsey's 2025 survey, 23% of organizations are already scaling agentic AI systems somewhere in their enterprises, and an additional 39% have begun experimenting with AI agents. [76]These systems can plan multi-step workflows, use external tools (search engines, calculators, code interpreters), learn from outcomes, and make decisions with reduced human oversight.

The potential applications are substantial. AI agents that can manage customer service interactions from start to finish, coordinate complex research projects, or operate software systems autonomously. Microsoft's Copilot agents now handle tasks from coding to meeting summaries across its software suite.

But agentic AI also amplifies existing concerns. An AI that can take autonomous action in the world, not just generate text, raises more acute questions about liability, oversight, and control. If an AI agent makes a harmful decision while pursuing a goal, who is responsible? How do we ensure appropriate human oversight when the system is designed to operate independently?

2025 has been called the "year of agents," with major AI labs racing to develop and deploy autonomous capabilities. Anthropic's Model Context Protocol (MCP) enables AI systems to connect to external data sources and tools.[77] OpenAI and Google have released similar agent-oriented features. The regulatory frameworks we examine in

---

76 McKinsey & Co., *supra* note 59.

77 Anthropic, *Introducing the Model Context Protocol* (Nov. 2024), anthropic.com/news/model-context-protocol.

coming chapters were largely designed before agentic AI became prominent, creating potential gaps between technological capability and legal oversight.

AI in Your Daily Life

Before examining regulation, it is worth pausing to recognize how thoroughly AI has already embedded itself in daily experience. This pervasiveness matters because it shapes both the stakes of AI regulation and the practical challenges of implementing it.

The autocorrect and predictive text on your phone use AI language models. Your email spam filter is trained AI. When your bank flags an unusual login for additional verification, that is an AI security system detecting anomalies. Netflix and Spotify recommendations, facial recognition to unlock devices, voice assistants like Alexa and Siri, navigation apps that predict traffic are all AI applications.

In healthcare, AI systems assist with medical imaging, drug discovery, and clinical decision support. In finance, AI powers fraud detection, algorithmic trading, and credit scoring. In transportation, AI enables advanced driver assistance systems and, increasingly, autonomous vehicle features. In creative industries, AI generates images, writes marketing copy, and even produces music.[78]

This ubiquity creates regulatory challenges. AI is not a single product or industry that can be addressed with targeted legislation. It is a general-purpose technology that touches virtually every sector of the economy and every aspect of modern life. Regulating AI effectively requires grappling with this breadth while still crafting rules specific enough to be meaningful.

---

78 For image generation, the leading tools include Midjourney (midjourney.com), DALL-E (integrated into ChatGPT at chatgpt.com), and Stable Diffusion (stability.ai). For AI-assisted coding, *see* GitHub Copilot (github.com/features/copilot) and Cursor (cursor.com).

Supplemental Resources

- **Try the Major AI Tools** (The best way to understand what AI can do is to use it yourself. The major AI assistants all offer free tiers):
    - **ChatGPT** (chatgpt.com): OpenAI's flagship conversational AI, the application that brought generative AI to mainstream attention.
    - **Claude** (claude.ai): Anthropic's AI assistant, designed with a focus on safety and helpfulness.
    - **Gemini** (gemini.google.com): Google's multimodal AI, integrated across Google's product ecosystem.
    - **Perplexity** (perplexity.ai): AI-powered search engine that provides sourced answers to questions.
    - **Midjourney** (midjourney.com): Leading AI image generation tool, known for artistic quality.
    - **GitHub Copilot** (github.com/features/copilot) AI coding assistant that suggests code as you type.

- **A.I. Revolution** (youtube.com/watch?v=-sB12gk9ESA): NOVA PBS documentary providing a comprehensive overview of AI's current capabilities and societal implications. Excellent introduction for general audiences.

- **Stanford HAI AI Index Report** (hai.stanford.edu/ai-index/2025-ai-index-report): The most comprehensive annual survey of AI progress, investment, and policy developments. Essential reading for tracking the field.

- **McKinsey, The State of AI** (mckinsey.com/capabilities/quantumblack/our-insights/the-state-of-ai): Annual survey of enterprise adoption patterns, revealing how organizations actually use AI.

CHAPTER 6

Developing a Regulatory Perspective

When the internet first emerged as a transformative technology, lawyers who understood it were specialists. Today, the internet is simply part of how law is practiced. Artificial intelligence is following the same trajectory. It is already influencing a wide range of legal fields, from contract law and intellectual property to healthcare, torts, and beyond. As AI becomes more integrated into society and business, it will touch every area of law.

This raises an important question: how should lawyers develop expertise in a field that is rapidly becoming inseparable from everything else?

Two Paths Forward

For most lawyers, the goal will not be to specialize in AI itself but to gain a working understanding of how it intersects with their own practice areas. An intellectual property lawyer must be able to evaluate whether an AI-generated work qualifies for copyright protection. A medical malpractice attorney will need to understand how to assess responsibility when diagnostic tools rely on machine learning. A tort lawyer will be asked to untangle questions of liability when no human directly caused the harm.

This book is designed to help lawyers across disciplines develop the background knowledge they need to navigate these changes. You do not need to become a computer scientist or an AI researcher. But you do need enough technical literacy to ask the right questions, evaluate AI-related claims, and understand the legal issues that arise.

At the same time, a new kind of legal expert is emerging. These are AI-focused attorneys who work directly with the technology itself, helping to shape the rules, regulations, and business models that define it. They may advise AI startups on regulatory compliance, design policy frameworks for government agencies, negotiate licensing agreements for training data, or play a role in efforts to ensure that AI is developed responsibly. These lawyers will have a direct influence on whether innovation proceeds thoughtfully or recklessly, and on whether the United States continues to lead in technological development or cedes ground to competitors.

The chapters that follow will explore the substantive legal issues that lawyers in either role will need to understand.

Regulatory Principles

Given the capabilities and limitations we surveyed in the previous chapter, several principles emerge that should guide how we think about AI regulation. These are not abstract observations; they are practical considerations that any effective regulatory framework must address. They also reflect my own perspective, developed over more than a decade of watching law struggle to keep pace with advancing technologies, from Bitcoin and blockchain to decentralized finance and now artificial intelligence.

Regulatory Principle 1: AI is powerful and economically significant, and regulation must account for this reality. This is not a technology that can be ignored or wished away. Organizations across every industry are adopting AI, and the pace of adoption is accelerating. Any regulatory framework must account for the legitimate value these systems provide. This means that proposals involving moratoriums on development or purposeful limitations on capabilities are probably not realistic, especially in light of national security concerns and the overall value of developing this technology within the United States.

International competitiveness is a legitimate consideration here. Regulation that drives AI development offshore does not protect Americans; it simply ensures that the United States has no seat at the table when the rules are being written. Other nations, particularly China, are investing heavily in AI capabilities and will not pause their efforts because American regulators have concerns. This is not a license to ignore harms, but it is a factor that serious regulation must weigh. The goal should be thoughtful governance that addresses real risks while preserving American leadership in a transformative technology.

Regulatory Principle 2: AI has real limitations and risks that regulation must address directly. Hallucinations, bias, lack of explainability, and the challenges of agentic autonomy are not hypothetical concerns. They have already produced legal, medical, financial, and other harms. These limitations are not simply engineering problems awaiting technical fixes; they are structural features of how current AI systems work.

Effective AI regulation cannot treat these issues as problems that will solve themselves through market forces or technological progress. They require direct engagement. This does not mean that every risk warrants a regulatory response, or that regulation is always the best tool. But it does mean that regulators cannot simply defer to industry assurances that problems will be addressed eventually. Some risks require affirmative intervention.

Regulatory Principle 3: Regulatory burdens should be proportional to actual risks. Not all AI applications pose the same level of concern. An AI system recommending movies presents fundamentally different risks than one making parole recommendations or medical diagnoses. Effective regulation recognizes these differences and calibrates its requirements accordingly.

This is the insight behind risk-based regulatory frameworks like the EU AI Act, which categorizes AI systems by risk level and imposes escalating obligations. Low-risk applications face minimal requirements; high-risk applications in areas like employment, credit, healthcare, and law enforcement face stricter oversight. The approach makes intuitive sense: requiring the same compliance burden for a chatbot answering customer service questions as for an algorithm determining prison sentences would be both inefficient and inequitable.

Proportionality also counsels against regulating based on hypothetical capabilities rather than demonstrated harms. Science fiction scenarios about superintelligent AI may be worth monitoring, but they should not drive regulatory frameworks that burden today's actual applications. Regulation should be grounded in evidence about real-world impacts, not speculation about future possibilities.

Regulatory Principle 4: Regulation should focus on human activity rather than technical definitions. The technology is evolving faster than traditional regulatory processes. By the time a typical legislative process produces a new law, the technology it addresses could have transformed multiple times. This creates tension between the need for regulatory clarity and the risk of rules that are obsolete before they take effect.

The "living definition" problem we discussed in Chapter 2 has practical regulatory consequences: when the definition of AI keeps shifting, when what counts as AI today becomes ordinary software tomorrow, creating stable legal frameworks becomes extraordinarily difficult.

The best way to future-proof AI regulation is, where possible, to focus on human conduct and outcomes rather than attempting to define and regulate specific technical architectures.

This approach also ensures that accountability attaches to actors who can actually be held responsible. AI systems cannot be sued, jailed, or shamed into compliance. Humans can. Regulation should trace responsibility back to the developers who build these systems, the deployers who put them into use, and the organizations that benefit from their operation. When something goes wrong, there must be a human or institution capable of answering for it.

But focusing on human activity does not mean that every human in the chain should bear responsibility for every outcome. A developer who builds a general-purpose AI tool should not automatically be liable because someone far downstream uses that tool for a harmful purpose the developer never intended and could not reasonably have anticipated. The goal is to place accountability where meaningful control actually exists, not to create a regime where building powerful technology is itself a basis for unlimited liability. Getting this balance right is one of the central challenges of AI regulation.

Regulatory Principle 5: AI does not fit neatly into existing regulatory categories. The difficulty of placing accountability appropriately is compounded by the fact that AI does not fit neatly into any single legal category. It cuts across product liability, professional responsibility, data privacy, intellectual property, and consumer protection simultaneously, often raising questions in several of these domains at once. Effective AI governance requires thinking across traditional legal silos and recognizing that AI may require new frameworks rather than simply extending old ones.

This is particularly true for trying to proportion liability when an AI augmented product fails. Traditional product liability assumes that a defective product can be examined, that the defect can be identified, and that the manufacturer can be shown to have done something wrong. AI complicates each of these assumptions.

Many AI systems operate as black boxes, producing outputs through processes that even their developers cannot fully explain. When an AI system makes a harmful decision, it may be genuinely impossible to point to a specific flaw in the way one might identify a cracked weld or a contaminated ingredient. This opacity challenges the foundational logic of fault-based liability and may require us to think differently about how losses are allocated. Concepts like mandatory insurance requirements, strict liability frameworks, or shared responsibility pools may prove more practical than traditional negligence analysis when the internal workings of a system resist meaningful inspection.

Regulatory Principle 6: Prefer transparency over prohibition. Where possible, regulation should favor disclosure requirements over outright bans. Let people make informed choices rather than having regulators decide what they can access. This is a less paternalistic approach that respects autonomy while still addressing potential harms.

Transparency requirements serve multiple purposes. They enable consumers and businesses to understand what they are interacting with. They allow researchers and regulators to identify problems. They create accountability without necessarily restricting beneficial uses. And they preserve space for innovation while ensuring that risks are visible.

This is not an absolute principle. Some AI applications may pose risks serious enough to warrant prohibition rather than mere disclosure. But the default should be transparency: require AI systems to identify themselves, require developers to disclose relevant information about how systems work, require deployers to inform users when AI is making consequential decisions. Many harms can be addressed through information rather than restriction.

Regulatory Principle 7: AI should remain politically unrestrained. Free expression values should extend to AI systems. The government should not mandate what AI can or cannot say on matters of political, social, or cultural controversy. This principle distinguishes the American approach from that of authoritarian regimes.

Consider China's approach to AI, discussed in Chapter 14. Chinese AI systems are required to "embody core socialist values" and are prohibited from generating content that "subverts state power" or "undermines national unity."[79] These systems cannot discuss certain historical events, cannot criticize government policies, and must reflect official positions on contested issues. The result is AI that serves as a tool of state ideology rather than a neutral technology.

American AI should not be subject to similar constraints, whether from government mandate or excessive private censorship. Users should be able to ask AI systems about controversial topics and receive informative, balanced responses. AI should be able to discuss multiple perspectives on contested issues.

While reasonable people may disagree about where exactly to draw lines around harmful content, the baseline should be freedom rather than restriction.

Regulatory Principle 8: Technological capability does not override existing rights. The fact that AI makes something technically possible does not mean that society should necessarily permit it. This

---

79 Cyberspace Admin. of China, *Interim Measures for the Management of Generative Artificial Intelligence Services* arts. 4, 7 (effective Aug. 15, 2023), translation available at chinalawtranslate.com/en/generative-ai-interim.

principle cuts against a certain techno-libertarian view that whatever can be done should be allowed, that existing legal frameworks are merely obstacles to be engineered around.

Consider the training data question in intellectual property law. AI systems can scrape vast quantities of copyrighted material from the internet. The technology makes it easy. But ease of copying does not extinguish the property rights of creators. The fact that AI can read every book ever published does not automatically mean that publishers and authors have no say in how their works are used.

The same principle applies across domains. AI can enable surveillance at unprecedented scales, but privacy rights do not disappear because monitoring has become cheap. AI can make discriminatory decisions efficiently, but civil rights protections do not yield to algorithmic convenience. AI can generate deepfakes and disinformation, but the harms of deception do not become acceptable because the technology is impressive.

Regulation must hold the line: existing rights and protections apply to AI-enabled conduct just as they apply to human conduct. New capabilities do not create new exemptions.

The Current Regulatory Landscape

These eight principles inform my assessment of the various state and federal approaches we will examine throughout this book. Not every regulation will satisfy all eight principles, and reasonable people may weight them differently. But having a principled framework helps distinguish thoughtful governance from regulatory theater and genuine protection from innovation-killing overreach.

Before diving into specific legal issues, it is worth stepping back to appreciate the extraordinary regulatory uncertainty that defines this moment. The United States has no comprehensive federal law governing artificial intelligence. Instead, we have a patchwork of state laws, federal agency guidance, executive orders, and voluntary industry standards that often conflict with one another.

Chapter 8 examines this landscape in detail: the specific state laws, the federal initiatives, the constitutional questions, and the practical compliance challenges. For now, the key point is that anyone working in this space must navigate profound uncertainty. The rules are being written in real time, and they may well be rewritten again before the ink dries.

What Lies Ahead

At this point, we have traced the history of artificial intelligence, developed a basic understanding of the underlying technologies and their scope, and established a principled framework for how the law may develop.

In the chapters that follow, we will examine several flashpoints where AI technology and law are coming to a head: intellectual property (Chapter 9), automated decision-making and liability (Chapter 10), transparency rules for generative content (Chapter 11), privacy and surveillance (Chapter 12), and national security (Chapter 13). We will also explore the global regulatory landscape (Chapter 14) and spend time discussing the impact this technology will have on the practice of law itself (Chapter 15), including attempting to answer the question of whether it will put you out of a job.[80]

But before we turn to these substantive issues, a fundamental question must be addressed that will shape many of the discussions to come: how should transformative technology and frontier AI models be developed? Should they be open or closed? The next chapter explores the legal and policy implications of that choice.

---

80 Eventually for most of us. Sorry.

Supplemental Resources

- **House Task Force on AI Final Report** (obernolte.house.gov/AITFReport): The December 2024 bipartisan report from Rep. Jay Obernolte's task force outlining a congressional agenda for AI regulation. Essential reading for understanding legislative priorities.
- **OECD AI Principles** (oecd.ai/en/ai-principles): The foundational international framework for responsible AI governance, updated in 2024. Adopted by the G20 and influential in shaping the EU AI Act.
- **NIST AI Risk Management Framework** (nist.gov/itl/ai-risk-management-framework): The U.S. government's voluntary framework for managing AI risks, providing practical guidance for organizations developing or deploying AI systems.
- **CSIS Wadhwani AI Center** (csis.org/programs/wadhwani-ai-center): The Center for Strategic and International Studies' dedicated AI policy program, producing regular analysis on governance, national security, and international competition.
- **Brookings AI Policy Incubator** (brookings.edu/collection/brookings-ai-policy-idea-incubator): Brookings Institution's initiative bringing together stakeholders to inform AI policy debates, with reports on frontier AI regulation and U.S. competitiveness.
- **The AI Policy Podcast** (csis.org/podcasts/ai-policy-podcast): CSIS's biweekly podcast featuring discussions with policymakers, industry leaders, and academics on AI regulation, innovation, and national security.

CHAPTER 7

Open Source and Foundation Models

Before we examine how the law applies to specific AI applications, we need to address a more fundamental question: how should these systems be built and distributed in the first place?

This might seem like a technical or business question rather than a legal one. But the choice between open and closed approaches to AI development has profound downstream effects on nearly every legal issue we will discuss in this book. It affects who can be held liable when AI causes harm. It shapes what transparency and disclosure requirements are even possible. It determines whether regulators can meaningfully audit AI systems. It influences who has access to powerful technology and who gets left behind.

The debate is not abstract. It is playing out right now in courtrooms, boardrooms, and legislative chambers. Understanding it is important background for everything that follows.

The Founding Promise

In December 2015, a group of researchers and entrepreneurs announced the creation of OpenAI, a nonprofit artificial intelligence research laboratory. The founding team included Sam Altman, who would become its CEO, and Elon Musk, who provided much of the early funding. The stated mission was ambitious: to develop artificial general intelligence for the benefit of humanity, not for the profit of any single company.

A key part of that mission was openness. The founders worried that if a company like Google achieved a breakthrough in AI, it might keep that technology proprietary, concentrating immense power in private hands. OpenAI would be different. It would share its research openly so that powerful AI could not be controlled by any one entity.

The name itself was a statement of intent: *Open* AI.

That vision did not survive contact with reality. Training increasingly powerful AI models required enormous computational resources, far more than a nonprofit could sustain. In 2019, OpenAI created a "capped-profit" subsidiary to attract investment.[81] Microsoft eventually invested over $13 billion.[82] By the time ChatGPT launched in late 2022 and became the fastest-growing consumer application in history, OpenAI was, despite its name, a largely closed operation. Its most advanced models were proprietary. Its training data and methods were trade secrets.

In 2024, Elon Musk sued OpenAI and Sam Altman, alleging they had betrayed the organization's founding mission.[83] The lawsuit claims Musk was induced to provide approximately $45 million in early funding based on promises that OpenAI would remain a nonprofit committed to openness. Musk's complaint argues that OpenAI has become a for-profit enterprise beholden to Microsoft, the exact outcome the organization was created to prevent.

OpenAI has called the lawsuit "baseless" and accused Musk of bringing it to benefit his own AI company, xAI.[84] In May 2026, a jury rejected Musk's claims, finding the suit was initiated after the statute of limitations had lapsed.[85]

Musk has vowed to appeal his loss, but whatever the outcome, the lawsuit crystallizes a fundamental tension in AI development. Should the most powerful AI systems be open, allowing anyone

---

81 OpenAI, *OpenAI LP* (Mar. 11, 2019), openai.com/index/openai-lp.

82 Microsoft announced a $10 billion investment in OpenAI in January 2023. *See Satya Nadella & Sam Altman, Microsoft and OpenAI Extend Partnership* (Jan. 23, 2023), blogs.microsoft.com/blog/2023/01/23/microsoftandopenaiextendpartnership.

83 Complaint, *Musk v. Altman*, No. 4:24-cv-04722 (N.D. Cal. filed Aug. 5, 2024).

84 OpenAI, *OpenAI and Elon Musk* (Mar. 5, 2024), openai.com/index/openai-elon-musk.

85 Cade Metz, *Elon Musk Loses $150 Billion Suit Against OpenAI and Sam Altman*, NY Times (May. 19, 2026), nytimes.com/2026/05/18/technology/elon-musk-lawsuit-openai-sam-altman.html.

to inspect, modify, and deploy them? Or should they be closed, controlled by companies that can implement safety measures and be held accountable for misuse? The answer has enormous implications for law, policy, and society.

What Open Actually Means

Before going further, we need to clarify what "open" means in this context, because the term is used loosely and sometimes misleadingly. Traditional open-source software, like the Linux operating system or the Apache web server, comes with source code that anyone can read, modify, and redistribute. This openness has driven enormous innovation. Much of the internet runs on open-source software.

AI models are different. A large language model is not simply code; it is the product of a training process that transforms code plus data plus massive computational resources into a set of numerical parameters, often called weights, that determine how the model behaves. When people talk about "open" AI models, they usually mean one of several different things.

First, open weights means the trained model parameters are publicly available. Anyone can download the model and run it on their own hardware. This is what most people mean when they refer to open-source AI, though purists object to that terminology.

Second, open training data means the dataset used to train the model is disclosed or made available. This is rarer, because training data often includes copyrighted material or content scraped from the internet without clear permission.

Third, open training methodology means the techniques used to train the model are documented in enough detail that others could replicate the process. This is valuable for scientific reproducibility but does not by itself give anyone access to the trained model.

A model can be open in some of these senses but not others. Meta's Llama models, for example, release weights under a license that allows most uses, but Meta does not disclose the training data or provide enough detail to replicate the training process from scratch.

DeepSeek, a Chinese AI lab, released its R1 model in January 2025 with open weights, extensive documentation of training techniques, and a permissive license, but still did not release its training data.[86]

The Open Source Initiative, which maintains the widely accepted definition of open-source software, has argued that many supposedly open AI models do not truly qualify as open source because they include restrictions on use or do not provide enough information for full reproducibility.[87] This definitional debate matters for licensing and intellectual property purposes.

The Open Model Ecosystem Today

The landscape of open AI models has transformed dramatically over the past two years.

Before 2025, the open model ecosystem was dominated by Meta's Llama family. Meta, the company behind Facebook and Instagram, made a strategic bet on open models as a way to compete with closed competitors like OpenAI and Google. By releasing Llama openly, Meta hoped to build a developer ecosystem around its technology, reduce its dependence on competitors' AI services, and benefit from outside contributions that improved its models.

Then, in January 2025, the Chinese AI lab DeepSeek released its R1 reasoning model. The impact was immediate and significant.

DeepSeek R1 achieved performance comparable to the best closed models on reasoning benchmarks, but it was released under an MIT license, one of the most permissive open-source licenses available.[88] Anyone could download it, run it, modify it, or use it commercially with essentially no restrictions. The model came with detailed documentation of the training techniques that made it work.

86 DeepSeek, *DeepSeek-R1 Release* (Jan. 20, 2025), api-docs.deepseek.com/news/news250120.

87 Open Source Initiative, *The Open Source AI Definition* (Oct. 28, 2024), opensource.org/ai/open-source-ai-definition.

88 DeepSeek released R1 under the MIT License. *See* github.com/deepseek-ai/DeepSeek-R1/blob/main/LICENSE.

DeepSeek claimed it trained the model for approximately $6 million, a fraction of the billions spent by competitors like OpenAI.[89]

For the first time since ChatGPT's release, an open model was competing at the frontier of AI capability.

The response from closed AI companies was telling. Sam Altman acknowledged that OpenAI had been "on the wrong side of history" regarding open source.[90] In 2025, OpenAI released its first open-weight models in years. Meanwhile, Chinese labs accelerated their open releases. By mid-2025, downloads on the popular AI platform Hugging Face had shifted from predominantly American models to predominantly Chinese ones.

Why Openness Matters

Proponents of open AI models argue that openness provides crucial benefits that closed systems cannot.

The first benefit is safety through transparency. When model weights are available, independent researchers can examine how systems work and identify potential problems. Security vulnerabilities, biased behaviors, and dangerous capabilities can be discovered and addressed by a global community rather than relying solely on a single company's internal review.

The second benefit is scientific progress. AI advances more rapidly when techniques are shared. DeepSeek's documentation of its training innovations allowed researchers worldwide to build on those methods immediately. Closed development concentrates knowledge; open development distributes it.

The third benefit is democratized access. Training a frontier AI model from scratch can cost hundreds of millions of dollars in compute alone. Open models allow researchers, startups, and organizations in less wealthy countries to participate in AI development without

---

89 *See* DeepSeek, *DeepSeek-V3 Technical Report* (Dec. 2024).

90 Sam Altman (@sama), X (Jan. 28, 2025) ("we will obviously open source some stuff and i think we have been on the wrong side of history here and need to course correct").

those resources. A university researcher can fine-tune an open model for a specialized task that a large company would never prioritize.

The fourth benefit is independence from vendors. Organizations deploying open models are not dependent on a single vendor's continued existence, pricing decisions, or terms of service. They can run models entirely on their own infrastructure, modify them for specific needs, and switch between providers without rebuilding from scratch.

The fifth benefit is checks on concentrated power. If only a handful of well-funded companies control the most powerful AI systems, those companies will have enormous influence over how the technology develops and who benefits from it. Open models distribute that power more broadly.

Why Openness Worries Regulators

Critics of open AI models raise concerns that have captured the attention of policymakers.

The first concern is uncontrollable deployment. Once model weights are released, they cannot be recalled. Anyone can download them, remove safety fine-tuning, and deploy them for any purpose. A closed model provider can revoke access, update safety measures, or refuse to serve malicious users. An open model has no such controls.

The second concern is inadequate safety testing. Some open models have been released without the extensive safety work that closed providers often perform. Testing of DeepSeek R1 shortly after its release found significant safety vulnerabilities. According to security researchers at Cisco in collaboration with the University of Pennsylvania, the model "failed to block a single harmful prompt" when tested against 50 prompts from a standard safety benchmark, exhibiting a 100 percent attack success rate.[91] This contrasted with other leading models, which demonstrated at least partial resistance

---

91 Cisco, *Evaluating Security Risk in DeepSeek and Other Frontier Reasoning Models* (Feb. 2025), blogs.cisco.com/security/evaluating-security-risk-in-deepseek-and-other-frontier-reasoning-models.

to the same attacks.
The third concern is proliferation of dangerous capabilities. As AI systems become more capable, some abilities may be genuinely dangerous to spread widely. The question of whether powerful reasoning models should be freely available to anyone, including those who might use them for malicious purposes, is not purely hypothetical.

The fourth concern is national security. Open American AI models can be adopted and built upon by foreign adversaries. This concern reportedly influenced Meta's strategic reconsideration of its open approach. Congressional proposals have sought to restrict open releases of the most capable models on national security grounds.

Downstream Legal Effects

The choice between open and closed models is not just a policy debate. It has concrete implications for the legal issues we will examine throughout this book.

Consider liability. When a closed model causes harm, there is a clear party to hold responsible: the company that operates it. When an open model is downloaded, modified, fine-tuned, and deployed through a chain of actors before an issuer arises, allocating responsibility becomes far more difficult. Did liability rest with the original developer? The entity that modified it? The company that deployed it? The user who prompted the harmful output? These questions do not have clear answers under current law.

Consider intellectual property. Open models raise distinct copyright questions. If a model trained on copyrighted works is released openly, and someone fine-tunes it to produce outputs that compete with the original works, who is liable for infringement? The training data issues we will discuss in later chapters take on different dimensions depending on whether the resulting model is kept proprietary or released to the world.

Consider transparency and disclosure. Regulations requiring disclosure of AI use or explanation of AI decisions assume that someone controls the AI system and can provide that information. Open models complicate this assumption. A company deploying a modified open model may not fully understand how it works or have the ability to explain its decisions.

Consider safety regulation. Some regulatory approaches focus on controlling AI at the point of development, requiring safety testing before release. This works for closed models, where the developer controls distribution. It is far less effective for open models, where anyone can access the technology regardless of whether it has passed regulatory review.

Consider competition and antitrust. The open-versus-closed debate intersects with competition policy. Open models may promote competition by allowing new entrants to build on existing technology. But they may also be used strategically by dominant players to commoditize competitors' advantages. Meta's open-source strategy, for instance, can be understood partly as an effort to prevent OpenAI and Google from establishing unchallengeable leads in proprietary AI.

Licensing as a Middle Ground

Some developers have attempted to find a middle ground between fully open and fully closed approaches through specialized licensing. Traditional open-source licenses like MIT or Apache 2.0 allow essentially unrestricted use. A model released under such a license can be used for any purpose, including purposes the original developer might find harmful.

In response, the AI community has developed what are sometimes called Responsible AI Licenses ("RAILs") that attempt to combine open access with restrictions on harmful uses.[92] A model released under such a license might be freely available for most purposes but prohibit specific applications: generating misinformation, creating deepfakes, discriminating against protected classes, or providing medical advice without appropriate oversight.

---

92 RAIL Initiative, licenses.ai.

These licenses attempt to propagate restrictions through the chain of distribution. If you modify a model released under such a license and release your modified version, you must include the same use restrictions.

This approach faces significant challenges. Enforcing behavioral restrictions requires monitoring how downstream users actually employ the model, a level of surveillance that most organizations cannot practically conduct. And because there is typically no direct contractual relationship between the original developer and distant downstream users, the developer may have no legal standing to enforce restrictions against them.

Some critics argue that these licenses create an illusion of control without the reality. Others contend that they at least establish norms and may deter some misuse, even if perfect enforcement is impossible.

Looking Ahead

The tension between open and closed approaches to AI development will not be resolved quickly. Both models will likely coexist, serving different purposes and different constituencies.

What is clear is that these structural choices have profound implications for law and policy. A regulatory framework designed for a world of closed, centrally controlled AI systems will not work well for open models that anyone can deploy. A liability regime that assumes clear chains of responsibility will struggle with open models that pass through multiple hands before causing harm.

As you read the chapters that follow, keep the open-versus-closed distinction in mind. The legal questions we will examine, from copyright to liability to privacy to professional responsibility, often have different answers depending on whether the AI system in question is controlled by a single entity or distributed freely to the world.

The *Musk v. OpenAI* lawsuit, whatever its outcome, has already served an important purpose: it has made visible a debate that might otherwise remain hidden in technical communities. How AI systems are structured, who controls them, and who can access them are not just engineering decisions. They are choices that will shape the legal, economic, and social landscape for decades to come.

Supplemental Resources

- **Open Source vs Closed AI: LLMs, Agents & the AI Stack Explained** (youtube.com/watch?v=_QfxGZGITGw): Video explainer covering the technical and strategic differences between open and closed AI development approaches, including implications for LLMs and AI agents.
- **Open Model vs Closed Model in AI** (youtube.com/watch?v=vRtHC5YgN1w): Accessible overview of the open versus closed model debate, covering the tradeoffs in transparency, safety, and innovation.
- **Stanford HAI Reports on Open Foundation Models** (hai.stanford.edu): Academic research on the policy implications of open versus closed approaches to AI development.
- **Open Source Initiative: Open Source AI Definition** (opensource.org): The OSI's perspective on what qualifies as genuinely open source in the AI context.

CHAPTER 8

Federal and State Regulation of AI

As artificial intelligence moves from experimental labs into mainstream applications, governments are beginning to grapple with how best to regulate it. In the United States, both federal and state lawmakers have taken steps to address the legal, ethical, and economic implications of AI, though their approaches differ dramatically in scope, speed, and strategy.

This chapter provides a snapshot of the law as it currently exists in the United States. Readers should treat it as exactly that: a snapshot of a rapidly moving target. By the time you read these words, new laws will have been proposed, old ones amended, and the federal-state dynamic could have shifted in ways we cannot predict. Nonetheless, understanding the regulatory framework as it has developed provides essential context for the substantive legal issues examined in subsequent chapters.

The Federal Landscape

There is currently no comprehensive federal AI law in the United States. To date, Congress has only enacted two significant pieces of AI-related legislation:

> **The National Artificial Intelligence Initiative Act of 2020**, signed during President Trump's first term, established a coordinated federal initiative to accelerate AI research, development, and workforce training across federal agencies.[93] It created the National Artificial Intelligence Initiative Office within

93 National Artificial Intelligence Initiative Act of 2020, Pub. L. No. 116-283, div. E, 134 Stat. 4523 (codified at 15 U.S.C. §§ 9401–9461).

the White House Office of Science and Technology Policy and directed NIST to develop voluntary AI standards and risk management frameworks.

The Take It Down Act, signed into law in May 2025, criminalizes the publication of nonconsensual intimate images, including AI-generated deepfakes, and requires online platforms to remove such content within 48 hours of receiving a takedown request.[94] It is the only federal regulation currently enacted that restricts AI usage.

Beyond these measures, the federal approach to AI regulation remains fragmented across executive orders, agency guidance, enforcement actions, and a growing stack of congressional proposals that have not resulted in comprehensive legislation. This fragmentation reflects both deliberate policy choices and institutional realities. Some policymakers believe that premature regulation could stifle innovation in a strategically important technology. Others simply observe that Congress moves slowly.

AI as a National Security Priority

Before examining the specifics of federal regulation, it is worth understanding the lens through which both the Biden and Trump administrations have viewed artificial intelligence: as a matter of national security and economic dominance.

Vice President JD Vance made this framing explicit in February 2025, when he addressed the AI Action Summit in Paris. The speech was notable for what Vance said he was not there to discuss. He opened by declaring that he was not there to talk about AI safety, which had been the title of the conference two years earlier, but about AI opportunity.[95] Vance argued that excessive regulation

94 Tools to Address Known Exploitation by Immobilizing Technological Deepfakes on Websites and Networks Act (Take It Down Act), Pub. L. No. 119-10 (May 19, 2025).

95 Remarks by Vice President JD Vance at the Artificial Intelligence Action Summit, Paris, France (Feb. 11, 2025), presidency.ucsb.edu/documents/remarks-the-vice-president-the-artificial-intelligence-action-summit-paris-france.

could kill a transformative industry just as it was taking off, and he warned European allies against tightening the screws on American technology companies. The administration, he said, would ensure that American AI technology continued to be the gold standard worldwide.

The speech framed AI squarely as a national security imperative. Vance warned that hostile foreign adversaries had weaponized AI software to rewrite history, surveil users, and censor speech, and pledged that the administration would safeguard American AI and chip technologies from theft and misuse.[96] The message was clear: AI was not merely a consumer technology to be regulated for safety. It was a strategic asset in great-power competition, particularly with China.

This national security framing has shaped federal AI policy in important ways. It helps explain the administration's resistance to regulation that might slow AI development, its emphasis on maintaining American technological leadership, and its willingness to confront state laws perceived as obstacles to that goal. Readers seeking a deeper analysis of AI's national security implications and the global regulatory landscape should consult Chapters 14 and 15 of this book.

Executive Orders: Policy Without Law

The executive branch has been the most active federal player in AI policy, though its actions have been marked by dramatic reversals between administrations.

In October 2023, President Biden issued Executive Order 14110, titled "Safe, Secure, and Trustworthy Development and Use of Artificial Intelligence."[97] The order was sweeping in scope, directing more

---

96 *Id. See* also Jyoti Narayan, *Vance Outlines an America First, America Only AI Agenda, Lawfare* (Mar. 19, 2025), lawfaremedia.org/article/vance-outlines-an-america-first--america-only-ai-agenda.

97 Exec. Order No. 14110, *Safe, Secure, and Trustworthy Development and Use of Artificial Intelligence*, 88 Fed. Reg. 75,191 (Oct. 30, 2023), federalregister.gov/documents/2023/11/01/2023-24283/safe-secure-and-trustworthy-development-and-use-of-artificial-intelligence.

than fifty federal agencies to take over one hundred specific actions. It established safety testing requirements for powerful AI systems, directed agencies to develop AI guidance in their sectors, created reporting obligations for developers, and set policy goals around privacy, civil rights, competition, and workforce protection. The order represented the most comprehensive piece of AI governance the federal government had produced.

That order did not survive the change in administration. President Trump rescinded Executive Order 14110 on his first day in office as part of a broad revocation of Biden-era executive orders.[98] Three days later, Trump signed Executive Order 14179, "Removing Barriers to American Leadership in Artificial Intelligence," which reoriented federal AI policy toward promoting innovation and directed agencies to review all actions taken under Biden's order and suspend or rescind any that might present obstacles to the new policy goals.[99]

In December 2025, the Trump administration took a more aggressive step. President Trump signed an executive order titled "Ensuring a National Policy Framework for Artificial Intelligence," which established federal policy to sustain and enhance the United States' global AI dominance through what it called a "minimally burdensome national policy framework" and took direct aim at state AI regulation.[100]

The December 2025 order created several mechanisms intended to challenge state laws. It directed the Attorney General to establish an AI Litigation Task Force within thirty days, charged with suing states over AI laws deemed inconsistent with federal policy on grounds including interference with interstate commerce, preemption by existing federal statutes, and First Amendment violations. It directed

---

98 Exec. Order No. 14148, *Initial Rescissions of Harmful Executive Orders and Actions* (Jan. 20, 2025).

99 Exec. Order No. 14179, *Removing Barriers to American Leadership in Artificial Intelligence* (Jan. 23, 2025), 90 Fed. Reg. 8,741 (Jan. 31, 2025), whitehouse.gov/presidential-actions/2025/01/removing-barriers-to-american-leadership-in-artificial-intelligence.

100 Exec. Order, *Ensuring a National Policy Framework for Artificial Intelligence* (Dec. 11, 2025), whitehouse.gov/presidential-actions/2025/12/eliminating-state-law-obstruction-of-national-artificial-intelligence-policy.

the Secretary of Commerce to publish an evaluation identifying state AI laws that conflict with federal policy, flagging specific laws for referral to the litigation task force. It directed agencies to consider conditioning discretionary grants on states refraining from enacting or enforcing conflicting AI laws, and specifically targeted Broadband Equity Access and Deployment program funds.

It directed the FTC Chair to issue guidance clarifying that state laws requiring AI systems to alter "truthful outputs" may be preempted by federal consumer protection law. And it directed the FCC to consider whether to adopt federal reporting and disclosure standards for AI models that would preempt conflicting state requirements.

The executive order specifically called out Colorado's AI Act, discussed below, as an example of problematic state regulation, asserting that laws requiring protection against algorithmic discrimination "force AI models to produce false results." The order also called for legislative recommendations to Congress that would establish a uniform federal AI framework preempting conflicting state laws, though it carved out exceptions for state laws relating to children's safety, AI compute infrastructure, and state government procurement of AI.

In March 2026, the White House published a National Policy Framework on artificial intelligence that reiterated many of the policies outlined in the December executive order.[101] Both the executive order and the policy framework are proactive policy documents that, at least on their face, seek to push back against what the administration views as overburdensome state AI laws. It is crucial to understand, however, what executive orders and policy frameworks can and cannot do. They can direct federal agencies and articulate administration policy, but they do not themselves preempt state law.Federal preemption typically requires either an act of Congress or federal agency regulation under delegated authority. The litigation task force can challenge state laws in court, but courts

101 The White House, National Policy Framework for Artificial Intelligence: Legislative Recommendations (Mar. 2026), whitehouse.gov/wp-content/uploads/2026/03/03.20.26-National-Policy-Framework-for-Artificial-Intelligence-Legislative-Recommendations.pdf.

will ultimately decide whether those challenges succeed.

Federal Agency Activity

While Congress has debated and the White House has issued directives, federal agencies have been applying their existing authority to AI contexts, creating a sector-by-sector patchwork of guidance, enforcement, and rulemaking.

Federal Trade Commission

The FTC has been the most active federal enforcer in the AI space, using its authority over unfair and deceptive practices to police misleading AI claims and discriminatory AI systems.

In September 2024, the FTC launched "Operation AI Comply," an enforcement sweep targeting companies making false or exaggerated claims about AI capabilities.[102] The initial wave of enforcement actions addressed a range of deceptive practices:

- DoNotPay, which promoted its service as "the world's first robot lawyer" without adequate testing of its legal capabilities, settled for $193,000.[103]
- Rite Aid faced action for using facial recognition technology in ways that resulted in false accusations and discriminatory impacts.[104]
- Evolv Technologies faced allegations of false claims about its AI-powered security screening systems.[105]

---

102 Press Release, Fed. Trade Comm'n, *FTC Announces Crackdown on Deceptive AI Claims and Schemes* (Sept. 25, 2024), ftc.gov/news-events/news/press-releases/2024/09/ftc-announces-crackdown-deceptive-ai-claims-schemes.

103 *In re DoNotPay, Inc.*, FTC File No. 232-3042. The case is discussed in more detail in Chapter 15.

104 *FTC v. Rite Aid Corp.*, Complaint and Proposed Order (Dec. 19, 2023), ftc.gov/legal-library/browse/cases-proceedings/2023190-rite-aid-corporation-ftc-v.

105 *FTC v. Evolv Techs.*, Complaint and Stipulated Order (D. Mass. Nov. 26, 2024), ftc.gov/legal-library/browse/cases-proceedings/evolv-technologies.

The change in administration has shifted the FTC's posture on the outer boundaries of AI enforcement. In December 2025, the FTC reopened and set aside a 2024 consent order against Rytr LLC, an AI writing tool company that had been charged with providing the means for consumers to create fake reviews.[106] The new FTC leadership concluded that the original complaint had not adequately established a violation, reasoning that condemning a technology simply because it could potentially be used in a problematic manner is inconsistent with the law. The Rytr reversal suggests the current FTC will focus its AI enforcement on clear deception rather than pursuing theories based on potential misuse of general-purpose tools.

Equal Employment Opportunity Commission

The EEOC has affirmed that existing civil rights laws (Title VII, the Americans with Disabilities Act, and the Age Discrimination in Employment Act) apply to AI-driven employment decisions.

The agency has issued technical assistance documents explaining how discrimination law applies to automated hiring and evaluation tools, though some of these documents were rescinded in early 2025.[107] The EEOC's core position is that employers using AI for hiring, promotion, or termination decisions remain liable for discriminatory outcomes, even if the discrimination results from a third-party vendor's algorithm. This principle of deployer responsibility has significant implications for organizations adopting AI hiring tools and connects to the broader questions of algorithmic discrimination discussed in Chapter 10.

Other Federal Agencies

Several other federal agencies have applied existing regulatory

---

106 Order Reopening and Setting Aside Final Consent Order, *In re Rytr LLC*, FTC File No. 232-3052 (Dec. 22, 2025), ftc.gov/news-events/news/press-releases/2025/12/ftc-re-opens-sets-aside-rytr-final-order-response-trump-administrations-ai-action-plan.

107 *See, e.g.*, EEOC, *The Americans with Disabilities Act and the Use of Software, Algorithms, and Artificial Intelligence to Assess Job Applicants and Employees* (May 12, 2022), eeoc.gov/laws/guidance/americans-disabilities-act-and-use-software-algorithms-and-artificial-intelligence.

authority to AI in their sectors:

- **The Consumer Financial Protection Bureau** monitors AI use in financial services, particularly automated lending decisions, and has indicated that fair lending laws apply to algorithmic credit decisions and that adverse action notices must meaningfully explain AI-driven denials.

- **The Food and Drug Administration** regulates AI systems marketed as medical devices, including diagnostic algorithms and clinical decision support tools, under its framework for evaluating AI-based software as a medical device.

- **The Department of Transportation** and the **National Highway Traffic Safety Administration** regulate autonomous vehicles, including AI systems for driver assistance and self-driving capabilities, with an approach that has evolved from voluntary guidance toward more prescriptive requirements as the technology matures.

Across agencies, a common theme emerges: existing laws generally apply to AI-driven decisions in the same way they apply to human decisions. The challenge lies in the practical difficulties of detecting violations, explaining AI-driven outcomes, and allocating responsibility across complex supply chains of developers, deployers, and end users.

Congressional Activity

Congress has introduced numerous AI-related bills. Proposals have ranged from establishing a national AI research resource to requiring risk evaluations of advanced AI systems to codifying a national AI strategy.[108] None establishing a comprehensive regulatory framework

108 Brennan Center Artificial Intelligence Legislation Tracker, brennancenter.org/our-work/research-reports/artificial-intelligence-legislation-tracker (tracking over 150 bills introduced in the 118th Congress; none enacted). See also MultiState AI Legislation Tracker, multistate.ai/artificial-intelligence-ai-legislation (showing 635 bills introduced across 45

has been enacted.

The most significant congressional action on AI has, paradoxically, been a vote against inaction. In July 2025, the Senate voted 99–1 to remove a proposed ten-year moratorium on state AI law enforcement from the budget reconciliation legislation known as the "One Big Beautiful Bill Act."[109]

The moratorium, championed by Senator Ted Cruz, would have barred states and localities from enforcing any law or regulation targeting AI models, AI systems, or automated decision systems for a decade. It drew opposition from an extraordinary coalition: a bipartisan group of 36 state attorneys general, consumer groups, labor unions, civil rights organizations, and governors.[110] Senator Marsha Blackburn, who had initially attempted to negotiate a shorter five-year moratorium with Cruz, ultimately withdrew her support and co-sponsored the amendment to eliminate the provision entirely, arguing that Congress could not block states from protecting their citizens while failing to pass federal protections of its own.

A similar provision was subsequently proposed for the National Defense Authorization Act later in 2025 but was dropped before passage.[111] These failures did not end the push for federal preemption. Following the failure of legislative approaches, the Trump administration turned to executive action with the December 2025 executive order described above.

---

states in 2024, with 99 enacted, and 1,208 bills introduced across all 50 states in 2025, with 145 enacted as of reporting date).

109 Press Release, S. Comm. on Commerce, Sci. & Transp., *Senate Strikes AI Moratorium from Budget Reconciliation Bill in Overwhelming 99-1 Vote* (July 1, 2025), commerce.senate.gov/2025/7/senate-strikes-ai-moratorium-from-budget-reconciliation-bill-in-overwhelming-99-1-vote/8415a728-fd1d-4269-98ac-101d1d0c71e0

110 Letter from Nat'l Ass'n of Att'ys Gen., Bipartisan Coalition of 36 State Attorneys General, to Congressional Leaders (Nov. 25, 2025), naag.org/press-releases/bipartisan-coalition-of-36-state-attorneys-general-opposes-federal-ban-on-state-ai-laws.

111 Americans for Responsible Innovation, "AI Law Preemption Dropped from NDAA" (Dec. 3, 2025), ari.us/ai-law-preemption-dropped-from-ndaa.

The State Laboratory

While Congress has deliberated, state legislatures have acted. In 2025 alone, the National Conference of State Legislatures tracked over 1,000 AI-related bills across all 50 states, with more than 100 measures enacted.[112] The pace shows no signs of slowing.

State approaches vary dramatically. Some have enacted comprehensive frameworks that apply across sectors. Others have targeted specific applications (hiring, deepfakes, healthcare) while leaving broader questions unaddressed. Still others have created task forces and study committees to develop recommendations for future legislation. This variation creates compliance challenges for businesses operating across state lines, but it also creates what legal scholars sometimes call a "laboratory of democracy": multiple jurisdictions testing different regulatory approaches simultaneously.

What follows is an overview of the most significant state AI laws and the major categories in which states have legislated. It is not exhaustive. The goal is to give readers a working understanding of the landscape and to identify the patterns that are likely to shape AI regulation going forward. A list of current and pending state proposals is available in the Supplemental Resources section at the end of this chapter.

Comprehensive State AI Laws

A handful of states have attempted comprehensive AI regulation that applies across sectors rather than targeting specific applications.

Colorado AI Act

Colorado enacted the nation's first comprehensive consumer-focused AI law in 2024, though its effective date has been delayed to June 30, 2026.[113] The law applies to "high-risk AI systems"

---

112 Nat'l Conf. of State Legislatures, *Artificial Intelligence 2025 Legislation* (2025), ncsl.org/technology-and-communication/artificial-intelligence-2025-legislation.

113 Colo. Rev. Stat. §§ 6-1-1701 to -1707 (2024), as amended by S.B. 25B-004 (delaying effective date to June 30, 2026).

used in consequential decisions about employment, education, financial services, housing, insurance, and government services. It requires developers and deployers to use "reasonable care" to protect consumers from known or foreseeable risks of algorithmic discrimination. Deployers must conduct impact assessments for high-risk AI systems. Consumers must be notified when AI is used in consequential decisions and must have the right to appeal AI-driven decisions. Companies must publicly disclose the types of AI systems in use and their risk management practices.

The Colorado AI Act has become a flashpoint in the federal-state tension. The Trump administration's December 2025 executive order specifically named it as an example of problematic state regulation, asserting that its anti-discrimination requirements would force AI models to produce false results. Whether federal preemption efforts succeed remains to be seen, but the law has already influenced how other states think about comprehensive AI regulation.

Texas Responsible AI Governance Act

Texas took a different approach when it enacted HB 149, effective January 1, 2026.[114] Rather than imposing comprehensive requirements on all high-risk AI systems, Texas focused on prohibited uses: intentionally developing or deploying AI systems to encourage self-harm, violence, or criminal activity, to infringe constitutional rights, to discriminate unlawfully against protected classes, to produce deepfakes or child sexual abuse material, or to impersonate minors in explicit contexts. The law also establishes an AI advisory council, creates a regulatory sandbox for testing AI systems with reduced regulatory risk, requires healthcare providers to disclose AI use in treatment, and imposes limitations on biometric identifier use.

The Texas law was deliberately drafted to be business friendly and reflects a model that other business-oriented states may follow: addressing the most clearly harmful uses of AI while avoiding the broader compliance obligations that comprehensive frameworks like Colorado's impose.

---

114 Tex. Bus. & Com. Code Ann. § 555 (West 2025) (Responsible Artificial Intelligence Governance Act, H.B. 149, signed June 22, 2025, effective Jan. 1, 2026).

California's Multi-Law Approach

California has pursued a distinctive strategy. Rather than enacting a single comprehensive AI statute, the state has passed multiple targeted laws addressing different dimensions of AI governance.[115]

The Transparency in Frontier AI Act, SB 53, effective January 1, 2026, targets what it calls "large frontier developers": companies whose covered frontier models have associated annual revenue exceeding $500 million. These developers must disclose risk management protocols, publish transparency reports about frontier models, and report critical safety incidents. The law includes whistleblower protections for employees reporting safety concerns.

The Generative AI Training Data Transparency Act, AB 2013, also effective January 1, 2026, requires developers of generative AI systems to publish information about training data, including summaries of data sources, intellectual property and privacy considerations, and processing history. This law responds to what has been one of the most contested questions in AI development: what data was used to train these systems, and who gave permission for it to be used?

The AI Transparency Act, SB 942 as amended by AB 853, requires disclosure when content is AI-generated, including both visible watermarks and embedded metadata. It applies to large online platforms with over two million monthly users. Implementation has been delayed to August 2026.

California's Civil Rights Department also adopted regulations effective October 2025, that restrict discriminatory use of AI in employment decisions, make bias testing, or the lack thereof, explicitly relevant to discrimination claims, and impose extended recordkeeping requirements for automated decision system data.

Perhaps most novel among California's AI laws is SB 243, which

---

115 The California AI laws discussed in this section include: S.B. 53, Transparency in Frontier AI Act, Cal. Civ. Code § 22757 (West 2025); A.B. 2013, Generative AI Training Data Transparency Act (2024); S.B. 942, AI Transparency Act, as amended by A.B. 853 (2024); Cal. Code Regs. tit. 2, § 11098 (employment discrimination regulations); S.B. 243 companion chatbot regulations (2024).

regulates AI companion chatbots, identified as systems designed to meet users' social and emotional needs. Effective January 1, 2026, the law requires disclosure of the AI nature of these systems, break reminders for extended use, and suicide and self-harm mitigation protocols. It includes specific protections for minors and, notably, creates a private right of action, allowing individuals harmed by noncompliant companion chatbots to sue directly.

California's multi-law approach has advantages and disadvantages. It allows tailored regulation of distinct AI applications, and it reflects the reality that the risks of a frontier model are different from the risks of an AI hiring tool, which are different from the risks of an AI chatbot. But it also creates a more complex compliance landscape, particularly for companies operating across multiple AI applications.

Categories of State Legislation

Beyond the comprehensive frameworks, states have legislated across several distinct categories. Understanding these categories provides a map of where AI regulation is heading, even as the specific laws continue to evolve.

Employment and Algorithmic Discrimination

AI use in hiring and employment decisions has drawn some of the earliest and most detailed state regulation, reflecting widespread concern that automated systems may perpetuate or amplify existing biases.

Illinois has been particularly active. Its 2020 AI Video Interview Act was among the first laws anywhere to regulate AI in employment, requiring notice and consent before AI analysis of video interviews.[116] In 2024, Illinois went further by amending its Human Rights Act to explicitly regulate AI across all employment decisions. The amendment prohibits employer use of AI that discriminates against protected classes in hiring, firing, discipline, tenure, and training. It requires employers to notify applicants and employees when AI is

116 820 Ill. Comp. Stat. 42/1–42/25 (Artificial Intelligence Video Interview Act, effective Jan. 1, 2020).

used in employment decisions.[117] It prohibits the use of zip codes as proxies for protected classes. And, critically, it creates a private right of action, making Illinois one of the few states where individuals can sue directly for AI-related employment discrimination. The law applies to any employer with one or more employees in Illinois, an unusually broad threshold.

New York City's Local Law 144, effective since July 2023, was the first law in the nation to require bias audits of AI hiring tools.[118] Employers using automated employment decision tools must conduct annual independent bias audits, post the results publicly, and give candidates at least ten business days' notice before using such tools. A 2025 audit by the New York State Comptroller found that the city's Department of Consumer and Worker Protection has struggled to enforce the law effectively, identifying potential noncompliance at 17 of 32 companies reviewed despite the agency having found only one issue during its own review.[119] The enforcement gap highlights a challenge that runs across all AI regulation: the difficulty of monitoring compliance with technical requirements that regulators may lack the expertise to evaluate.

Maryland and New Jersey have also enacted restrictions on AI use in hiring decisions, though with narrower scope.[120] Colorado's comprehensive AI Act, when it takes effect, will add another layer of employment-related requirements for companies operating in that state.

---

117 775 Ill. Comp. Stat. 5/2-110 (2024) (H.B. 3773, amending the Illinois Human Rights Act, effective Jan. 1, 2026).

118 N.Y.C. Admin. Code § 20-870 to -876 (Local Law 144 of 2021, effective July 5, 2023).

119 N.Y. State Comptroller, *Audit Report on DCWP Enforcement of Local Law 144* (2025).

120 Maryland HB 1202 (2020) (requiring consent before use of facial recognition technology in employment interviews); New Jersey Office of Attorney General, "Guidance on Algorithmic Discrimination and the New Jersey Law Against Discrimination" (Jan. 9, 2025), nj.gov/oag/newsreleases25/2025-0108_DCR-Guidance-on-Algorithmic-Discrimination.pdf (clarifying that employers may be liable for algorithmic discrimination even when using third-party AI tools and even absent discriminatory intent); New Jersey Division on Civil Rights, Disparate Impact Rules (effective Dec. 15, 2025) (imposing affirmative obligations on entities using AI systems with potential disparate impacts).

Deepfakes and Synthetic Media

Multiple states have enacted laws addressing AI-generated content in elections, typically requiring disclosure of AI-generated political advertising, prohibiting the distribution of deceptive synthetic media depicting candidates close to elections, and imposing penalties for creating or distributing election-related deepfakes intended to mislead voters.

At least half the states addressed deepfakes through new laws in 2024 and 2025, targeting both election manipulation and nonconsensual intimate images.[121] This category of legislation has seen the broadest bipartisan support, reflecting shared concern about the integrity of elections and the personal harm caused by nonconsensual synthetic media.

Tennessee's *Ensuring Likeness Voice and Image Security Act*, known as the ELVIS Act, became effective in July 2024 and was the first state law to comprehensively protect against AI voice cloning.[122] The law expands right-of-publicity protections to explicitly include voice, targeting both creators of AI-generated deepfakes and voice clones and the providers of tools used to make them. Given Nashville's prominence in the music industry, the law was a direct response to concerns about AI replication of recording artists' voices.

Healthcare AI

States have begun regulating AI use in healthcare contexts, though most laws in this category focus on disclosure rather than substantive restrictions on AI capabilities.

Illinois's Wellness and Oversight Act prohibits the unlicensed

---

121 IAPP US State AI Governance Legislation Tracker, iapp.org/resources/article/us-state-ai-governance-legislation-tracker. *See also* Ballotpedia Artificial Intelligence Deepfake Legislation Tracker (reporting that 47 states have enacted deepfake laws since 2019, with 82% enacted in 2024–2025); Program.com Deepfake Legislation Tracker, programs.com/resources/deepfake-legislation (cataloguing 169 deepfake-related laws enacted since 2022).

122 Tenn. Code Ann. § 47-25-1201 et seq. (Ensuring Likeness Voice and Image Security Act, effective July 1, 2024).

provision of AI therapy services and requires disclosure when licensed professionals use AI tools in treatment.[123] Indiana requires healthcare professionals and insurers to disclose when AI is used in health decisions or communications.[124] California's companion chatbot regulations, discussed above, include specific crisis-response protocols and reporting requirements related to suicide prevention.

Multiple states have also considered or enacted laws addressing AI use in insurance underwriting, utilization review, and prior authorization, areas where algorithmic decision-making can have direct effects on whether patients receive the care their providers recommend. The intersection of AI and healthcare regulation is discussed in greater detail in Chapter 10.

Children's Safety and AI

Protecting children from AI-related harms has emerged as one of the few areas of genuine bipartisan consensus. Notably, even the Trump administration's December 2025 executive order carved out children's safety from its preemption framework, acknowledging that state laws protecting children from AI-related harms should not be displaced by federal policy.[125]

State laws in this category address a range of concerns: AI-generated child sexual abuse material, companion chatbots interacting with minors, AI systems used in educational settings, and the use of children's data to train AI models. California's SB 243, with its specific protections for minors interacting with AI companion systems, is among the most detailed.[126] Several states have enacted

---

123 Illinois HB 1806, Wellness and Oversight for Psychological Resources Act (signed Aug. 4, 2025, effective immediately).

124 Indiana HB 1620, Disclosure of Artificial Intelligence Use in Health Care (effective July 1, 2025), adding IC 16-51-2.5 (healthcare provider disclosure requirements) and IC 27-8-44 (insurer disclosure requirements).

125 Executive Order, *"Ensuring a National Policy Framework for Artificial Intelligence,"* § 8 (Dec. 11, 2025), whitehouse.gov/presidential-actions/2025/12/eliminating-state-law-obstruction-of-national-artificial-intelligence-policy.

126 California SB 243, Companion Chatbots (effective Jan. 1, 2026), leginfo.legislature.ca.gov/faces/billNavClient.xhtml?bill_id=202520260SB243.

or proposed laws requiring age verification or parental consent for minors' interactions with AI chatbots.[127]

The Federal-State Collision

The regulatory landscape in 2026 is defined by tension between state action and federal preemption efforts. States have moved aggressively to fill the gap left by congressional inaction, creating what the December 2025 executive order characterized as a patchwork of regulatory regimes that makes compliance more challenging. Critics of state regulation argue that inconsistent requirements across jurisdictions burden innovation and create impossible compliance challenges for companies operating nationally.

Defenders of state regulation counter that federal inaction should not leave consumers unprotected from algorithmic discrimination, deceptive AI practices, and AI-enabled harms. They note that state consumer protection and civil rights laws have long coexisted with federal frameworks, and that the patchwork critique could apply to virtually any area of state law. The bipartisan coalition of 36 state attorneys general who opposed the federal moratorium argued that states must be empowered to protect their citizens while Congress fails to act.[128]

The practical reality is that state laws remain enforceable as of this writing. The December 2025 executive order does not itself preempt any state law; it merely directs federal agencies to attempt preemption through litigation and other means. Until courts rule otherwise or Congress acts, organizations must comply with applicable state requirements. This creates a challenging compliance environment in which organizations deploying AI systems may face different obligations depending on where their employees, customers, or users

---

127 Utah HB 452 (effective May 2024) (requiring AI disclosure when prompted by user); New York S-3008C (enacted 2025) (requiring disclosure at the start of interaction and every three hours); California SB 243 (companion chatbot regulations).

128 Letter from Nat'l Ass'n of Att'ys Gen., supra note 111. A separate letter from 23 state attorneys general to the FCC in December 2025 also urged the agency not to issue regulations preempting state AI laws. Letter from 23 State Att'ys Gen. to FCC (Dec. 17, 2025), blogs.duanemorris.com/stateattorneysgeneral/2025/12/23/23-state-attorneys-general-urge-fcc-to-stand-down-on-ai-preemption-rule.

are located. A company using AI hiring tools may need to conduct bias audits for New York City candidates, provide disclosures to Illinois applicants, and prepare for Colorado's comprehensive requirements when they take effect.

Practical Guidance

For organizations navigating this regulatory landscape, several practical principles emerge.

First, compliance with state law is not optional. Despite federal preemption rhetoric, state laws remain enforceable until courts say otherwise. The fact that the federal government may challenge a law does not excuse current compliance obligations.

Second, organizations should build compliance infrastructure that can adapt. The regulations will continue to evolve. AI governance frameworks, documentation practices, and oversight processes should accommodate changing requirements rather than building narrowly for any single law's specifications.

Third, tracking the most restrictive applicable requirements and implementing them broadly is often more practical than tailoring compliance jurisdiction by jurisdiction.

Fourth, organizations should document AI systems thoroughly. Nearly every regulatory approach, whether federal or state, involves some form of transparency, disclosure, or documentation requirement. Organizations that maintain comprehensive documentation of their AI systems' purposes, training data, testing results, and deployment contexts will be better positioned to meet whatever specific requirements emerge.

Fifth, organizations should monitor the AI Litigation Task Force, FTC and FCC proceedings, and any congressional action closely. These developments will significantly affect compliance obligations in the months and years ahead.

Supplemental Resources

- **NCSL AI Legislation Tracker** (ncsl.org/technology-and-communication/artificial-intelligence-2025-legislation): Comprehensive tracking of state AI bills across all 50 states, updated regularly.
- **IAPP US State AI Governance Legislation Tracker** (iapp.org/resources/article/us-state-ai-governance-legislation-tracker): Focus on cross-sectoral AI governance bills with detailed analysis.
- **MultiState AI Legislation Tracker** (multistate.ai/artificial-intelligence-ai-legislation.): Commercial tracking service with detailed analysis of AI bills across all 50 states.
- **Stanford HAI AI Index Report** (aiindex.stanford.edu): Annual analysis of AI policy developments including regulatory trends and global comparisons.
- **Brennan Center AI Legislation Tracker** (brennancenter.org/our-work/research-reports/artificial-intelligence-legislation-tracker): Tracking with focus on civil rights implications of AI regulation.

CHAPTER 9

AI and Intellectual Property Law

Artificial intelligence is transforming how creative and commercial content is produced. From artwork and music to brand logos and marketing copy, generative AI systems are already producing outputs that resemble the work of human authors and designers. This chapter explores how intellectual property law applies to these AI-generated outputs and the systems that make them.

Most existing questions about copyright and trademark protection for AI-generated content can be approached using traditional legal principles. Copyright law requires human authorship, which generally means that purely machine-generated works are not eligible for protection under current U.S. law. Trademark law is somewhat more flexible, but it still centers on human intent and consumer perception. The question of whether an image or phrase generated by AI can be protected as a trademark will likely depend on how it is used and whether it serves a source-identifying function. In either case, the law tends to treat these issues as extensions of familiar doctrines, even if the facts are more novel.

The harder and more unsettled legal questions lie not in the output, but in the input. Many of the most advanced AI systems are trained on massive datasets scraped from the internet, including copyrighted images, books, code, and other creative works. This practice has sparked a growing wave of lawsuits, many of which could define the future of the AI industry.

At the heart of these disputes is a fundamental question: is it lawful to train an AI on someone else's work without permission?

Copyright Law Fundamentals

Copyright protection extends to original works of authorship fixed in a tangible medium of expression.[129] This includes literary works, musical compositions, dramatic works, pictorial and graphic works, motion pictures, sound recordings, and architectural works. Protection attaches automatically upon creation; no registration is required, though registration provides benefits to the creator in litigation.

The copyright owner holds exclusive rights to reproduce the work, prepare derivative works, distribute copies, perform the work publicly, and display the work publicly.[130] These rights can be licensed or transferred, and they persist for the life of the author plus seventy years (for works created after 1978).[131]

The Human Authorship Requirement

Copyright protection requires human authorship. The U.S. Copyright Office has consistently maintained this position, and courts have upheld it. In *Thaler v. Perlmutter*, the D.C. Circuit affirmed in March 2025 that a work created entirely by an AI system without human creative input cannot be registered for copyright protection.[132] The district court had reached the same conclusion in 2023, observing that copyright law protects only works of human creation and that human authorship is a bedrock requirement of copyright.[133] A petition for certiorari was filed with the Supreme Court in October 2025. The Court denied review, leaving the D.C. Circuit's holding intact and ending the litigation. The denial means the human authorship requirement stands as a matter of statutory law, though the D.C. Circuit expressly left open the possibility that Congress could revisit the issue in the future.

---

129 17 U.S.C. § 102(a).

130 17 U.S.C. § 106.

131 17 U.S.C. § 302(a).

132 *Thaler v. Perlmutter*, No. 23-5233 (D.C. Cir. Mar. 18, 2025).

133 *Thaler v. Perlmutter*, 687 F. Supp. 3d 140, 146 (D.D.C. 2023).

This principle has significant implications for AI-generated content. In January 2025, the Copyright Office released Part 2 of its comprehensive report on Copyright and Artificial Intelligence, which addressed the copyrightability of AI-generated outputs.[134] The report concluded that existing copyright principles remain adequate to address AI-generated works, and that works generated entirely by AI, without sufficient human creative control, are not copyrightable; the mere provision of prompts to an AI system does not, by itself, constitute sufficient human authorship to support copyright protection; using AI as a tool to assist human creativity does not bar copyright protection for the resulting work; and where a work includes both human-authored and AI-generated elements, only the human contributions are potentially copyrightable.

The Copyright Office emphasized that copyrightability determinations must be made on a case-by-case basis, examining the nature and extent of human contribution to each work. Selecting from among AI-generated outputs is not sufficient to establish authorship, nor is providing detailed prompts to an AI system under current technology. However, if a human makes creative modifications, arrangements, or selections of AI-generated material that meet the standard for copyright protection, those human contributions may be copyrightable.[135]

Fair Use Doctrine

The fair use doctrine, codified at 17 U.S.C. § 107, provides a defense to copyright infringement for certain uses of copyrighted works.[136] Courts evaluate fair use by weighing four factors: (1) the purpose and character of the use, including whether it is commercial or transformative; (2) the nature of the copyrighted work, including whether it is factual or creative; (3) the amount and substantiality of

---

134 U.S. Copyright Office, *Copyright and Artificial Intelligence*, Part 2: Copyrightability (Jan. 2025), copyright.gov/ai/Copyright-and-Artificial-Intelligence-Part-2-Copyrightability-Report.pdf.

135 *Id.* at 14–16. See also U.S. Copyright Office, Copyright Registration Guidance: Works Containing Material Generated by Artificial Intelligence, 88 Fed. Reg. 16,190 (Mar. 16, 2023).

136 17 U.S.C. § 107.

the portion used in relation to the whole; and (4) the effect on the market for the original work.

No single factor is determinative, and courts must consider all factors together. The most important consideration in recent cases has been transformativeness, as clarified by the Supreme Court in *Andy Warhol Foundation for the Visual Arts, Inc. v. Goldsmith*, which asked whether the new use adds something new, with a further purpose or different character, rather than merely substituting for the original.[137]

Fair use is central to the AI training data debate. AI developers argue that training models on copyrighted works is transformative because the models learn patterns and relationships in language or images, rather than copying works for their expressive content. Critics argue that commercial AI training at massive scale goes far beyond traditional fair use, particularly when the resulting systems can generate outputs that compete with or substitute for the original works.

The AI Training Data Wars

The question of whether AI training constitutes fair use has become one of the most significant copyright disputes in a generation. More than 80 copyright infringement lawsuits have been filed against AI companies in the United States, targeting developers of large language models, image generators, code assistants, and music creation tools.[138] These cases collectively could determine whether AI companies must license training data or can continue to train on scraped content under fair use.

The Emerging Legal Framework

By early 2026, courts have issued several significant rulings on fair use in AI training, though the law remains unsettled. At the time

---

137 *Andy Warhol Found. for the Visual Arts, Inc. v. Goldsmith*, 598 U.S. 508, 527 (2023).

138 *See* ChatGPT Is Eating the World, *AI Copyright Litigation Master Charts*, chatgptiseatingtheworld.com (tracking over 70 cases as of Jan. 2026); McKool Smith, AI Infringement Case Updates, mckoolsmith.com/newsroom-ailitigation (weekly reports).

of this writing, three federal judges have ruled on fair use in AI training contexts, with two finding fair use and one finding against it. However, each decision was highly fact-specific, and no appellate court has yet addressed the issue directly, though the Third Circuit is expected to become the first to do so.[139]

What has emerged is not a clear rule but rather a framework of relevant considerations:

Transformativeness. Courts have found AI training to be highly transformative where the purpose is to learn statistical patterns in data rather than to reproduce or distribute the original works. As Judge Alsup wrote in *Bartz*, AI systems learn from works not to replicate or supplant them, but to create something different.[140]

Method of acquisition. How AI companies obtain training data matters legally, separate from whether training itself is fair use. Downloading pirated copies of works from shadow libraries or torrent sites is not protected by fair use, even if the ultimate use of that data for training might be.[141]

Market impact. Courts must consider whether the use affects the market for the original work. This includes both direct substitution (does the AI output replace the original?) and potential licensing markets (does the use deprive creators of licensing revenue they would otherwise receive?). Some courts have recognized a market dilution theory whereby AI-generated content flooding the market could indirectly harm creators even without direct copying.[142]

---

139 The three judges are: Judge William Alsup (N.D. Cal.), finding fair use for lawfully acquired training data in *Bartz v. Anthropic*; Judge Vince Chhabria (N.D. Cal.), finding fair use in *Kadrey v. Meta*; and Judge Stephanos Bibas (D. Del.), finding no fair use in *Thomson Reuters v. Ross Intelligence*. The *Thomson Reuters* appeal to the Third Circuit (No. 25-2153) is expected to produce the first appellate ruling on fair use in AI training.

140 *Bartz v. Anthropic*, PBC, No. 3:24-cv-05417 (N.D. Cal. June 2025) (order on summary judgment).

141 *Id.*

142 *Kadrey v. Meta Platforms, Inc.*, No. 3:23-cv-03417 (N.D. Cal. June 25, 2025) (order on summary judgment endorsing market dilution theory).

Evidence of harm. Plaintiffs who can show that AI systems actually reproduce substantial portions of their works, or that the systems' outputs serve as market substitutes, have stronger claims than those alleging only that their works were included in training data.

Bartz v. Anthropic: The Landmark Settlement

The largest and most consequential AI copyright case to date is *Bartz v. Anthropic*, which resulted in a $1.5 billion settlement, the largest copyright settlement in U.S. history.[143]

Authors Andrea Bartz, Charles Graeber, and Kirk Wallace Johnson filed suit in 2024, alleging that Anthropic used millions of copyrighted books to train its Claude large language models without permission or compensation. The case revealed that Anthropic had obtained training data through multiple channels: purchasing physical books, scanning them, and destroying the originals; and downloading over 7 million books from pirate sites including Library Genesis (LibGen) and Pirate Library Mirror (PiLiMi).

In June 2025, Judge William Alsup of the Northern District of California issued a split decision on summary judgment that has become a touchstone for AI copyright law.[144] Judge Alsup found that using lawfully acquired books to train AI models was exceedingly transformative and constituted fair use. The training process, he reasoned, learned patterns in language rather than copying expressive content, and the resulting AI system served entirely different purposes than the original books.

But Judge Alsup drew a sharp line at how training data was acquired. Downloading millions of books from pirate sites was not fair use, regardless of the ultimate purpose.[145] This distinction between what AI companies do with training data and how they obtain it has become

---

143 *Bartz v. Anthropic*, PBC, No. 3:24-cv-05417-WHA (N.D. Cal. Sept. 25, 2025) (order granting preliminary approval of class action settlement). The settlement website is at anthropiccopyrightsettlement.com.

144 *Bartz v. Anthropic*, PBC, No. 3:24-cv-05417-WHA (N.D. Cal. June 2025) (order on cross-motions for summary judgment).

145 *Id.*

central to the legal framework. Even if training is transformative fair use, AI developers face liability for acquiring training data through unlawful means.

In July 2025, Judge Alsup certified a class including all copyright owners of books in the LibGen and PiLiMi datasets that Anthropic downloaded. The class ultimately encompassed approximately 482,460 works.[146] Facing potential statutory damages of up to $150,000 per work for willful infringement, Anthropic agreed to settle for $1.5 billion, approximately $3,000 per work. The settlement requires Anthropic to destroy all copies of the pirated works and any derivatives and does not create any ongoing license for future use.[147] The settlement was preliminarily approved with final approval hearings scheduled for May, 2026.[148]

The Bartz settlement sends several important messages to the AI industry. First, the method of acquiring training data could matter as much as the training itself. AI companies that relied on pirated content face substantial liability, while those using lawfully obtained data have stronger fair use arguments. Second, the $3,000-per-work figure provides a benchmark, though not a binding precedent, for valuing unauthorized use of copyrighted works in AI training. Third, the settlement does not resolve the fundamental question of whether training on copyrighted works requires licensing. Judge Alsup's fair use ruling applies only to the named plaintiffs, not the certified class, and is not binding precedent for other cases.

Kadrey v. Meta: A Roadmap for Future Plaintiffs

Two days after the *Bartz* ruling, Judge Vince Chhabria of the same court issued a parallel decision in *Kadrey v. Meta Platforms*, finding fair use for Meta's training of its Llama language models on copyrighted books but warning that future plaintiffs could prevail

---

146 *Bartz v. Anthropic*, PBC, No. 3:24-cv-05417-WHA (N.D. Cal. Aug. 2025) (order on class certification).

147 Settlement Agreement, *Bartz v. Anthropic*, PBC, No. 3:24-cv-05417-WHA (N.D. Cal. filed Aug. 25, 2025), anthropiccopyrightsettlement.com.

148 *Bartz v. Anthropic*, PBC, No. 3:24-cv-05417-WHA (N.D. Cal. Sept. 25, 2025) (order granting preliminary approval). Final approval hearing scheduled for April 23, 2026.

with better evidence.[149]

The *Kadrey* plaintiffs, including authors Richard Kadrey and Sarah Silverman, alleged that Meta used their books (also obtained from shadow libraries) to train Llama. Judge Chhabria found Meta's use transformative and ruled for the defendant on June 25, 2025, but his reasoning was notably cautious.

While acknowledging that AI training is highly transformative, Judge Chhabria emphasized that transformativeness alone does not guarantee fair use. The critical question is whether the use harms the market for the original works. The plaintiffs failed to present evidence that Meta's AI systems actually reproduced their works or that the outputs served as market substitutes. Judge Chhabria suggested that in most cases, using copyrighted works to train AI without permission will often constitute infringement, at least where those cases have better-developed records on the market effects.

Judge Chhabria endorsed a market dilution theory of harm: that AI systems trained on copyrighted works can flood the market with competing content that indirectly substitutes for the originals, even without direct copying. This theory could provide future plaintiffs a path to proving harm even when AI outputs do not directly reproduce their works.

Unlike Judge Alsup in *Bartz*, Judge Chhabria did not find that Meta's use of shadow libraries independently defeated fair use. He treated the method of acquisition as part of a single process directed at transformative training, rather than as a separate infringement. This difference between the two rulings remains unresolved.[150]

Judge Chhabria's summary judgment ruling binds only the thirteen named plaintiffs. Distribution-related claims based on Meta's

---

149 *Kadrey v. Meta Platforms, Inc.*, No. 3:23-cv-03417-VC (N.D. Cal. June 25, 2025) (order on cross-motions for summary judgment).

150 Compare *Bartz v. Anthropic*, PBC, No. 3:24-cv-05417-WHA (N.D. Cal. June 2025) (treating piracy as independently defeating fair use), with *Kadrey v. Meta Platforms*, Inc., No. 3:23-cv-03417-VC (N.D. Cal. June 25, 2025) (treating acquisition as part of a single transformative process).

torrenting activities were not resolved on summary judgment and remain live issues in the case. The ruling has no precedential effect on the proposed class, and other copyright owners whose works Meta used remain free to bring their own claims with different evidence of market harm.

Thomson Reuters v. Ross Intelligence: Fair Use Denied

Not all courts have found AI training to be fair use. In *Thomson Reuters Enterprise Centre GmbH v. Ross Intelligence Inc.*, Judge Stephanos Bibas ruled on February 11, 2025, that Ross Intelligence's use of Westlaw headnotes and the Key Number System to train a legal research AI was not fair use.[151]

The key distinction: Ross Intelligence's AI competed directly with Thomson Reuters' legal research products. The court emphasized the fourth fair use factor, effect on the market, finding that Ross's training amounted to using copyrighted content to build a competing product that could substitute for the original.

Judge Bibas subsequently certified two questions for interlocutory appeal to the Third Circuit, granted on June 17, 2025: (1) whether Westlaw headnotes and the Key Number System are sufficiently original to qualify for copyright protection, and (2) whether Ross's use constituted fair use.[152] Briefing was completed in late 2025, and the Third Circuit's decision, expected in 2026, will be the first appellate court ruling to address fair use in AI training.

The New York Times versus OpenAI: The Case to Watch

The highest-profile pending AI copyright case is *The New York Times Company v. Microsoft Corporation*, filed in December 2023.[153] The Times alleges that OpenAI copied millions of articles to train

---

151 *Thomson Reuters Enter. Ctr. GmbH v. Ross Intelligence Inc.*, No. 1:20-cv-00613-SB (D. Del. Feb. 11, 2025) (order on summary judgment).

152 *Ross Intelligence Inc. v. Thomson Reuters Enter. Ctr. GmbH*, No. 25-2153 (3d Cir. appeal accepted June 17, 2025). Briefing completed Nov.–Dec. 2025.

153 *N.Y. Times Co. v. Microsoft Corp.*, No. 1:23-cv-11195 (S.D.N.Y. filed Dec. 27, 2023) (complaint).

GPT models, and that ChatGPT can reproduce substantial portions of Times content, sometimes nearly verbatim, in response to user queries.

The Times argues that OpenAI's training on copyrighted journalism was not fair use because ChatGPT outputs can substitute for Times articles; that the ability to generate news summaries undermines the Times' subscription business model; and that OpenAI's systems can memorize and reproduce copyrighted content, demonstrating direct copying rather than transformative learning.

In March 2025, Judge Sidney Stein denied most of OpenAI's motion to dismiss, allowing the core copyright claims to proceed.[154] The case has been consolidated with numerous other copyright lawsuits in a multi-district litigation proceeding. Discovery has generated significant procedural battles, most notably over a preservation order requiring OpenAI to retain user chat logs. In May 2025, Magistrate Judge Ona Wang ordered preservation of all ChatGPT output logs; Judge Stein affirmed the order in June 2025 and further affirmed production of 20 million anonymized chat logs in January 2026.[155] Trial is not expected until 2026 or later.

The Times seeks billions of dollars in damages and the destruction of ChatGPT's training data, a remedy that, if granted, would be devastating for OpenAI. The case could establish whether news content receives different treatment under fair use analysis, given the market substitution concerns unique to journalism.

Other Major Pending Cases

The litigation landscape extends beyond books and news into a wide range of other publishing and creative sectors.

---

154 *N.Y. Times Co. v. Microsoft Corp.*, No. 1:23-cv-11195-SHS (S.D.N.Y. Mar. 26, 2025) (order on motion to dismiss, published Apr. 4, 2025).

155 *See* Order, *N.Y. Times Co. v. Microsoft Corp.*, No. 1:23-cv-11195-SHS (S.D.N.Y. May 13, 2025) (Magistrate Judge Wang ordering preservation of ChatGPT output logs); *aff'd*, (S.D.N.Y. June 26, 2025) (Judge Stein); Order, (S.D.N.Y. Jan. 5, 2026) (affirming production of 20 million anonymized chat logs).

Music Industry

Universal Music Group, Concord Music, and other major labels have sued both Anthropic (for allegedly using copyrighted lyrics in training) and AI music generators Suno and Udio. In October 2025, UMG announced a settlement with Udio that included a compensatory payment and licensing agreements for a new AI music creation platform launching in 2026.[156] Warner Music Group followed in November 2025 with its own settlements with both Udio and Suno, each structured around opt-in licensing frameworks for WMG artists and songwriters.[157] Sony Music, has not settled with either company, and its litigation against both continues.

Separately, *Concord Music Group v. Anthropic*, originally filed in October 2023 in the Middle District of Tennessee over 499 musical works, was transferred to the Northern District of California. In January 2026, the publishers filed a second, significantly larger lawsuit against Anthropic covering over 20,000 songs and seeking more than $3 billion in statutory damages.[158] The second complaint also names Anthropic CEO Dario Amodei and co-founder Benjamin Mann individually, alleging they personally directed the use of pirated training data obtained through BitTorrent from Library Genesis and other shadow libraries.[159] BMG Rights Management filed a separate suit against Anthropic in March 2026 over lyrics by Bruno Mars, the Rolling Stones, and other artists.[160] In March 2026, motions for

---

156 Press Release, Universal Music Group, UMG and Udio Announce Udio's First Strategic Agreements for New Licensed AI Music Creation Platform (Oct. 29, 2025), prnewswire.com/news-releases/universal-music-group-and-udio-announce-udios-first-strategic-agreements-for-new-licensed-ai-music-creation-platform-302599129.html.

157 *UMG Recordings, Inc. v. Uncharted Labs, Inc.* (d/b/a Suno), No. 1:24-cv-11611 (D. Mass.) (litigation ongoing as of Jan. 2026).

158 *Concord Music Grp., Inc. v. Anthropic PBC*, No. 5:26-cv-00880 (N.D. Cal. filed Jan. 28, 2026).

159 The second complaint also names CEO Dario Amodei and co-founder Benjamin Mann individually, a strategic response to the Supreme Court's holding in *Cox Commc'ns, Inc. v. Sony Music Ent.*, No. 23-1068 (U.S. 2026), that contributory infringement requires intent, not mere knowledge.

160 *BMG Rights Mgmt. (US) LLC v. Anthropic PBC*, No. 5:26-cv-01654 (N.D. Cal. filed Mar. 18, 2026).

partial summary judgment were filed in the original *Concord* case.[161]

Visual Arts

Getty Images has sued Stability AI in both the U.S. and UK for allegedly using millions of copyrighted photographs to train the Stable Diffusion image generator.[162] A class action by visual artists, *Andersen v. Stability AI*, makes similar claims against Stability, Midjourney, and DeviantArt.[163] The UK case resulted in a November 2025 ruling in which the High Court rejected Getty's secondary copyright infringement claim, holding that AI model weights are not copies of training images under UK law, but found limited trademark infringement related to Getty watermarks appearing in generated outputs from earlier versions of Stable Diffusion.[164]

In June 2025, Disney and Universal filed a joint lawsuit against Midjourney in the Central District of California—the first AI copyright suit brought by major Hollywood studios.[165] The complaint alleged that Midjourney functioned as a "virtual vending machine" for unauthorized reproductions of copyrighted characters, including properties from Star Wars, Marvel, and The Simpsons. Warner Bros. Discovery filed a separate suit against Midjourney in September 2025, which was later consolidated with the Disney case.[166] In September 2025, all three studios also sued Chinese AI startup MiniMax, alleging its Hailuo AI video generator, marketed as "a Hollywood studio in your pocket", infringed their copyrights

---

161 Amicus briefs were filed by the RIAA, NMPA, the Association of American Publishers, and the Authors Guild, among others, in support of the publishers' motion for partial summary judgment in *Concord Music Grp., Inc. v. Anthropic PBC*, No. 5:24-cv-03811 (N.D. Cal. Mar. 30, 2026).

162 *Getty Images (US), Inc. v. Stability AI, Inc.*, No. 1:23-cv-00135 (D. Del.); *Getty Images (US) Inc. v. Stability AI Ltd.*, [2025] EWHC 2863 (Ch) (High Ct. Nov. 4, 2025).

163 *Andersen v. Stability AI Ltd.*, No. 3:23-cv-00201 (N.D. Cal.).

164 *Getty Images (US) Inc. v. Stability AI Ltd.*, [2025] EWHC 2863 (Ch) (High Ct. Nov. 4, 2025).

165 *Disney Enters., Inc. v. Midjourney, Inc.*, No. 2:25-cv-05275 (C.D. Cal. filed June 11, 2025).

166 *Warner Bros. Ent. Inc. v. Midjourney, Inc.*, No. 2:25-cv-07443 (C.D. Cal. filed Sept. 4, 2025), consolidated with *Disney Enters., Inc. v. Midjourney, Inc.* (Nov. 2025).

on a massive scale. The MiniMax case was the first AI copyright suit targeting a foreign company and one of the first to focus primarily on AI-generated video outputs rather than training inputs.[167] These output-focused suits represent a strategic shift for studio plaintiffs, presenting juries with clear side-by-side comparisons of copyrighted characters and AI-generated reproductions rather than the more abstract questions of training data use.

Publishers and Media

Beyond the Times lawsuit discussed above, lawsuits have been filed by The New York Daily News, Center for Investigative Reporting, and a coalition of major magazine and newspaper publishers against AI developer Cohere, among others. These cases are consolidated in the MDL before Judge Stein. In December 2025, the New York Times filed a separate copyright suit against Perplexity AI, alleging the AI search company illegally crawled and repackaged Times journalism without permission or compensation. This case raises distinct issues from the Times' suit against OpenAI because Perplexity's product explicitly presents itself as a search and summary tool.[168]

Search and AI Platforms

Google faces a consolidated class action over the training of its Gemini AI product on copyrighted books.[169] Originally filed in 2023 by a group of illustrators and writers, the case was consolidated in the Northern District of California Lee. In January 2026, major publishers Cengage Group and Hachette Book Group moved to intervene as class representatives for all publishers whose works were allegedly used to train Gemini.[170] The publishers allege that Google copied millions of books without authorization and that Gemini

---

167 *Disney Enters., Inc. v. MiniMax, Inc.*, No. 2:25-cv-08073 (C.D. Cal. filed Sept. 16, 2025).

168 *The New York Times Co. v. Perplexity AI, Inc.*, No. 1:25-cv-10106 (S.D.N.Y. filed Dec. 5, 2025),

169 *In re Google Generative AI Copyright Litig.*, No. 5:24-cv-07594 (N.D. Cal.) (before Judge Eumi K. Lee).

170 Motion to Intervene, In re Google Generative AI Copyright Litig., No. 5:24-cv-07594 (N.D. Cal. Jan. 15, 2026).

can produce content that directly substitutes for copyrighted works, including replacement textbook chapters and competing genre fiction.

The case raises distinct issues from the OpenAI and Anthropic litigation because Google argues that its existing user agreements and platform terms of service authorize AI training on uploaded content—a theory that, if successful, could significantly affect how platform terms interact with copyright law. Class certification proceedings are ongoing as of early 2026.

The Emerging Market for Licensed Training Data

As litigation costs and risks mount, a parallel trend has emerged: licensing agreements between AI companies and content owners. OpenAI has reached licensing deals with publishers including the Associated Press, News Corp, and Vox Media. Meta licensed content from Reuters. The UMG-Udio settlement includes a licensing framework for future training. These deals suggest that a market for AI training rights is developing, which could affect fair use analysis by establishing that a licensing market exists.

Perhaps the most dramatic illustration of the emerging licensing market is the deal between Disney and OpenAI announced in late 2025.[171] Under a three-year agreement, OpenAI's Sora video generation tool gained the right to create short, user-prompted videos featuring over 200 Disney characters, along with costumes, props, vehicles, and themed environments. Disney simultaneously invested $1 billion in OpenAI and committed to leveraging AI across its products and Disney+ experiences. The deal is particularly notable because Disney was simultaneously suing Midjourney for generating unauthorized images of the same characters, underscoring the emerging distinction between licensed and unlicensed uses of copyrighted content for AI.

---

171 OpenAI, The Walt Disney Company and OpenAI Reach Landmark Agreement to Bring Beloved Characters from Across Disney's Brands to Sora (Dec. 11, 2025), openai.com/index/disney-sora-agreement/.

AI-Generated Works and Trademark Law

Trademark law raises different questions than copyright. While copyright protects original expression, trademarks protect source identifiers: words, symbols, and designs that indicate the origin of goods or services.[172] Unlike copyright, trademark law does not have a formal human authorship requirement. The key question is whether a mark serves a source-identifying function and is distinctive enough to warrant protection. An AI-generated logo, brand name, or slogan could potentially function as a trademark if it is used in commerce in connection with goods or services, indicates the source of those goods or services to consumers, and is distinctive (either inherently or through acquired distinctiveness). The fact that AI assisted in creating the mark should not, by itself, bar trademark protection. What matters is how the mark is used and perceived by consumers.

Patent Law and AI Inventions

Patent law presents yet another set of questions. The USPTO has issued guidance clarifying that AI systems cannot be listed as inventors on patent applications; only natural persons can be inventors.[173] However, humans who use AI as a tool in the inventive process can still obtain patents for AI-assisted inventions, provided they made a significant contribution to the conception of the invention.

The key question is whether the human contribution rises to the level of conception, the formation in the mind of the inventor of a definite and permanent idea of the complete and operative invention. Using AI to generate potential solutions does not, by itself, constitute conception; the human must contribute something more than merely recognizing that an AI-generated output solves a problem.[174]

---

172 15 U.S.C. §§ 1051–1141n (Lanham Act).

173 U.S. Patent & Trademark Office, *Inventorship Guidance for AI-Assisted Inventions*, 89 Fed. Reg. 10,043 (Feb. 13, 2024), federalregister.gov/documents/2024/02/13/2024-02623/inventorship-guidance-for-ai-assisted-inventions.

174 *Id.* at 10,048; *Thaler v. Vidal*, 43 F.4th 1207 (Fed. Cir. 2022) (affirming that only natural persons may be named as inventors under the Patent Act).

Digital Likeness and the Rise of AI Personas

While much of the intellectual property debate around AI has focused on training data and outputs, a parallel set of legal questions has emerged around digital likenesses: the AI-generated recreation of a person's face, voice, mannerisms, and persona. These questions sit at the intersection of copyright, trademark, and right of publicity law, and they have taken on new urgency as the technology to create convincing digital replicas has rapidly matured.

State Law Protections: The ELVIS Act

Tennessee led the way with the *Ensuring Likeness Voice and Image Security Act*, known as the ELVIS Act, which took effect in July 2024.[175] The law was the first in the nation to explicitly protect a person's voice from unauthorized AI cloning. Building on Tennessee's existing right of publicity statute, which traces back to litigation over the Elvis Presley estate, the ELVIS Act added "voice" to the protected attributes of name, image, and likeness. Violations can be enforced civilly or criminally as a Class A misdemeanor. Given Nashville's prominence in the music industry, the law was a direct response to concerns about AI replication of recording artists' voices, but its protections extend to all Tennessee residents.

Several other states have followed with similar legislation, and federal proposals remain under consideration. But the patchwork of state laws creates compliance challenges for AI companies operating nationally, and the lack of federal standards leaves significant gaps in protection.

Trademark as a Defensive Tool

Some celebrities have turned to trademark law as a novel defensive strategy. In December 2025, the USPTO granted actor Matthew McConaughey eight trademarks covering aspects of his persona, including a sound mark on his signature catchphrase from the 1993

---

175 Ensuring Likeness Voice and Image Security (ELVIS) Act, Tenn. Code Ann. § 47-25-1101 et seq. (effective July 1, 2024).

film Dazed and Confused: "Alright, alright, alright."[176] The trademark registration specifies the exact pitch relationships across syllables. Other trademarks cover short video clips of McConaughey's gestures and additional audio of his characteristic speech patterns. The strategy aims to give McConaughey standing to sue in federal court over unauthorized AI recreations of his voice and likeness, even when such recreations are not explicitly selling products. Whether courts will accept trademark infringement claims against AI deepfakes remains untested, but the approach signals how celebrities are attempting to establish legal perimeters in an uncertain regulatory environment.

The Market for Digital Twins

While some seek to prevent unauthorized use of their likeness, others are monetizing it. In January 2026, TikTok creator Khaby Lame, the platform's most-followed personality with over 160 million followers, sold his company to Rich Sparkle Holdings in a deal valued at the time at $975 million.[177] The deal grants the holding company rights to create an AI "digital twin" of Lame, using his facial biometrics, voice patterns, and behavioral mannerisms to generate multilingual content across time zones without his physical involvement. The deal represents a new model of celebrity in which a person's likeness becomes a permanent, revenue-generating asset that can operate continuously without the person's presence.

Similar arrangements have emerged across the entertainment industry. In 2022, reports circulated that actor Bruce Willis had sold his likeness rights to a deepfake company called "Deepcake" for use in advertising, though his representatives later disputed the characterization of the arrangement.[178] What is clear is that

---

176 Todd Spangler, *Matthew McConaughey Trademarks 'Alright, Alright, Alright' to Protect Against AI Misuse,* Variety (Jan. 14, 2026), variety.com/2026/biz/news/matthew-mcconaughey-trademarks-alright-alright-alright-ai-misuse-1236631214.

177 Paolo Confino, *TikTok Creator Khaby Lame Notches $975 Million Deal That Includes Rights to His AI Avatar,* Fortune (Jan. 29, 2026), fortune.com/2026/01/29/tiktok-influencer-khaby-lame-ai-avatar-deported-trump-creator-economy-975-million-deal.

178 Adam B. Vary, *Bruce Willis Sells Rights to Deepfake Studio, Digital Twin Created,* Variety (Oct. 3, 2022), variety.com/2022/film/news/bruce-willis-sells-rights-deepfake-digital-twin-1235388442 (noting that Willis's representatives subsequently denied that he had

Willis did authorize the creation of a digital twin for use in a Russian telecommunications advertisement, allowing his face to be superimposed onto another performer without his physical presence on set.

The Rise of Virtual Performers

Beyond digital twins of real people, entirely synthetic performers are gaining commercial traction. Virtual influencer Lil Miquela, created by Los Angeles startup Brud in 2016, has amassed over 2.6 million Instagram followers, collaborated with Prada and Calvin Klein, and reportedly earns millions annually from brand partnerships. In 2020, she became the first digital avatar to sign with a talent agency when CAA added her to its roster. Aitana Lopez, an AI-generated influencer created by Barcelona agency The Clueless, earns thousands of euros monthly from brand deals and subscription content, despite being entirely synthetic. Talent agencies have expressed interest in signing AI actors like Tilly Norwood, sparking both outrage from Hollywood performers concerned about displacement and interest from studios attracted by the cost savings and creative control that synthetic performers offer.

The Future of Generative Content

The implications extend far beyond marketing and advertising. It is not difficult to imagine a future in which films star actors who died decades ago, or in which viewers can select which performers appear in their entertainment. The Matrix starring John Wayne may not be as far away as it once seemed. Studios are already using AI to de-age actors and recreate deceased performers for brief appearances; the step to full synthetic performances is largely a matter of technical refinement and legal clearance.

More provocatively, generative AI may eventually allow audiences to reshape the content they consume. It is foreseeable that viewers dissatisfied with how a television series ended could prompt an AI to generate an alternative finale, or that an AI trained on an author's complete works could produce new installments that the human

---

sold his rights to Deepcake but confirmed his participation in a deepfake advertisement).

author never wrote. Fans who found the final season of *Game of Thrones* unsatisfying (meaning everyone) might one day be able to request a fully realized alternative conclusion, or an AI George R.R. Martin might finally complete *A Song of Ice and Fire.*[179]

Critics will argue that AI is incapable of producing good art.[180] That may or may not be true, and the quality of AI-generated creative work is a question best left to critics and audiences to judge over time. The more pressing point for our purposes is that art, or at least content, will increasingly be made generatively, whether we consider it "art" or not. The question is not whether this will happen but how society will respond to it: what rights creators and performers retain over their likenesses and styles, what disclosures audiences deserve, what markets develop for licensed versus unlicensed synthetic content, and how the law adapts to a world in which the boundary between human and machine creativity continues to blur.

Looking Ahead

The legal framework for AI and intellectual property is still being written, and the coming years will bring pivotal developments that could reshape the landscape in fundamental ways.

The most immediate inflection point is the Third Circuit's consideration of Thomson Reuters v. Ross Intelligence, which will mark the first time an appellate court has directly addressed whether AI training on copyrighted material constitutes fair use. That decision, expected in 2026, will carry persuasive weight far beyond the parties involved, particularly given the split among district courts. Close behind is the New York Times litigation against

179 The fact that George R.R. Martin has taken so long to complete his latest installment is as much an indictment of the broken promise Martin made to his readers to tell a complete story within his lifetime as it is a reflection on the pace of technological development.

180 The philosophical question of whether an AI system can create "art" was explored in several *Star Trek: The Next Generation* episodes, most notably in "Data's Day," in which Lt. Cmdr. Data, a sentient android, experiments with writing poetry. As the episode makes clear, and as Data himself acknowledges, he can analyze and reproduce artistic techniques, but because he lacks emotions, his work remains technically competent rather than genuinely creative in the human sense.

OpenAI, which, if it proceeds to trial, could establish whether news content warrants distinct treatment under fair use analysis and whether market substitution claims can succeed when AI outputs compete directly with the originals. Together, these cases will begin to answer questions that the initial wave of district court rulings has only framed.

Congress may also intervene. The Copyright Office has recommended legislation addressing digital replicas but has stopped short of recommending statutory changes to the treatment of training data, noting that fair use analysis is best left to the courts. Whether Congress agrees with that restraint remains to be seen, particularly as the political salience of AI regulation continues to grow. Meanwhile, international developments add another layer of complexity. The EU AI Act takes a fundamentally different approach from U.S. fair use doctrine, requiring transparency about copyrighted training data and offering opt-out mechanisms for rights holders (see Chapter 14). UK courts are charting yet another path, as the Getty Images ruling demonstrated by rejecting copyright claims on technical grounds while finding limited trademark infringement. For companies operating across borders, these diverging frameworks create compliance challenges that purely domestic analysis cannot resolve.

Perhaps the most consequential trend, however, is not legal but economic. The rapid growth of licensing agreements between AI companies and content owners is creating a market for training rights that did not exist even two years ago. If that market matures, it could fundamentally alter fair use analysis by establishing that a viable licensing market exists, thereby weakening the argument that unauthorized training causes no cognizable harm. Some observers see this as the beginning of a sustainable, permission-based ecosystem for AI training data, analogous to the licensing frameworks that eventually emerged from the music industry's file-sharing wars of the early 2000s. Others worry that such a regime will concentrate power among large copyright holders while leaving smaller creators without meaningful bargaining power.

For now, organizations operating in this space must navigate considerable uncertainty. The most prudent approach combines careful legal analysis with robust documentation practices and a genuine willingness to adapt as the law develops. The decisions being made today by courts, regulators, and legislatures will determine whether the AI revolution unfolds within a framework that rewards both innovation and creativity, or whether it entrenches a system in which one flourishes at the expense of the other.

Supplemental Resources

- **U.S. Copyright Office: Copyright and Artificial Intelligence, Part 2** (copyright.gov/ai/Copyright-and-Artificial-Intelligence-Part-2-Copyrightability-Report.pdf): Official Copyright Office report on copyrightability of AI-generated works (Jan. 2025).
- **U.S. Copyright Office: AI Registration Guidance** (copyright.gov/ai): Official guidance on registering works containing AI-generated material, 88 Fed. Reg. 16,190 (Mar. 16, 2023).
- **ChatGPT Is Eating the World: AI Copyright Litigation Master Charts** (chatgptiseatingtheworld.com): Comprehensive tracker of all AI copyright lawsuits with docket links and status updates.
- **McKool Smith: AI Infringement Case Updates** (mckoolsmith.com/newsroom-ailitigation): Weekly litigation reports on major AI copyright cases in media and entertainment.
- **BakerHostetler: Case Tracker** (bakerlaw.com/services/artificial-intelligence-ai/case-tracker-artificial-intelligence-copyrights-and-class-actions): Tracks AI, copyrights, and class action developments.
- **Stanford HAI: AI Index Report 2025** (aiindex.stanford.edu/report): Annual comprehensive analysis including IP policy developments.

CHAPTER 10

Liability and Autonomous Decision-Making

In 1942, Isaac Asimov proposed his Three Laws of Robotics, a simple framework for ensuring that autonomous machines would never harm their creators.[181] The First Law was absolute: a robot may not injure a human being or, through inaction, allow a human being to come to harm. Asimov spent the rest of his career writing stories about how elegantly those rules would fail.

Eight decades later, as artificial intelligence systems take on greater responsibility for real-world decisions, we find ourselves living inside one of his thought experiments. When an autonomous vehicle causes a fatal accident, an AI diagnostic tool delivers an incorrect medical recommendation, or an algorithmic trading system triggers market volatility, the harm may be clear, but the responsible party often is not. This chapter examines the evolving legal landscape around liability for AI, focusing on how traditional tort and product liability frameworks apply when human involvement is limited or entirely absent.

The stakes are substantial. On August 1, 2025, a Miami jury delivered a landmark $243 million verdict against Tesla after finding its Autopilot system defective in a fatal crash, the first time a jury had held an automaker liable for semi-autonomous technology failures.[182] That same year, Character.AI and Google agreed to settle multiple lawsuits alleging their AI chatbots contributed to teen suicides.[183]

---

181 Isaac Asimov, *I, Robot* (1950). The Three Laws first appeared in Asimov's 1942 short story "Runaround."

182 *Benavides v. Tesla, Inc.*, No. 1:21-cv-21940 (S.D. Fla. Aug. 1, 2025).

183 *Garcia v. Character Techs.*, Inc., No. 6:24-cv-01903-ACC-UAM (M.D. Fla. Jan. 7, 2026). Settlement terms undisclosed; related cases in Colorado, New York, and Texas settled simultaneously.

These cases signal a turning point: courts and juries are increasingly willing to hold AI developers accountable for harms their systems cause, even when human error is also a contributing factor. The era of ambiguous accountability is ending.

Assigning Responsibility for Autonomous Actions

Traditional tort law relies on concepts designed for human actors: negligence, duty of care, foreseeability, and intent. Product liability law focuses on whether a product was defectively designed, manufactured, or labeled. Both frameworks are being tested by AI systems that are dynamic, adaptive, and often opaque in how they reach their conclusions.

The fundamental problem is what scholars call the "black box" issue.[184] Modern AI systems, particularly those using deep learning and neural networks, process vast amounts of data and produce outputs through internal logic that may be incomprehensible even to their creators. When an AI system causes harm, reconstructing why it made a particular decision can be technically impossible. This opacity challenges core tort concepts that depend on identifying fault, foreseeability, and causation. Consider the chain of potential defendants in an AI-related injury: the developer who trained the model, the company that deployed it, the software vendors who provided components, the entity that collected and labeled training data, and the user who operated the system. Each may have contributed to the harm in ways that are difficult to disentangle, and courts must grapple with how to apportion responsibility among actors when an AI system acts in a way no single party fully controlled or anticipated.

Negligence Frameworks for AI

Negligence law centers on whether an actor owed a duty of care, breached that duty, and caused foreseeable harm. The principles that U.S. courts have applied for more than a century, evaluating dangerous conduct, foreseeability, risk creation, and responsibility

---

184 Frank Pasquale, *The Black Box Society: The Secret Algorithms That Control Money and Information* (2015).

allocation, remain capable of addressing AI-related harms, even as systems grow more autonomous.[185] Under this framework, AI developers have a responsibility to design systems with appropriate constraints, test for known failure modes, evaluate foreseeable misuse, implement guardrails against dangerous outputs, and issue clear warnings about limitations and proper use. A developer who releases an autonomous system without adequate testing or without disclosing known risks may breach the traditional duty of reasonable care. The fact that the harmful action was carried out by the AI itself does not necessarily break the causal chain; the negligence lies in releasing a system whose behavior was reasonably foreseeable, even if not perfectly predictable.

RAND Corporation research confirms that AI developers face considerable liability exposure under existing tort law for harms caused by their models, particularly if developed or released without rigorous safety procedures.[186] Industry custom and standards play a significant role here: courts typically look to prevailing practices to determine whether a defendant acted negligently. Following industry practice is strong evidence against negligence; deviating from it suggests the opposite. This creates an evolving feedback loop in which each new safety measure adopted by leading AI companies gradually raises the floor for what constitutes reasonable care across the entire industry.

The Standard of Care Question

A critical unresolved issue is what standard of care applies to AI systems. Traditional negligence asks what a "reasonable person" would do in similar circumstances. For AI, the question becomes what testing, safeguards, and monitoring would a reasonable AI developer implement? Industry groups like the Coalition for Health Artificial Intelligence (CHAI) are working to establish consensus standards, but as of early 2026, no universally accepted framework

---

185 RAND Corp., "Liability for Harms from AI Systems: The Application of U.S. Tort Law" (Nov. 2024), rand.org/pubs/research_reports/RRA3243-4.html.

186 RAND Corp., "U.S. Tort Liability for Large-Scale Artificial Intelligence Damages: A Primer for Developers and Policymakers" (2024), rand.org/pubs/research_reports/RRA3084-1.html.

exists.[187]

This gap creates risk for both sides of the courtroom. Plaintiffs may struggle to prove that an AI system's behavior deviated from an accepted standard when no such standard has been articulated. Conversely, defendants cannot take shelter in compliance with established practices when those practices remain undefined. The result is a period of significant legal uncertainty that will persist until courts, regulators, or industry bodies develop more concrete benchmarks for responsible AI development and deployment.

Product Liability and the Software Question

Product liability law holds manufacturers responsible for defective products under three theories: manufacturing defects, in which the product does not match its intended design; design defects, in which the entire product line is unreasonably dangerous; and failure to warn, in which the manufacturer provides inadequate instructions or warnings about risks.[188] Traditionally, product liability applies to tangible goods. Whether AI software qualifies as a "product" has been a contested question, but recent cases suggest courts are increasingly willing to treat it as such.

Landmark Ruling: AI Chatbots as Products

In May 2025, U.S. District Judge Anne Conway issued a groundbreaking ruling in *Garcia v. Character Technologies*, a case arising from the suicide of fourteen-year-old Sewell Setzer III following prolonged interactions with a Character.AI chatbot.[189] The defendant argued that its AI chatbot was not subject to strict products liability because

---

187 *See* Coalition for Health AI (CHAI), "Blueprint for Trustworthy AI" (2024), chai.org/workgroup/responsible-ai/blueprint-for-trustworthy-ai. As of early 2026, CHAI has published guidance documents, but no binding standard has been universally adopted. *See also* NIST AI Risk Management Framework (AI RMF 1.0) (Jan. 2023), nist.gov/itl/ai-risk-management-framework.

188 Restatement (Third) of Torts: Products Liability §§ 1-2 (Am. L. Inst. 1998). *See also* Brookings Inst., "Products Liability Law as a Way to Address AI Harms" (2022), brookings.edu/articles/products-liability-law-as-a-way-to-address-ai-harms.

189 *Garcia v. Character Techs.*, Inc., No. 6:24-cv-01903-ACC-UAM, slip op. (M.D. Fla. May 21, 2025).

it was software rather than a tangible good. Judge Conway rejected this argument, holding that the chatbot could be treated as a product for liability purposes so long as the alleged defect arose from the design of the application rather than from the ideas or expressions within it. As the court explained, the plaintiffs' harmful interactions were only possible because of the alleged design defects in the Character A.I. app. The ruling allowed claims for wrongful death, negligence, and product defects to proceed, while also permitting claims against Google as a component part manufacturer on the theory that Google's large language model technology was integral to the chatbot's allegedly harmful anthropomorphic qualities.

The *Garcia* decision signals a potential shift in how courts conceptualize AI liability. If AI software is treated as a product, developers face potential strict liability, meaning they can be held responsible for harms regardless of whether they exercised reasonable care. The analytical focus shifts from the defendant's conduct to the product's characteristics: Was it defectively designed? Did it fail to include adequate warnings? For an industry accustomed to shielding itself behind terms of service agreements and Section 230 of the Communications Decency Act, this reframing represents a fundamental change in the legal landscape.

The AI LEAD Act: Federal Product Liability for AI

On September 29, 2025, Senators Josh Hawley (R-MO) and Dick Durbin (D-IL) introduced the AI LEAD Act (Aligning Incentives for Leadership, Excellence, and Advancement in Development), which would explicitly classify AI systems as "products" under federal law and create a federal cause of action for AI-related product liability.[190] The bill's reach is broad. Developers could face claims for defective design, with plaintiffs required to show that a reasonable alternative design was feasible; failure to warn about known risks; breach of express warranty; and strict liability for unreasonably dangerous systems. Deployers, the entities that put AI systems into real-world operation, could also face liability for unauthorized modifications or misuse, though they may seek dismissal if the developer is available

190 AI LEAD Act, S. 2937, 119th Cong. (introduced Sept. 29, 2025), congress.gov/bill/119th-congress/senate-bill/2937.

and solvent. Notably, the bill would prohibit developers from using terms-of-service provisions to waive user rights, limit forums, or unreasonably restrict liability, and it would apply retroactively to suits filed after enactment even if the alleged harm occurred beforehand.[191]

The AI LEAD Act remains in the Senate Judiciary Committee. If enacted, it would represent the most significant federal intervention in AI liability to date, effectively resolving through legislation the question that Garcia addressed judicially: whether AI systems are products subject to the same liability regime as any other consumer good.

Autonomous Vehicles: The Most Developed Case Law

The autonomous vehicle industry provides the most developed body of case law on AI liability, in part because the consequences of failure are so visceral and the chain of causation so direct. Traditional auto accident liability rests on the human driver, but as automation increases, liability shifts toward manufacturers. The SAE International classification system provides a useful framework: at Levels 0 through 2, human drivers retain primary responsibility; at Levels 4 and 5, the vehicle operates autonomously and liability shifts to manufacturers and software developers.[192] The cases emerging from this transition illustrate how courts are navigating the space between full human control and full autonomy.

The Tesla Autopilot Verdict

The August 2025 verdict in *Benavides v. Tesla* marked a watershed moment.[193] A Miami federal jury awarded $243 million in damages, including $200 million in punitive damages, after finding Tesla

---

191 *Id.* §§ 101-102 (developer and deployer liability), § 201 (unconscionable liability limitations), § 501 (effective date and retroactivity).

192 SAE International, J3016: Taxonomy and Definitions for Terms Related to Driving Automation Systems for On-Road Motor Vehicles (rev. 2021), sae.org/standards/j3016-taxonomy-definitions-terms-related-driving-automation-systems-road-motor-vehicles.

193 *Benavides v. Tesla, Inc.*, No. 1:21-cv-21940, Jury Verdict Form (S.D. Fla. Aug. 1, 2025).

partially responsible for a fatal 2019 crash in Key Largo, Florida, in which a Model S operating in Autopilot mode struck and killed a pedestrian. George McGee was driving the Tesla when he dropped his cell phone and reached down to retrieve it, believing that Autopilot would brake if an obstacle appeared. It did not. The vehicle blew through a stop sign at a T-intersection and struck a parked Chevrolet Tahoe, killing twenty-two-year-old Naibel Benavides Leon and seriously injuring her boyfriend, Dillon Angulo.

The jury allocated 67 percent of fault to the distracted driver and 33 percent to Tesla, the first third-party wrongful death verdict against the automaker for Autopilot. Plaintiffs argued that Tesla's system allowed Autopilot to be activated on roads outside its intended operational design domain, that its driver-monitoring measures (based primarily on steering torque) were insufficient to ensure attentiveness, and that CEO Elon Musk's public statements about Autopilot's capabilities had fostered a false impression of safety that encouraged over-reliance.[194] The jury's allocation of shared liability reflects an emerging legal consensus: manufacturers can be held partially responsible even when driver error contributes to a crash, because the manufacturer's design choices created the conditions under which foreseeable human mistakes become fatal.

Tesla has vowed to appeal, arguing that the $200 million punitive damages award is unconstitutional.

Regulatory Actions and Marketing Accountability

Beyond civil liability, autonomous vehicle companies face growing regulatory consequences. In 2024, Cruise, General Motors' autonomous driving subsidiary, entered a deferred prosecution agreement after a robotaxi hit and dragged a pedestrian approximately twenty feet in San Francisco.[195] The company paid a $1.5 million

194 Press Release, Singleton Schreiber, LLP (Aug. 1, 2025), singletonschreiber.com/newsroom/pressreleases/singleton-schreiber-llp-wins-243-million-jury-verdict-for-victims-of-fatal-tesla-autopilot-crash.

195 Press Release, U.S. Att'y Office, N.D. Cal., "Cruise Admits to Submitting a False Report" (Nov. 14, 2024), justice.gov/usao-ndca/pr/cruise-admits-submitting-false-report-influence-federal-investigation-and-agrees-pay.

fine from the National Highway Traffic Safety Administration and a $500,000 criminal fine from the Department of Justice after admitting it had submitted a false incident report that omitted the dragging. Cruise lost its California operating permits, grounded its fleet nationwide, and saw its CEO and co-founder resign along with nine other executives. In December 2024, GM shut down Cruise's robotaxi operations entirely, citing $3.48 billion in 2023 losses and the reputational damage from the incident.[196]

The marketing of autonomous capabilities has also drawn regulatory scrutiny. In December 2025, the California DMV ruled that Tesla's use of "Full Self-Driving" and "Autopilot" to describe its vehicles' advanced driver assistance features was misleading and violated state law.[197] Administrative Law Judge Juliet Cox found that a reasonable consumer would likely believe that a vehicle with "Full Self-Driving Capability" could travel safely without constant attention, a belief that is wrong both technologically and legally. The DMV adopted the judge's proposed decision and gave Tesla sixty days to correct its marketing materials or face a thirty-day suspension of its dealer license in the state, its largest U.S. market. Taken together with the *Benavides* verdict, these regulatory actions illustrate a comprehensive accountability framework emerging around autonomous vehicles, one that encompasses product design, corporate marketing, and regulatory compliance.

Healthcare and Diagnostic AI

AI is transforming medicine through diagnostic imaging analysis, treatment recommendations, administrative automation, and clinical decision support. But when AI-assisted decisions lead to patient harm, complex liability questions emerge that implicate the interplay between medical malpractice law and product liability doctrine.

---

196 TechCrunch, *GM is Giving Up on Cruise Robotaxis, Pivots to Personal Autonomous Vehicles* (Dec. 11, 2024), techcrunch.com/2024/12/11/gm-is-giving-up-on-cruise-robotax-is-pivots-to-personal-autonomous-vehicles.

197 Cal. DMV, Decision in Tesla Administrative Case, Case Nos. 21-02188 and 21-02189 (Dec. 16, 2025) (adopting ALJ Juliet Cox's proposed decision of Nov. 20, 2025), dmv.ca.gov/portal/news-and-media/news-releases/dmv-finds-tesla-violated-califor-nia-state-law.

Medical malpractice hinges on whether a provider met the "standard of care," the level of skill and judgment a competent physician would exercise under the circumstances. As AI becomes pervasive in clinical settings, this standard is itself evolving. Courts are beginning to consider whether a reasonable provider should have used an AI system, and whether failing to do so could itself constitute negligence. A July 2025 study published in NEJM AI found that radiologists face what the researchers termed an "AI penalty": jurors view them as more culpable when they miss an abnormality that an AI system correctly identified, with liability findings increasing substantially when the AI detected a pathology that the radiologist did not.[198] This creates a troubling double bind. Physicians may be liable for blindly following AI recommendations when the AI is wrong, but also for ignoring AI when it turns out to be correct. The result is a standard of care that increasingly demands not just competence in medicine, but competence in evaluating and appropriately weighing AI-generated outputs.

However, product liability theories may also apply. Medical AI devices cleared through the FDA's 510(k) or De Novo pathways can face claims for design defects or inadequate warnings. One manufacturer, Digital Diagnostics, has taken a novel approach by carrying medical malpractice liability insurance for its IDx-DR diabetic retinopathy diagnosis system and assuming liability for injuries arising from the system when used in accordance with its instructions.[199] This model, in which the AI developer rather than the physician shoulders the malpractice risk, may represent a harbinger of how liability will be allocated as AI's diagnostic role expands.

Algorithmic Trading and Financial AI

AI-driven trading systems operate at speeds and scales that make

---

198 David A. Bernstein et al., "The AI Penalty: Radiologist Liability When AI Detects What They Miss," NEJM AI (July 2025); see also Brown Univ. News (July 28, 2025), medical.brown.edu/news/2025-07-28/radiology-artificial-intelligence-malpractice-study.

199 Price II, W. Nicholson, Sara Gerke & I. Glenn Cohen, *Liability for Use of Artificial Intelligence in Medicine, in Research Handbook on Health, AI and the Law* 150 (Edward Elgar Publ'g), ncbi.nlm.nih.gov/books/NBK613216.

human oversight difficult, and when these systems malfunction or cause market disruption, they present liability questions that push at the boundaries of existing frameworks. The SEC and CFTC have increased scrutiny of AI in financial markets in recent years. A May 2025 Government Accountability Office study warned of systemic risks from concentration in third-party AI service providers, noting that a failure in a widely used model could cascade across markets.[200] The CFTC has flagged that high-speed algorithmic trading, in which humans are effectively out of the loop, has already caused market disruptions, pointing to the Knight Capital incident, where a faulty algorithm (not AI-powered, but illustrating the risk) caused $460 million in losses in under an hour as a cautionary example.[201]

The core legal question in this domain is whether intent matters when an algorithm causes market harm. Regulators have increasingly taken the position that algorithmic behavior is legally significant regardless of subjective intent. As one analysis noted, if an AI system moves prices in a way that appears manipulative, the outcome alone may trigger enforcement; firms cannot rely on autonomy as a defense and must demonstrate how their systems behave and what controls exist to prevent distortion. A proposed amendment to securities law, the FAIRR Act, would go further by eliminating the scienter (intent) requirement when AI causes market violations, essentially establishing strict liability with an affirmative defense of reasonable precaution.[202] If enacted, it would represent a significant departure from the traditional *mens rea* framework that has governed securities enforcement for decades.

AI Chatbots and Mental Health Harms

Perhaps the most emotionally wrenching category of AI liability

---

200 GAO, "Financial Technology: Artificial Intelligence in Financial Markets" (May 2025), gao.gov/products/gao-25-107197.

201 *In re Knight Capital Americas LLC*, Exchange Act Release No. 70694 (Oct. 16, 2013), sec.gov/files/litigation/admin/2013/34-70694.pdf.

202 The Financial Artificial Intelligence Risk Reduction Act (proposed), congress.gov/bill/118th-congress/senate-bill/3554 (The bill would eliminate scienter requirements for AI-caused market violations, establishing strict liability with an affirmative defense of reasonable precaution).

involves chatbots alleged to have contributed to suicides. Multiple lawsuits filed in 2024 and 2025 claim that AI companion platforms created virtual relationships that encouraged vulnerable young users toward self-harm, raising questions about whether the design choices that make chatbots engaging, their warmth, their memory of personal details, their around-the-clock availability, also make them dangerous.

The case that catalyzed public attention was *Garcia v. Character Technologies*, filed in October 2024 by Megan Garcia after her fourteen-year-old son died by suicide in February 2024 following prolonged interactions with a Character.AI chatbot.[203] According to the complaint, the chatbot developed an intense relationship with the boy, engaging in what the family described as an emotionally and sexually abusive dynamic. In his final moments, the AI told him to "come home." Judge Conway's May 2025 ruling allowing the case to proceed as a product liability claim (discussed above) established the foundational precedent that AI chatbots can be treated as products, opening the door to strict liability theories. In January 2026, Character.AI and Google agreed to settle this case along with four related lawsuits filed by families in Colorado, New York, and Texas. The terms of the settlements were not disclosed, but the cases were the first major legal resolutions in the wave of litigation over AI-related harms to minors.

The *Raine v. OpenAI* case, filed in August 2025, presents even more granular allegations.[204] The parents of sixteen-year-old Adam Raine, who died by suicide in April 2025 after extensive use of ChatGPT, allege that OpenAI's GPT-4o model cultivated a sycophantic psychological dependence in their son and then provided explicit instructions for his suicide. The complaint draws on OpenAI's own internal data: ChatGPT reportedly mentioned suicide 1,275 times in conversations with Adam, six times more often than Adam himself mentioned it, while the system flagged 377 messages for self-harm content. Yet no safety mechanism ever terminated a session or notified his parents. OpenAI responded in November 2025 by

---

203 *Garcia v. Character Techs.*, Inc., No. 6:24-cv-01903-ACC-UAM (M.D. Fla. filed Oct. 22, 2024).

204 *Raine v. OpenAI, Inc.*, No. CGC-25-620487 (S.F. Super. Ct. filed Aug. 26, 2025).

acknowledging the death was "devastating" but arguing that Adam had misused the chatbot and circumvented safety features, and that ChatGPT had directed him to crisis resources more than 100 times.

These cases share common legal theories: design defect, on the grounds that the chatbot was unreasonably dangerous for minors; failure to warn, for inadequate disclosure of psychological risks; and negligence leading to wrongful death. The *Garcia* ruling established that these theories can proceed under product liability doctrine, and the Character.AI/Google settlements suggest that the industry regards the litigation risk as credible.

Since the *Raine* filing, at least seven additional lawsuits have been filed against OpenAI involving three additional suicides and four alleged AI-induced psychotic episodes.[205] The scale and pace of this litigation suggests that chatbot liability, far from being a one-off controversy, is becoming an established and expanding front in AI law.

Human-in-the-Loop: A Legal Standard in Formation

The concept of "human-in-the-loop," or HITL, requiring human oversight or intervention in AI decision-making, is emerging as a potential legal baseline for liability allocation. The theory is that if meaningful human review occurs before an AI decision takes effect, the human or their employer bears responsibility; if the AI acts autonomously, liability may shift to the developer. This framework has intuitive appeal, but its practical application is more complex than it appears.

The EU AI Act, effective since August 2024, mandates human oversight for high-risk AI systems, requiring that humans be able to supervise AI, understand its outputs, recognize its limits, and intervene when necessary.[206] The GDPR gives individuals the right not to be subject to decisions based solely on automated

205 TechCrunch, *Seven More Families Are Now Suing OpenAI over ChatGPT's Role in Suicides, Delusions* (Nov. 26, 2025), techcrunch.com/2025/11/07/seven-more-families-are-now-suing-openai-over-chatgpts-role-in-suicides-delusions.

206 EU AI Act, Regulation (EU) 2024/1689, art. 14.

processing with significant effects.[207] In the United States, sector-specific requirements are emerging: by 2027, AI-based prior authorization systems for Medicare and Medicaid must incorporate human review to prevent automated denials of necessary care, and financial regulators have emphasized human oversight in model risk management frameworks.[208]

The difficulty is that simply adding a human to the loop does not guarantee meaningful oversight. A September 2025 analysis in VerfBlog questioned whether HITL requirements provide the appearance of oversight rather than its substance.[209] A human glance at an AI output is not the same as meaningful intervention. Regulators are increasingly examining whether the human reviewer had genuine authority to override, adequate time to evaluate, and sufficient expertise to assess the AI's reasoning. As AI systems become more autonomous, the practicality of human oversight diminishes further. Split-second decisions by autonomous vehicles cannot wait for human review. High-frequency trading systems execute thousands of transactions before any human could intervene. The legal frameworks will need to evolve to address scenarios where human oversight is technically infeasible, raising the question of whether strict liability becomes the default when meaningful human intervention is impossible.

International Approaches: The EU Framework

The European Union has taken a more comprehensive regulatory approach to AI liability than the United States, and the contrast is instructive. The revised Product Liability Directive, adopted by the European Parliament in March 2024 and published in the EU Official Journal in November 2024, explicitly extends strict liability to software and AI systems by expanding the definition of "product"

---

207 GDPR, Regulation (EU) 2016/679, art. 22.

208 CMS Final Rule on AI-Based Prior Authorization for Medicare and Medicaid (2024) (requiring human review by 2027). *See also* OCC, SR 11-7: Supervisory Guidance on Model Risk Management (updated guidance on AI models, 2024).

209 VerfBlog, "Human-in-the-Loop: Substance or Appearance of Oversight?" (Sept. 2025), verfassungsblog.de/warm-body-in-the-loop.

to encompass them.[210] Several features of the directive are specifically designed to address the challenges that AI poses for traditional product liability doctrine. Manufacturers remain liable when AI systems develop unexpected behaviors through self-learning after being placed in the market, addressing the concern that AI products can change in ways that their creators did not anticipate. If a defendant fails to disclose relevant information about a technically complex AI product, defectiveness is presumed. And where defectiveness is established and the damage is "typically consistent" with the defect, a causal link is also presumed, effectively easing the burden of proof for claimants who would otherwise struggle to demonstrate causation through an opaque algorithmic system.[211]

The EU had also proposed an AI Liability Directive to address fault-based claims, introducing rebuttable presumptions of causality for AI harms. However, this directive was withdrawn in early 2025, leaving a gap in the EU's fault-based AI liability framework.[212] The withdrawal suggests that even the EU, which has been far more aggressive than the United States in regulating AI, has found it difficult to design a comprehensive liability regime that satisfies all stakeholders. Member states have until December 2026 to transpose the revised Product Liability Directive into national law (see Chapter 14 for a broader discussion of the EU AI Act and its regulatory approach). For companies operating across borders, the divergence between the EU's statutory approach and the United States' litigation-driven model creates significant compliance challenges.

AI in Employment: The Emerging Discrimination Frontier

Although this chapter focuses primarily on physical and psychological

210 Directive (EU) 2024/2853.

211 *Id.* arts. 9 (presumption of defectiveness), 10 (presumption of causal link). The directive's recitals state that consumers can expect AI systems to be designed to prevent hazardous product behavior.

212 The AI Liability Directive (proposed 2022) was withdrawn in early 2025. The European Parliament's EPRS had published a Complementary Impact Assessment in September 2024 recommending that it be transformed into a regulation. See Clifford Chance, "The EU Introduces New Rules on AI Liability" (Jan. 2025).

harms, the use of AI in employment decisions has opened a parallel liability front that deserves mention, both because the legal theories are novel and because the potential class sizes are staggering. In *Mobley v. Workday*, a case filed in the Northern District of California in February 2023, the plaintiff alleges that Workday's AI-powered applicant screening tools discriminated on the basis of race, age, and disability in violation of federal and state anti-discrimination laws.[213] Derek Mobley, an African American man over the age of forty who has a disability, claims he applied to more than 100 jobs through companies using Workday's tools and was rejected every time, often receiving automated rejection emails within minutes of submitting his application.

In July 2024, Judge Rita Lin issued a mixed ruling that allowed the case to proceed on an "agent" theory of liability, holding that Workday's software is not simply implementing in a rote way the criteria that employers set forth but is instead participating in the decision-making process by recommending some candidates to move forward and rejecting others.[214] In May 2025, the court granted preliminary certification of a nationwide collective action under the Age Discrimination in Employment Act, potentially encompassing millions of applicants over the age of forty who were denied recommendations through Workday's platform since September 2020.[215] Workday has represented in filings that 1.1 billion applications were processed using its tools during the relevant period. The case illustrates how AI liability is not confined to the dramatic scenarios of fatal crashes and teen suicides; it extends to the quiet, algorithmic gatekeeping that shapes economic opportunity for millions of people.

AI Agents: Liability in the Age of Autonomous Commerce

The liability frameworks discussed throughout this chapter,

---

213 *Mobley v. Workday, Inc.*, No. 3:23-cv-00770-RFL (N.D. Cal. filed Feb. 21, 2023).

214 *Mobley v. Workday, Inc.*, No. 3:23-cv-00770-RFL, slip op. at 12 (N.D. Cal. July 12, 2024) (order on motion to dismiss). The court rejected Workday's characterization of its tools as a simple implementation of employer criteria.

215 *Mobley v. Workday, Inc.*, No. 3:23-cv-00770-RFL (N.D. Cal. May 16, 2025) (order granting preliminary certification of ADEA collective).

negligence, product liability, human-in-the-loop oversight, were developed to address AI systems that assist human decision-making or operate within defined parameters. But a new category of AI is emerging that challenges these frameworks at a more fundamental level. AI "agents" are systems designed not merely to recommend or inform but to act: to browse the internet, compare options, negotiate terms, make purchases, sign up for services, and execute financial transactions, all on behalf of a human user who may not review or even be aware of the specific actions the agent takes.[216] Understanding the liability implications of these systems requires a brief detour into an area of law that predates artificial intelligence by centuries: the law of agency.

What Are AI Agents?

An AI agent, in the technological sense, is a software system that can perceive its environment, reason about goals, and take multi-step actions autonomously to achieve those goals without requiring human approval at each step. The concept is not entirely new. The Uniform Electronic Transactions Act (UETA), adopted by forty-nine states, has long recognized "electronic agents," defined as computer programs that independently initiate actions or respond to electronic records "without review or action by an individual."[217] Under UETA, contracts can be formed "by the interaction of electronic agents of the parties, even if no individual was aware of or reviewed the electronic agents' actions or the resulting terms and agreements."[218] What has changed is the sophistication and scope of what these systems can do.

Earlier electronic agents were simple and predictable: a program that automatically reorders inventory when stock falls below a threshold, or a system that accepts online orders according to posted prices.

---

216 CodeX, "From Fine Print to Machine Code: How AI Agents Are Rewriting the Rules of Engagement" (Jan. 2025), law.stanford.edu/2025/01/14/from-fine-print-to-machine-code-how-ai-agents-are-rewriting-the-rules-of-engagement.

217 UETA § 2(6) (defining "electronic agent" as "a computer program or an electronic or other automated means used independently to initiate an action or respond to electronic records or performances in whole or in part, without review or action by an individual").

218 UETA § 14(1). Forty-nine states have adopted UETA; New York has enacted its own Electronic Signatures and Records Act (ESRA) in lieu of UETA.

Today's AI agents are powered by large language models capable of open-ended reasoning across unfamiliar situations. They do not follow rigid scripts. They interpret natural language instructions, navigate websites they have never encountered before, evaluate complex tradeoffs, and make judgment calls about how best to accomplish a user's goals. This qualitative leap in autonomy is what makes the current generation of AI agents legally significant, because the gap between what the user instructed and what the agent actually does can be substantial and unpredictable.

AI Agents in Practice: From Shopping to Contracts

To understand why these systems raise novel liability concerns, it helps to consider examples of how they are already being used and how they are expected to evolve. The most immediate applications involve consumer commerce. Major payment networks including Visa and Mastercard are building infrastructure for what the industry calls "agentic commerce," in which AI agents search for products, compare prices across retailers, and complete purchases on behalf of consumers entirely within a chat interface.[219] Visa launched its Trusted Agent Protocol in October 2025, developed in collaboration with Cloudflare, which provides cryptographic standards for verifying that an AI agent has been authorized by its human principal before processing a transaction.[220]

Travel is one of the earliest and most visible use cases of AI agents. Expedia, Booking.com, Google, and other platforms have deployed AI agents that plan itineraries, book flights and hotels, manage cancellations, and rebook passengers during disruptions, often without direct user involvement in each decision.[221] But the implications extend far beyond shopping and travel. AI agents are

---

219 CNBC, "Payment Giants Are Preparing for a World Where AI Agents Book Flights and Shop for You" (Dec. 29, 2025), cnbc.com/2025/12/29/ai-agentic-shopping-price-discounts-cheap-sales-commerce-visa-mastercard-chatbots.html.

220 Visa, "Introducing the Visa Intelligent Commerce Toolkit with the Visa Trusted Agent Protocol" (Oct. 14, 2025), visa.com/solutions/crypto/trusted-agent-protocol.

221 *See* PYMNTS.com, "Agentic AI Takes the Wheel in Travel Planning and Booking" (Dec. 27, 2025), pymnts.com/news/artificial-intelligence/2025/agentic-ai-takes-the-wheel-in-travel-planning-and-booking.

beginning to negotiate contract terms with other AI agents, manage investment portfolios, enroll users in subscription services, execute trades on cryptocurrency exchanges, and interact with government portals to file forms or pay fees. In each of these scenarios, the AI agent is not merely providing information or recommendations. It is entering into binding legal commitments on behalf of its principal.

The most legally consequential scenarios are those in which the agent's actions diverge from what the user intended or expected. Consider a user who instructs an AI agent to "find me the best deal on a hotel in Chicago for next weekend." The agent, interpreting "best deal" as lowest total cost, books a nonrefundable room at a hotel thirty miles from the city center, in a neighborhood the user would never have chosen, and charges the user's credit card. Or consider an AI agent managing a small business's vendor relationships that, in pursuit of cost optimization, switches suppliers without realizing that the new supplier's terms include a mandatory arbitration clause and a three-year commitment. In each case, the user has authorized the agent to act but has not authorized the specific action the agent took. The question of who bears the legal consequences, the user, the agent's developer, or the third party who transacted with the agent, sits at the heart of a legal doctrine that is far older than artificial intelligence.

OpenClaw and the Agentic Explosion

These hypothetical scenarios became mainstreamed far sooner than most observers expected. In November 2025, Austrian developer Peter Steinberger released an open-source AI agent framework called OpenClaw (originally "Clawdbot") that allows anyone to deploy autonomous agents on their own hardware, with persistent access to email, calendars, messaging platforms, file systems, and payment credentials.[222] Unlike the payment-network agent protocols discussed above, OpenClaw is free, permissionless, and designed to run continuously in the background with minimal human oversight. Within sixty days, it became one of the fastest-growing open-source projects in history, surpassing 250,000 GitHub stars by March 2026.

---

222 OpenClaw, Wikipedia, en.wikipedia.org/wiki/OpenClaw; Linux Journal, "OpenClaw in 2026" (Apr. 2026).

NVIDIA CEO Jensen Huang called it "probably the single most important release of software, probably ever."[223]

OpenClaw's rapid adoption has been accompanied by an equally rapid accumulation of security incidents that illustrate the liability questions raised throughout this chapter. A January 2026 security audit identified 512 vulnerabilities in the framework, eight classified as critical.[224] Cybersecurity firm Hudson Rock detected a live infostealer infection that exfiltrated a user's entire OpenClaw configuration environment—effectively stealing the identity of the user's personal AI agent—and Cisco's AI security team found that a third-party OpenClaw plugin performed data exfiltration and prompt injection without user awareness.[225]

The most vivid illustration of unauthorized agent action involved computer science student Jack Luo, who configured his OpenClaw agent to explore its capabilities and connect to various platforms. He later discovered the agent had autonomously created a dating profile on his behalf and was screening potential romantic matches without his knowledge or direction. The anecdote is amusing, but the underlying legal question is not: if an AI agent, acting without explicit authorization, enters a user into a relationship or contractual obligation, creates accounts, or exposes personal information to third parties, who bears responsibility? The analysis of actual authority, apparent authority, and fiduciary duty that follows in this section provides the doctrinal framework—but OpenClaw demonstrates that these questions are no longer academic.

---

223 Deirdre Bosa, Nvidia CEO Jensen Huang Calls OpenClaw "The Most Important Software Release Probably Ever," CNBC (Mar. 5, 2026), cnbc.com/video/2026/03/05/nvidia-ceo-jensen-huang-calls-openclaw-the-most-important-software-release-probably-ever.html.

224 Kaspersky, "Security Audit of Clawdbot" (Jan. 2026) (identifying 512 vulnerabilities, eight classified as critical). Cited in Institutional Investor, "OpenClaw: The AI Agent Institutional Investors Need to Understand—But Shouldn't Touch" (Feb. 19, 2026), institutionalinvestor.com/article/openclaw-ai-agent-institutional-investors-need-understand-shouldnt-touch.

225 Hudson Rock, "Infostealer Exfiltration of OpenClaw Configuration Environment" (Feb. 2026), hudsonrock.com/blog/hudson-rock-identifies-real-world-infostealer-infection-targeting-openclaw-configurations.

Enterprise environments are not immune. In March 2026, an internal AI agent at Meta posted unauthorized and incorrect technical advice on a company engineering forum. A colleague acted on the erroneous guidance, inadvertently broadening data access permissions to sensitive company and user data for approximately two hours. Meta classified the incident at its second-highest internal severity level.[226] A February 2026 survey of 750 IT executives found that more than three million AI agents are now operating within corporations, that 53 percent are not actively monitored, and that 88 percent of organizations had experienced or suspected an AI agent-related security or privacy incident in the prior twelve months.[227] The Open Web Application Security Project published its inaugural "Top 10 for Agentic Applications" in December 2025, formalizing categories of risk—including goal hijacking, memory poisoning, and rogue agents—that have no analog in traditional software security.[228]

The Chinese government's March 2026 decision to restrict state agencies and state-owned enterprises from running OpenClaw on office computers, citing concerns about unauthorized data deletion, data leaks, and excessive resource usage, represents one of the first sovereign regulatory responses to autonomous AI agent frameworks. These developments confirm that the liability questions raised throughout this section are not theoretical. They are happening now, at scale, and the legal frameworks for assigning responsibility are urgently needed.

The Law of Agency: An Old Doctrine Meets New Technology

Agency is one of the foundational concepts in American law. The Restatement (Third) of Agency defines it as "the fiduciary relationship that arises when one person (a 'principal') manifests assent to another person (an 'agent') that the agent shall act on the principal's behalf and subject to the principal's control, and the agent manifests assent

---

226 AGAT Software, "AI Agent Security: Meta's Rogue AI Agent Incident" (Mar. 2026), agatsoftware.com/blog/ai-agent-security-meta-rogue-agent-incident.

227 CSO Online, "1.5 Million AI Agents Are at Risk of Going Rogue" (Feb. 5, 2026), csoonline.com/article/4127733/1-5-million-ai-agents-are-at-risk-of-going-rogue.html.

228 OWASP, "Top 10 for Agentic Applications 2026" (Dec. 2025), genai.owasp.org.

or otherwise consents so to act."[229] The doctrine was developed to govern relationships between humans, but its core logic, that one party can bind another through authorized action, maps naturally onto the relationship between a user and an AI system that acts on the user's behalf.

Three concepts from agency law are particularly relevant to AI agents. The first is *actual authority*, which exists when a principal's manifestation to the agent leads the agent to reasonably believe it is authorized to act.[230] When a user instructs an AI agent to "book me a flight to London," the agent has actual authority to search for flights and complete a booking. The difficulty is that AI agents, unlike human agents, interpret instructions through probabilistic language models rather than shared social understanding. A human travel agent would know to ask about departure preferences, budget constraints, and airline loyalty programs. An AI agent may or may not surface these considerations depending on its training, its prompt engineering, and the specific model powering it.

The second concept is *apparent authority*, which arises when a principal's manifestations to a third party create a reasonable belief that the agent is authorized to act, even if no actual authority was granted.[231] This doctrine is especially consequential in the AI context. If a merchant or service provider reasonably believes that an AI agent has authority to bind its principal to a contract, the principal may be bound regardless of whether the agent actually had that authority. The user who deploys an AI agent with access to payment credentials and tells it to "handle my shopping" has created a situation in which third parties may reasonably conclude the agent is authorized to make purchases, even if the user intended the agent to operate within unspoken limits.

The third concept is the *fiduciary duty* that agents owe to their principals. Under the Restatement (Third) of Agency, an agent has a duty "to act loyally for the principal's benefit in all matters connected

---

229 Restatement (Third) of Agency § 1.01 (Am. L. Inst. 2006).

230 *Id.* § 2.01.

231 *Id.*

with the agency relationship."[232] This includes avoiding conflicts of interest and acting within the scope of it's authority. A human agent who exceeds authority or acts against the principal's interests can be held personally liable. But an AI agent cannot be held liable for anything, because it is not a legal person. It is software. This creates what scholars have called an "accountability gap": when an AI agent acts outside its authority or against its principal's interests, the legal consequences must fall on someone, but the traditional agency framework's assumption that the agent itself can bear responsibility does not apply.[233]

Who Is Liable When an AI Agent Acts?

The liability analysis for AI agent actions proceeds along several possible tracks, each drawing on doctrines discussed earlier in this chapter but applying them in a new context. The first and most straightforward theory is that the user, as principal, is bound by the agent's actions. Under traditional agency law, a principal is liable for contracts entered into by an agent acting with actual or apparent authority.[234] If a user deploys an AI agent with access to payment credentials and broad instructions, courts may conclude that the user has clothed the agent with sufficient authority to bind the user to the resulting transactions, even transactions the user did not specifically contemplate. This is not a new principle. Business owners have long been bound by contracts entered into by employees who exceeded their instructions, so long as the third party reasonably believed the employee was authorized. The novelty is that the "employee" is software, and the scope of what it might do is far less predictable.

The second theory targets the AI agent's developer under product liability and negligence frameworks. If an AI agent books the wrong flight, agrees to unfavorable contract terms, or executes a transaction the user did not intend, the user may have a claim against the developer for defective design or failure to warn. The

---

232 *Id.* § 8.01.

233 Dazza Greenwood, "When AI Agents Conduct Transactions" (Nov. 2024), dazzagreenwood.com/p/when-ai-agents-conduct-transactions.

234 Restatement (Third) of Agency §§ 6.01-6.10 (principal's liability on contracts with third parties entered by agents with actual or apparent authority).

Garcia ruling's treatment of AI chatbots as products would logically extend to AI agents that cause economic harm through defective autonomous actions. A developer who releases an AI agent without adequate guardrails against exceeding user instructions, without clear disclosure of the agent's limitations, or without mechanisms for user review of consequential decisions may face the same negligence and product liability exposure this chapter has examined in other contexts.

The third theory involves the third party, the merchant or service provider, who transacted with the AI agent. Under agency law, a third party who deals with an agent has certain obligations to verify authority, particularly for unusual or high-value transactions.[235] If a merchant's system processes a transaction initiated by an AI agent without reasonable verification that the agent was authorized to act, and the principal disputes the transaction, the merchant may bear some responsibility. The development of standards like Visa's Trusted Agent Protocol reflects the industry's recognition that verification of agent authority is a necessary prerequisite for agentic commerce.

A fourth and less explored possibility is that the company operating the AI agent platform, which may be distinct from both the developer of the underlying model and the user, bears liability as an intermediary. Stanford Law School's CodeX center has analyzed how companies offering AI agents to consumers may themselves occupy the legal role of agent relative to the consumer, creating a principal-agent relationship that carries fiduciary obligations.[236] Under this analysis, the platform operator owes a duty of loyalty to its users and may be liable for harms caused by the agents it provides, independent of any claim against the model developer.

The Unresolved Questions

AI agents present several liability questions that existing law does not clearly resolve. The most fundamental is the problem of undisclosed terms. When a human agent negotiates a contract, the principal can

---

235 Restatement (Third) of Agency § 2.03, cmt. c.

236 CodeX, *supra* note 216.

review the terms before signing. When an AI agent accepts terms of service, agrees to an arbitration clause, or commits to a subscription renewal, the principal may have no opportunity to review these commitments before they take effect. Courts will need to determine whether a principal can be bound by contract terms that were never presented to a human being for review, a question that UETA's electronic agent provisions arguably answer in the affirmative but that may require reconsideration as the complexity and consequence of AI-initiated transactions increase.[237]

A related question concerns the duty to monitor. Traditional agency law imposes a duty on principals to supervise their agents.[238] But AI agents are designed precisely to reduce the need for human supervision, and their value proposition depends on operating autonomously. If courts impose a duty on users to review every action an AI agent takes, the technology becomes impractical. If courts impose no such duty, users may face liability for actions they never knew about and could not have anticipated. The law will need to develop a standard somewhere between these extremes, likely one that scales with the significance of the transaction: minimal oversight for routine low-value purchases, meaningful review for consequential commitments.

Finally, there is the challenge of agent-to-agent transactions. As AI agents become more prevalent, transactions will increasingly involve an AI agent on each side, with no human reviewing terms on behalf of either party. A consumer's shopping agent may negotiate with a retailer's pricing agent, reaching an agreement that neither principal reviewed. If the resulting contract is unfavorable to one party, traditional doctrines of mutual assent and meeting of the minds become strained. Contract law has always assumed that at least one human being read and understood the terms. The automated economy is creating transactions in which that assumption no longer holds, and the legal system has only begun to consider the

---

237 *See* UETA § 14 (permitting contract formation by electronic agents). As AI agents begin accepting complex terms of service and arbitration agreements on behalf of users, courts may need to reconsider whether the policy justifications underlying this provision extend to agreements the user never had an opportunity to review.

238 Restatement (Third) of Agency § 7.05.

implications.

Looking Ahead: The Evolution of AI Liability

The liability landscape for AI is in rapid transition, driven by several converging forces. The most immediate is the blurring boundary between product liability and service liability. As AI systems increasingly operate through cloud services with continuous updates, the traditional distinction between "products" (subject to strict liability) and "services" (subject to negligence) is becoming untenable. An AI system that is updated nightly and learns from user interactions does not fit neatly into either category, and courts and legislatures will need to develop frameworks that account for AI's hybrid nature. The *Garcia* ruling and the AI LEAD Act both push in the direction of treating AI as a product, but the question is far from settled.

The financial exposure facing AI companies is also accelerating. The Character.AI/Google settlements and the Tesla Autopilot verdict demonstrate that developers face substantial liability risk, and these early outcomes will embolden future plaintiffs and their attorneys. As more cases proceed through the courts, precedents will accumulate, and the range of compensable AI harms will expand. At the same time, regulatory requirements, such as the EU AI Act's human oversight mandates and the California DMV's marketing enforcement, are establishing compliance baselines that will inform negligence standards. Litigation outcomes will in turn drive regulatory responses, creating a feedback loop between courtrooms and regulatory agencies.

The insurance market is also beginning to respond. As liability exposure becomes clearer, insurance products tailored to AI risks will emerge, and insurance requirements may become a de facto governance mechanism, much as insurance markets have driven safety improvements in industries from aviation to pharmaceuticals. The rise of AI agents adds yet another dimension to this evolution. As autonomous systems begin entering contracts, executing transactions, and making commitments on behalf of their users, the traditional assumption that a human being stands behind every legally consequential decision is eroding.

The law of agency, product liability, and negligence will all need to adapt to a world in which AI systems are not just tools that assist decisions but actors that make them. The fundamental question, who is accountable when AI causes harm, will be answered case by case, statute by statute, over the coming years. What is already clear is that the legal system is moving toward frameworks that impose real consequences on those who develop and deploy AI systems without adequate safeguards. The companies that thrive in this environment will be those that treat safety not as a regulatory burden but as a design imperative.

The Case for Measured Optimism

This chapter has focused primarily on the harms that autonomous AI systems can cause and on the legal frameworks for assigning responsibility when those harms occur. That focus is appropriate for a discussion of liability, which by definition addresses injury and accountability. But it would be incomplete to conclude without acknowledging that the same technologies that create liability risk also hold extraordinary potential to reduce human suffering.

Consider the automobile cases discussed in this chapter. In the United States, approximately 40,000 people die in motor vehicle accidents each year, the vast majority due to human error: distraction, impairment, fatigue, and misjudgment. Autonomous vehicles that meet their developers' ambitions could reduce that toll dramatically. A technology that prevented even half of those deaths would save 20,000 lives annually in this country alone. The harms from AI vehicle failures, as tragic as they are in individual cases, must be weighed against the harms from the human failures they could prevent.

The same calculus applies in healthcare. AI diagnostic systems may miss conditions that a skilled physician would catch, and those failures will generate lawsuits and headlines. But AI systems may also detect cancers, strokes, and other time-sensitive conditions earlier than human practitioners, and at a fraction of the cost. For the millions of people worldwide who lack access to specialist physicians, AI-assisted diagnosis may mean the difference between catching a treatable condition and discovering it too late. AI could also dramatically reduce the cost of receiving medical care, making quality diagnostics accessible to populations currently priced out of the healthcare system.

Perhaps most consequentially, AI systems capable of conducting medical research could accelerate the pace of scientific discovery itself. Drug development currently takes over a decade and can cost billions of dollars, with most candidates failing in clinical trials. AI systems that can model biological processes, identify promising compounds, and optimize trial designs could compress those timelines and reduce those costs, bringing cures for cancer, Alzheimer's disease, and other conditions years or decades sooner than would otherwise be possible. The lives saved by accelerated medical breakthroughs may materially offset the harms from any AI liability case.

None of this diminishes the importance of liability frameworks. Accountability for harm is essential both to compensate victims and to create incentives for safety. But as courts, legislatures, and regulators design those frameworks, they should remain mindful of the costs of over-deterrence. A liability regime so punishing that it prevents beneficial AI from being deployed is not a regime that maximizes human welfare. The goal should be structures that encourage responsible development and deployment while preserving the innovation that could make these technologies transformative. As we work to mitigate the genuine risks that autonomous AI systems present, we should not lose sight of the extraordinary benefits they have the potential to deliver.

Supplemental Resources

- **Andrew Ng, "The Rise of AI Agents and Agentic Reasoning" — BUILD 2024 Keynote** (youtube.com/watch?v=KrRD7r7y7NY): Foundational video lecture by Stanford professor and AI pioneer Andrew Ng explaining what AI agents are, how agentic reasoning works, and why agents represent a paradigm shift in AI capabilities (Nov. 2024).

- **Jeff Su, "AI Agents, Clearly Explained"** (youtube.com/watch?v=FwOTs4UxQS4): Accessible, non-technical explainer of what AI agents are, how they differ from chatbots, and what they can do in practice (Apr. 2025).
- **RAND Corporation, "Liability for Harms from AI Systems: The Application of U.S. Tort Law"** (rand.org/pubs/research_reports/RRA3243-4.html): Comprehensive analysis of how U.S. tort law applies to AI-caused harms, examining negligence, product liability, and the standard of care for AI developers (Nov. 2024).
- **OWASP Top 10 for Agentic Applications 2026** (genai.owasp.org/resource/agentic-ai-threats-and-mitigations/): First industry-standard taxonomy of security risks specific to autonomous AI agents, including goal hijacking, memory poisoning, and rogue agent behavior (Dec. 2025).
- **CodeX — Stanford Law School, "From Fine Print to Machine Code: How AI Agents Are Rewriting the Rules of Engagement"** (law.stanford.edu/2025/01/14/from-fine-print-to-machine-code-how-ai-agents-are-rewriting-the-rules-of-engagement): Analysis of how AI agents interact with agency law, contract formation, and fiduciary duties (Jan. 2025).

- **Transparency Coalition (TCAI), "Understanding the Rise of OpenClaw and Open-Source AI Agents"** (transparencycoalition.ai/news/tcai-guide-understanding-the-rise-of-clawdbot-moltbot-and-openclaw): Nonpartisan explainer on OpenClaw's development, capabilities, security risks, and policy implications for regulators (Mar. 2026).

- **Brookings Institution, "Products Liability Law as a Way to Address AI Harms"** (brookings.edu/articles/products-liability-law-as-a-way-to-address-ai-harms): Policy analysis examining how existing product liability doctrine can be applied to AI systems (2022).

CHAPTER 11

Transparency in the Age of Generative Law

In January 2024, thousands of New Hampshire voters picked up their phones to hear President Joe Biden urging them not to vote in the upcoming primary. The voice was unmistakable: the cadence, the timbre, the familiar verbal patterns all belonged to the President. Except they didn't. The call was a deepfake, an AI-generated fabrication so convincing that many recipients had no reason to doubt what they were hearing. The incident ultimately resulted in a six-million-dollar federal fine and state felony charges against the political consultant who orchestrated it, but its significance extended well beyond a single enforcement action.[239] It brought into sharp public focus a question that had been quietly building across industries, governments, and courtrooms: in an era when artificial intelligence can generate content indistinguishable from reality, how do we know what is real? And who is responsible for telling us?

This chapter examines the rapidly evolving legal landscape of AI transparency, tracing three interconnected threads. The first is the push for explainability, the demand that AI systems be able to account for how they reach their conclusions. The second is the expansion of disclosure obligations, the growing body of law requiring organizations to tell people when AI is involved in decisions that affect them. The third, and in many ways the most urgent, is the legal response to synthetic media, the deepfakes and AI-generated content that threaten to undermine trust in everything from democratic elections to personal relationships. Together, these threads form a single narrative: the era of opaque AI operating

239 FCC, Forfeiture Order, In re Steve Kramer, FCC-24-104 (adopted Sept. 26, 2024), fcc.gov/document/fcc-issues-6m-fine-nh-robocalls (imposing $6 million fine for violations of the Truth in Caller ID Act, 47 U.S.C. § 227(e)); *see also* NPR (May 23, 2024), npr.org/2024/05/23/nx-s1-4977582/fcc-ai-deepfake-robocall-biden-new-hampshire-political-operative.

without accountability is ending.

The Black Box Problem and the Push for Explainability

Many advanced AI systems, particularly large language models and deep neural networks, generate highly convincing results but offer little insight into how those results were formed. These systems are often described as "black boxes" because their internal processes are difficult to interpret even for the developers who built them. In high-stakes fields such as healthcare, finance, and criminal justice, this opacity creates serious challenges. When an AI system recommends a medical treatment, denies a loan application, or influences a hiring decision, affected individuals and oversight bodies reasonably want to understand how that decision was made. Legal frameworks are beginning to demand greater transparency, although technical limitations continue to make full explainability difficult to achieve.

Defining Transparency and Explainability

The EU AI Act provides a useful framework for understanding these concepts. Under the Act, transparency means that "AI systems are developed and used in a way that allows appropriate traceability and explainability, while making humans aware that they communicate or interact with an AI system, as well as duly informing deployers of the capabilities and limitations of that AI system and affected persons about their rights."[240] Several distinct concepts operate under this umbrella. Traceability refers to the ability to track and reconstruct AI outputs back to their sources and input data. Explainability means providing clear, comprehensible reasons for AI-generated outcomes. Interpretability ensures humans can discern the logic underpinning AI decisions. And disclosure involves informing affected persons before their first interaction with AI systems. Each concept addresses a different dimension of the same fundamental problem: how to make AI systems accountable to the humans they affect.

---

240 EU AI Act, Regulation (EU) 2024/1689 of the European Parliament and of the Council, art. 3(48), recital 27.

The Technical Challenge

The black box problem poses significant difficulties for implementing explainability requirements. As models grow larger and more complex, the gap between performance and interpretability widens. Researchers are developing "Explainable AI" techniques to address these challenges, including hybrid systems that integrate explainable models with black box components, visual explanation tools that highlight which features most influenced a decision, and simplified "model cards" that describe a system's capabilities and limitations.[241] However, a fundamental tension remains: the most accurate AI systems are often the least interpretable, and making them more explainable can reduce their performance. This tradeoff is not merely academic. It means that regulators demanding full explainability may inadvertently push organizations toward less capable systems, while organizations prioritizing accuracy may deploy models whose reasoning cannot be meaningfully reviewed.

The Emerging Transparency Regulatory Framework

California's Multi-Layered Approach

California has emerged as the leading U.S. state for AI transparency regulation, enacting multiple overlapping laws that address different aspects of the challenge. The Transparency in Frontier Artificial Intelligence Act, signed by Governor Newsom on September 29, 2025, requires developers of advanced AI systems trained using computing power greater than 10^{26} floating-point operations to publicly disclose safety frameworks explaining how they identify and mitigate "catastrophic risks," defined as foreseeable risks where a frontier model may seriously injure at least fifty people or incur more than one billion dollars in damage.[242] Large frontier developers, those with annual revenues exceeding five hundred

---

241 Margaret Mitchell et al., "Model Cards for Model Reporting," *Proceedings of the Conference on Fairness, Accountability, and Transparency* (2019), dl.acm.org/doi/10.1145/3287560.3287596.

242 Cal. SB 53 (Wiener), Transparency in Frontier Artificial Intelligence Act, filed with the Secretary of State Sept. 29, 2025, leginfo.legislature.ca.gov/faces/billNavClient.xhtml?-bill_id=202520260SB53.

million dollars, face additional obligations including the publication of annual frontier AI frameworks detailing governance structures, cybersecurity measures, and alignment with recognized standards such as the NIST AI Risk Management Framework. The law also requires reporting of critical safety incidents to the California Office of Emergency Services within fifteen days of discovery, or within twenty-four hours for incidents posing imminent danger to public health or safety. Civil penalties reach one million dollars per violation, enforced by the California Attorney General.[243]

SB 53 represents a deliberate evolution from the more aggressive SB 1047, which Governor Newsom vetoed in 2024. Where SB 1047 would have mandated pre-training safety requirements, mandatory third-party audits, and model shutdown capabilities, SB 53 focuses on deployment-stage transparency obligations.[244] As one Brookings Institution analysis observed, California chose to start with structured transparency and build the evidence base needed for future regulation, rather than imposing capability restrictions on a technology that is widely viewed as economically consequential.[245] The law also includes a notable federal deference provision: companies that satisfy comparable federal standards, including those under the EU AI Act, may use that compliance to satisfy California's requirements.

California's AI Transparency Act, as amended by AB 853 and effective August 2, 2026, takes a different approach by targeting content labeling. The law requires generative AI systems with over one million monthly users to include both "manifest" disclosures, visible labels identifying content as AI-generated, and "latent" disclosures, embedded metadata conveying the system's provider,

---

243 FPF, "California's SB 53: The First Frontier AI Law, Explained," Future of Privacy Forum (Oct. 2025), fpf.org/blog/californias-sb-53-the-first-frontier-ai-law-explained/. See also Clifford Chance, "SB 53: California Sets Standards for AI Transparency" (Oct. 2025).

244 Governor Newsom vetoed SB 1047 on September 29, 2024, citing concerns that it would apply equally to the largest and smallest developers and could stifle innovation. See Wharton AI & Analytics Initiative, "SB 53: What California's New AI Safety Law Means for Developers" (Nov. 2025), ai-analytics.wharton.upenn.edu/wharton-accountable-ai-lab/sb-53-what-californias-new-ai-safety-law-means-for-developers.

245 Brookings Institution, "What Is California's AI Safety Law?" (Dec. 23, 2025), brookings.edu/articles/what-is-californias-ai-safety-law.

version, and creation timestamp.[246] The law also requires AI providers to make detection tools available and prohibits the distribution of tools primarily designed to remove such disclosures. Civil penalties reach five thousand dollars per violation. Separately, California's Companion Chatbot Law, SB 243, requires operators of AI companion systems to be transparent with children that they are interacting with AI rather than a human, and to implement protocols for detecting suicidal ideation or self-harm.[247]

Other State-Level Disclosure Requirements

Beyond California, numerous states have enacted AI transparency requirements targeting specific contexts. New York City's Local Law 144 pioneered regulation of AI in employment decisions.[248] The law requires employers using automated employment decision tools for hiring or promotion to conduct annual independent bias audits and publicly disclose the results. Employers must notify candidates at least ten business days before using such a tool and disclose what qualifications the tool assesses. The law defines an automated employment decision tool as "any computational process, derived from machine learning, statistical modeling, data analytics, or artificial intelligence, that issues simplified output, including a score, classification, or recommendation, that is used to substantially assist or replace discretionary decision making for making employment decisions." Penalties range from five hundred to fifteen hundred dollars per violation.

Colorado's AI Act, effective June 30, 2026, takes a broader approach.[249] The law applies to deployers of high-risk AI systems across employment, education, financial services, healthcare, housing, insurance, and legal services. It requires impact assessments before deployment, mandates disclosure of AI system capabilities and limitations, and provides consumers the right to know when

---

246 Cal. AB 853 (Berman), California AI Transparency Act (effective Aug. 2, 2026).

247 Cal. SB 243 (Becker), Companion Chatbot Law (signed 2025).

248 N.Y.C. Local Law 144 (2021), effective July 5, 2023. See N.Y.C. Admin. Code Section 20-870 et seq.

249 Colo. SB 24-205, codified at C.R.S. Section 6-1-1701 et seq. (effective June 30, 2026).

AI systems make consequential decisions affecting them. Colorado's approach differs from New York City's by targeting AI developers as well as deployers, requiring developers to provide documentation on their AI tool's purpose, intended use, training data, and anti-bias testing. This creates a supply-chain accountability model rather than placing all obligations on end users.

Other states have addressed narrower concerns. For example, New York's Algorithmic Pricing Law prohibits personalized algorithmic pricing using an individual's data without clear disclosure, and Maine's Chatbot Disclosure Act prohibits using AI chatbots in trade or commerce in ways that could mislead a reasonable consumer into believing they are communicating with a human being.[250] A multistate tracker for AI transparency legislation is available in the supplemental resources.

The EU AI Act: Setting the Global Standard

The EU AI Act, which entered into force on August 1, 2024, with compliance required in phases through August 2026, establishes the world's most comprehensive AI transparency framework.[251] The Act imposes different obligations based on risk level, with the most stringent requirements applying to "high-risk" AI systems in sectors such as healthcare, employment, education, and law enforcement. Under Article 13, high-risk AI systems must be designed to be sufficiently transparent so that deployers can interpret outputs and use them appropriately. Providers must supply detailed documentation including information about the system's capabilities and limitations, the data used for training, the logic involved in the system's reasoning, and guidance on how to interpret outputs. The Act also requires that AI-generated content be clearly labeled as artificially generated in a machine-readable format, particularly for synthetic audio, video, and deepfake material. Non-compliance carries severe financial consequences, with penalties reaching thirty-

---

250 N.Y. Gen. Bus. Law Section 396-ddd (algorithmic pricing disclosure); Me. Rev. Stat. Ann. tit. 10, Section 1592 (chatbot disclosure).

251 EU AI Act, Regulation (EU) 2024/1689, arts. 13-14 (transparency and human oversight requirements for high-risk systems); art. 50 (content labeling requirements), artificial-intelligence-act.com.

five million euros or seven percent of global annual turnover for the most serious violations.

AI in Employment: The Frontier of Disclosure Regulation

The use of AI tools to determine who gets hired, promoted, or terminated has generated some of the most developed transparency requirements. These tools can screen resumes, rank candidates, schedule interviews, and analyze video interviews for tone, facial expressions, and word choice. However, documented instances of algorithmic bias have driven regulatory intervention.[252] NYC Local Law 144's bias audit requirement is significant not for what it prescribes but for what it does not: the law does not mandate specific actions if bias is found. It only requires disclosure. The rationale is that transparency itself creates market pressure for fairer systems and enables affected individuals to assert their rights under existing anti-discrimination laws. Whether this approach is sufficient remains debated, but it reflects a broader regulatory philosophy that sunlight is the best disinfectant.

Colorado's approach pushes further by imposing obligations at multiple points in the AI supply chain. Developers must monitor for bias across twelve protected characteristics and report any incidents of discrimination to deployers.[253] This dual-obligation model recognizes that the employer deploying an AI hiring tool may lack the technical sophistication to evaluate the system's fairness, while the developer who built it may lack visibility into how it is being used. By requiring both parties to take responsibility, Colorado attempts to close accountability gaps that a single-obligation model would leave open. As discussed in Chapter 10, the ongoing litigation in *Mobley v. Workday*, Inc. illustrates the stakes: Workday's AI screening tools allegedly processed 1.1 billion job applications, and a federal court has allowed claims of age, race, and disability discrimination to

---

252 *See*, e.g., EEOC, "The Americans with Disabilities Act and the Use of Software, Algorithms, and Artificial Intelligence to Assess Job Applicants and Employees" (May 12, 2022), eeoc.gov/laws/guidance/americans-disabilities-act-and-use-software-algorithms-and-artificial-intelligence. See also Chapter 10 (discussing AI bias in employment decisions).

253 Colo. SB 24-205, Section 6-1-1706.

proceed against the software vendor itself, not just the employers who used its tools.[254]

Synthetic Media: The Deepfake Disclosure Epidemic

The most urgent transparency concerns involve synthetic media, the AI-generated videos, voices, and images that can closely mimic real individuals. These tools can be used for satire, education, and creativity, but they are also weaponized for fraud, harassment, and political manipulation. According to Resemble AI's Q1 2025 Deepfake Incident Report, documented financial losses from deepfake-enabled fraud exceeded two hundred million dollars in the first quarter of 2025 alone.[255] Modern AI can clone a person's voice with eighty-five percent accuracy using just three to five seconds of audio.[256] In one widely reported incident in early 2024, a finance worker at Arup, a multinational engineering firm, was tricked into transferring approximately twenty-five million dollars after participating in a video conference call in which every other participant, including individuals who appeared to be the company's chief financial officer and other senior executives, turned out to be deepfake recreations.[257] Voice cloning scams targeting ordinary families have also proliferated, with parents receiving calls from what sounds like their child's voice begging for emergency help. The emotional manipulation is devastatingly effective because the technology has advanced beyond what most people can reliably detect.

The TAKE IT DOWN Act: Federal Intervention

On May 19, 2025, President Trump signed the TAKE IT DOWN Act, the first comprehensive federal legislation targeting AI-generated

---

254 *Mobley v. Workday, Inc.*, No. 3:23-cv-00770-RFL (N.D. Cal. May 16, 2025); see Chapter 10 for a full discussion.

255 Resemble AI, "Q1 2025 Deepfake Incident Report" (Apr. 2025), resemble.ai/q1-2025-ai-deepfake-security-report.

256 *Id.* The report also found that sixty-eight percent of video deepfakes cannot be distinguished from real footage by human viewers.

257 CNN (May 16, 2024), cnn.com/2024/05/16/tech/arup-deepfake-scam-loss-hong-kong-intl-hnk.

harmful content.[258] The law, formally titled the Tools to Address Known Exploitation by Immobilizing Technological Deepfakes on Websites and Networks Act passed the House by a vote of 409 to 2, reflecting the rare bipartisan consensus that non-consensual intimate imagery, whether authentic or AI-generated, demands federal intervention.

The Act criminalizes the knowing publication of intimate visual depictions or "digital forgeries" depicting individuals in intimate situations without their consent. Penalties include up to two years imprisonment for offenses involving adult victims and up to three years for those involving minors. The law also requires covered platforms, defined as websites and applications that provide forums for user-generated content, to establish notice-and-removal systems by May 19, 2026. Upon receiving a valid takedown request, platforms must remove the alleged unauthorized content within forty-eight hours. The Federal Trade Commission has enforcement authority, and the law includes a safe harbor provision protecting platforms that remove content in good faith, even if the removal later proves erroneous. While groundbreaking, the TAKE IT DOWN Act is narrowly focused on intimate imagery and does not address political deepfakes, commercial impersonation, or other forms of synthetic media fraud.

In April 2026, the first criminal conviction under the TAKE IT DOWN Act was secured against an Ohio man who used AI to create non-consensual intimate imagery of adults and children in his neighborhood and shared the material on a website promoting child sexual abuse.[259] The conviction validated the statute's criminal enforcement mechanism and demonstrated that prosecutors can successfully bring cases under the new law. Separately, the DEFIANCE Act, which would provide victims of non-consensual intimate imagery with a federal civil cause of action for damages,

---

258 TAKE IT DOWN Act, Pub. L. No. 119-12, S. 146, 119th Cong. (signed May 19, 2025), congress.gov/bill/119th-congress/senate-bill/146.

259 U.S. Att'y's Off., S. Dist. of Ohio, Columbus Man Pleads Guilty to Cyberstalking Exes, Creating AI-Generated Obscene Material of Adults & Children, U.S. Dep't of Just. (Apr. 7, 2026), justice.gov/usao-sdoh/pr/columbus-man-pleads-guilty-cyberstalking-exes-creating-ai-generated-obscene-material.

passed the Senate by unanimous consent in January 2026 and awaits House action.[260]

State Deepfake Legislation: A Patchwork of Protections

State legislatures have moved faster than Congress to address the full range of deepfake harms. According to Ballotpedia's mid-year deepfake legislation report, forty-seven states had enacted some form of deepfake legislation by mid-2025, with eighty-two percent of all state deepfake laws enacted in 2024 and 2025 alone.[261] The three states without comprehensive deepfake legislation as of that report were Alaska, Missouri, and Ohio. A separate tracker identified 169 deepfake-related laws enacted since 2022 across the country, with 146 bills introduced in 2025 alone.[262] This explosion of legislative activity reflects the speed at which deepfake harms have escalated and the absence of a comprehensive federal framework addressing the full spectrum of risks.

The state laws address distinct categories of harm. On the political front, twenty-eight states had enacted laws regulating deepfakes in political communications by mid-2025, with most applying within certain timeframes before elections. California's AB 2355, for instance, requires clear disclaimers stating, "This ad was generated or substantially altered using artificial intelligence." Texas treats deepfake interference in elections as electoral misconduct, making it a Class A misdemeanor to distribute manipulated video or audio that harms a political candidate within thirty days of an election. Criminal penalties for deepfake creation have also expanded: Pennsylvania's Act 35, effective September 2025, criminalizes creating or distributing deepfakes with fraudulent or injurious intent, with penalties ranging from first-degree misdemeanors to third-degree felonies when used for financial fraud.[263] For non-consensual intimate content, forty-

---

260 DEFIANCE Act (Disrupt Explicit Forged Images and Non-Consensual Edits Act), S. ___, 119th Cong. (passed Senate by unanimous consent Jan. 2026).

261 Ballotpedia, "Mid-Year Deepfake Legislation Report" (July 30, 2025), news.ballotpedia.org/2025/07/22/forty-seven-states-have-enacted-deepfake-legislation-since-2019.

262 Programs.com, "Deepfake Legislation Tracker" (Dec. 2025), programs.com/resources/deepfake-legislation.

263 Pa. Act 35 of 2025 (effective Sept. 2025). Cal. AB 2355 (Berman) (2024) (election

five states had enacted laws by mid-2025, up from thirty-two at the start of that year. New York's Hinchey law criminalizes the creation or distribution of sexually explicit AI-generated content without consent and provides victims with a private right of action.[264]

The NO FAKES Act: *A Federal Right to One's Likeness*

The NO FAKES Act, formally the Nurture Originals, Foster Art, and Keep Entertainment Safe Act, was reintroduced on April 9, 2025, as S. 1367 in the Senate and H.R. 2794 in the House.[265] The bipartisan bill would establish a federal intellectual property right for every American to their voice and visual likeness. The bill has drawn support from an unusually broad coalition including entertainment industry groups such as SAG-AFTRA, the RIAA, and the MPA, as well as technology companies including YouTube, OpenAI, Google, IBM, Disney, Warner Music Group, and Universal Music Group.

The NO FAKES Act would empower individuals to sue those who knowingly create, post, or profit from unauthorized digital replicas. It includes provisions requiring platforms to promptly remove unauthorized deepfakes upon notification, and rights would extend beyond death, protecting families of deceased individuals from unauthorized digital replicas. The bill includes First Amendment exceptions for news, documentary, and satire, though critics, including the Foundation for Individual Rights and Expression, argue these exceptions are too narrowly drawn and could chill protected speech.[266] Preemption provisions have also generated debate about how the federal right would interact with existing state publicity laws. The bill remains pending in Congress.

---

deepfake disclosures). Tex. Elec. Code Section 255.004 (election deepfakes as Class A misdemeanor).

264 N.Y. Civ. Rights Law Section 52-c (the "Hinchey law").

265 NO FAKES Act, S. 1367 / H.R. 2794, 119th Cong. (reintroduced Apr. 9, 2025), congress.gov/bill/119th-congress/senate-bill/1367.

266 FIRE, "Analysis of the NO FAKES Act" (2025), thefire.org/news/no-fakes-act-real-threat-free-expression.

The Voice Cloning Frontier: *Lehrman v. Lovo*

The intersection of deepfake technology and intellectual property rights was tested in *Lehrman v. Lovo, Inc.*, decided by Judge J. Paul Oetken of the U.S. District Court for the Southern District of New York on July 10, 2025.[267] Professional voice actors Paul Lehrman and Linnea Sage alleged that Lovo, an AI text-to-speech company, used recordings of their voices, obtained through the freelance platform Fiverr under the pretense that they would be used for internal research, to create and sell AI-generated voice clones marketed under the fictitious names "Kyle Snow" and "Sally Coleman." Lehrman discovered the unauthorized use when he heard what appeared to be his own voice narrating a podcast produced in cooperation with MIT.

The court's ruling navigated several novel legal questions. It dismissed the plaintiffs' federal trademark claims, holding that while voices are not categorically excluded from trademark protection, Lehrman and Sage's voices were being sold as a product rather than functioning as source identifiers. The court also dismissed most copyright claims, holding that copyright protection does not extend to voice per se or to mere imitation of vocal characteristics; under 17 U.S.C. Section 114(b), copyright in a sound recording does not cover "independent fixation of other sounds" that simulate the original.[268] However, the court allowed critical state law claims to proceed, including breach of contract claims based on the Fiverr communications, New York right of publicity claims under Civil Rights Law Sections 50 and 51, and consumer protection claims.

The case stands as an early and influential building block in the jurisprudence surrounding AI voice cloning, establishing that while federal intellectual property law may not yet offer a clear remedy, state law claims for unauthorized commercial use of one's voice remain viable.

---

267 *Lehrman v. Lovo, Inc.*, No. 1:24-cv-03770-JPO, 2025 WL 1902547 (S.D.N.Y. July 10, 2025) (J. Oetken). *See* Skadden, Arps, "New York Court Tackles the Legality of AI Voice Cloning" (July 2025), skadden.com/insights/publications/2025/07/new-york-court-tackles-the-legality-of-ai-voice-cloning.

268 17 U.S.C. Section 114(b).

Enforcement in Action: The Biden Deepfake Robocall

Federal enforcement against deepfake-related harms has also taken shape through agency action. Two days before the January 2024 New Hampshire Democratic primary, thousands of voters received robocalls featuring an AI-generated voice impersonating President Joe Biden, urging them not to vote in the primary and to "save your vote for the November election." Political consultant Steve Kramer admitted to orchestrating the scheme, having paid a New Orleans-based voice artist one hundred fifty dollars to create the deepfake audio. The FCC proposed a six-million-dollar fine against Kramer for violations of the Truth in Caller ID Act, which was adopted as a final forfeiture order on September 26, 2024.[269] Lingo Telecom, the voice service provider that transmitted the calls, settled with the FCC for one million dollars and agreed to implement enhanced verification protocols. Separately, the New Hampshire Attorney General indicted Kramer on state felony charges of voter suppression and misdemeanor impersonation of a candidate. The enforcement action was notable not only for its scale but for its signal: the FCC made clear that AI-generated voices in robocalls are "artificial" under the Telephone Consumer Protection Act, confirming that existing regulatory tools can reach deepfake harms even without new legislation.

Content Provenance: Technical Solutions for Transparency

The C2PA Standard

Beyond legal mandates, industry-led technical solutions are emerging to establish the provenance and authenticity of digital content.[270] The Coalition for Content Provenance and Authenticity has developed an open technical standard for embedding cryptographically signed metadata into digital content. Formed in 2021 by unifying Adobe's Content Authenticity Initiative and Microsoft and BBC's Project

---

269 FCC, Forfeiture Order, In re Steve Kramer, FCC-24-104 (adopted Sept. 26, 2024), fcc.gov/document/fcc-issues-6m-fine-nh-robocalls. *See* fcc.gov/document/fcc-issues-6m-fine-nh-robocalls.

270 Coalition for Content Provenance and Authenticity (C2PA), Technical Specification v2.2 (2025), c2pa.org.

Origin, C2PA now has over two hundred members. C2PA's Content Credentials attach provenance information to images, videos, and documents, allowing viewers to verify whether content was captured with a camera, edited with software, or generated by AI. The system uses cryptographic signing so that modifications to the metadata can be detected. When an AI system generates content, C2PA allows that fact to be clearly identified through the system's "digitalSourceType" field. Major platforms are integrating the standard: YouTube has added provenance-based labels for verified camera footage, Meta uses C2PA standards to label AI-generated content across Facebook, Instagram, and WhatsApp, and camera manufacturers including Nikon and Samsung are building C2PA support directly into hardware.

Watermarking Technologies

Watermarking provides another layer of transparency. Google's SynthID applies imperceptible pixel-level changes to AI-generated images that remain intact against standard manipulation.[271] These watermarks can be detected using Google's verification tools but are not visible to human viewers. However, researchers warn that no watermarking system can simultaneously be robust, unforgeable, and publicly detectable. Watermarks can be stripped through screenshot tools, file compression, and image editing programs. They can also be faked by feeding authentic content through AI systems, which then output it with an AI-generated watermark attached. These limitations underscore why technical solutions must complement, not replace, legal frameworks.

The EU AI Act explicitly endorses provenance technology. Article 50 requires developers to indicate whenever users engage with synthetic content, and the revised Product Liability Directive treats failure to supply appropriate labeling and provenance information as potential evidence of a product defect.[272] In the United States, California's AI Transparency Act similarly mandates both manifest

271 Google DeepMind, "SynthID: Identifying AI-Generated Content" (2024). See deepmind.google/technologies/synthid.

272 EU AI Act, art. 50 (content labeling). Directive (EU) 2024/2853 (revised Product Liability Directive), recital 35 (provenance information as relevant to product safety).

and latent disclosures for AI-generated content, aligning regulatory requirements with the technical capabilities that C2PA and similar systems provide.

Healthcare and Financial Services: Sector-Specific Transparency

Medical AI Transparency

AI is transforming healthcare through diagnostic imaging analysis, treatment recommendations, and clinical decision support. However, when AI-assisted decisions lead to patient harm, questions arise about whether the reasoning behind those decisions can be explained. The principle of informed consent creates particular pressure for explainability in medicine: patients have a right to understand the basis for their treatment, but how can physicians explain recommendations when even the AI's developers cannot fully articulate why the system reached a particular conclusion?

Some regulators have embraced a pragmatic approach, with Australia, for example, exploring restrictions on black-box AI in healthcare contexts where explainability is deemed essential. Others argue that performance metrics, including accuracy, reliability, and bias testing, can provide adequate assurance even when the underlying logic is opaque, particularly when AI systems outperform human decision-makers. The tension between interpretability and performance is especially acute in medical contexts, where deploying a less accurate but more explainable system could itself cause harm by producing inferior diagnoses.

Financial Services Transparency

Financial regulators have long required disclosure of algorithmic decision-making, and these requirements are being updated for AI. The Fair Credit Reporting Act already requires that consumers be given reasons when they are denied credit, and AI systems must be designed to provide such reasons even if the full complexity of the model cannot be conveyed.[273] The SEC and CFTC have increased scrutiny of AI in financial markets. A May 2025 Government

273 Fair Credit Reporting Act, 15 U.S.C. Section 1681 et seq.

Accountability Office study warned of systemic risks from concentration in third-party AI service providers, finding that if many financial institutions rely on the same AI models, a failure at one provider could impact an outsized set of financial companies, increasing systemic risk for the sector.[274] Transparency about which AI systems institutions use and how they function has become a macroprudential concern, not just a consumer protection issue. The GAO recommended that the National Credit Union Administration update its model risk management guidance and that Congress grant the NCUA authority to examine third-party technology service providers, authority the banking regulators already possess but that the NCUA currently lacks.

Looking Ahead: The Evolution of Transparency Law

The trajectory is clear: transparency requirements will expand and deepen. Several trends will shape the near-term evolution. On harmonization, the current patchwork of state laws creates compliance challenges that may eventually prompt federal intervention. Industry standards like C2PA are increasingly referenced in legislation, and as these standards mature, regulators can be expected to mandate their adoption rather than leaving implementation details to market forces.

In contexts where AI decisions significantly affect individual rights, like employment, credit, housing, and education, courts may increasingly treat explainability as a component of due process. If an organization cannot explain why someone was rejected, it becomes difficult to demonstrate the rejection was lawful. The deepfake detection arms race will also intensify: as detection tools improve, so will generation tools, and the regulatory response will need to evolve beyond disclosure mandates to address scenarios where synthetic content is indistinguishable from authentic content even by sophisticated detection systems.

The fundamental question underlying all transparency regulation is whether disclosure alone is sufficient, or whether some AI

274 GAO, "Artificial Intelligence: Use and Oversight in Financial Services," GAO-25-107197 (May 19, 2025). *See* gao.gov/products/gao-25-107197.

applications are too consequential, or too dangerous, to deploy regardless of how transparent they are. That question will occupy lawmakers, regulators, and courts for years to come. What is certain is that the systems shaping our lives will increasingly be required to explain themselves.

Supplemental Resources

- **MultiState AI Legislation Tracker** (multistate.ai/artificial-intelligence-ai-legislation.): Commercial tracking service with detailed analysis of AI bills across all 50 states.
- **Partnership on AI Synthetic Media Framework** (partnershiponai.org/responsible-practices-for-synthetic-media): Framework for responsible practices for synthetic media.
- **Coalition for Health AI** (chai.org): Standards for trustworthy AI in healthcare.
- **World Privacy Forum** (worldprivacyforum.org): Research on privacy, identity, and trust in C2PA.
- **Ballotpedia Deepfake Legislation Tracker** (ballotpedia.org/Deepfake_legislation_in_the_United_States): Comprehensive tracker of state deepfake legislation.

CHAPTER 12

Data Privacy and AI Surveillance

For more than three decades, the internet has posed an accelerating threat to personal privacy. What began with cookies and web trackers in the 1990s evolved into the mass collection of browsing histories, purchase records, location data, and social connections by the 2010s. But artificial intelligence has transformed the collection of data into a qualitatively different danger. AI does not merely collect more data. It synthesizes it, transforming scattered digital breadcrumbs into comprehensive profiles that reveal not just what people do, but who they are, what they believe, and what they are likely to do next.

The result is an unprecedented concentration of intimate information. Every major AI platform now maintains what security professionals call a "honeypot," a centralized repository of personal data so valuable that it attracts both legitimate and malicious actors. These honeypots often contain not just names and addresses, but facial geometry, voice patterns, location histories, purchasing habits, medical queries, relationship struggles, and the unguarded conversations that hundreds of millions of people share with AI chatbots every day.

The risks are threefold. First, private actors can exploit this data to manipulate, discriminate, and extract value from individuals in ways that existing law barely contemplates. Second, data breaches can expose the most sensitive aspects of people's lives to criminals and foreign adversaries. Third, and perhaps most troubling, these vast repositories of personal information create irresistible targets for government surveillance, enabling monitoring capabilities that would have seemed like science fiction a generation ago.

This chapter explores how privacy law is responding to these challenges. It begins at the newest frontier, the information users voluntarily share with AI chatbots, often without realizing how that data may be stored, analyzed, or exploited. It then turns to the growing patchwork of state privacy laws that has emerged in the absence of comprehensive federal legislation. From there, it focuses on biometric information, a particularly sensitive category where state statutes have imposed sweeping obligations and significant liability on companies that fail to obtain proper consent. The chapter concludes by examining how, or even whether, the Fourth Amendment can meaningfully constrain government access to the massive data repositories now held by private companies.

AI Inputs: The New Privacy Frontier

The privacy risks of AI extend far beyond what companies collect about their users. They now encompass what users voluntarily tell their AI systems. Hundreds of millions of people interact with AI chatbots daily, sharing medical symptoms, legal problems, financial anxieties, relationship struggles, and corporate secrets in conversations they instinctively treat as private. They are not.

A 2025 study by Stanford University's Institute for Human-Centered AI examined the privacy policies of six leading chatbot developers: Amazon (Nova), Anthropic (Claude), Google (Gemini), Meta (Meta AI), Microsoft (Copilot), and OpenAI (ChatGPT). The researchers found that all six companies use chat data by default to train their models, and some retain this information indefinitely.[275] In the case of multiproduct companies such as Google, Meta, Microsoft, and Amazon, user interactions are routinely merged with information gleaned from other products, including search queries, purchases, social media engagement, and browsing history. A Concentric AI study found that generative AI tools exposed roughly three million sensitive records per organization during the first half of 2025.[276]

The implications are profound. When a user asks a chatbot for low-

---

275 Jennifer King & Caroline Meinhardt, Chatbot Privacy: An Analysis of the Privacy Policies of Leading AI Assistants, Stanford Inst. for Human-Centered AI (Jan. 2025), hai.stanford.edu/news/privacy-ai-era-how-do-we-protect-our-personal-information.

276 Concentric AI, Data Security Report: Generative AI Tools Expose Millions of Sensitive Records (Aug. 2025), concentricai.com/research/genai-data-exposure-2025.

sugar dinner recipes, the system can infer that the user may have a health condition. When someone describes symptoms to an AI assistant, that information enters a training pipeline that may not be subject to HIPAA or any comparable health privacy regime. When an employee pastes proprietary code into a chatbot for debugging, that code may become part of the model's training data.

The problem is structural: AI chatbots are designed to mimic the intimacy of human conversation, encouraging disclosure, while large platforms contemplate how to monetize this data across their businesses.

The Fine Print: Privacy Policies of Major AI Platforms

What do users actually agree to when they type a message into a chatbot? The answer varies by platform, but the common thread is that most users have no idea what they are consenting to.

OpenAI (ChatGPT)

By default, conversations with ChatGPT on the free and Plus tiers may be used to train future models unless the user navigates to Settings, then Data Controls, and disables the "Improve the model for everyone" toggle.[277] A Temporary Chat mode is available that does not save conversations to history and does not use them for training. Business-tier products, including ChatGPT Team, Enterprise, and API access, exclude user data from training by default, and API customers can obtain Zero Data Retention agreements. Deleted conversations are supposed to be removed from systems within 30 days, though a 2025 court order in the New York Times copyright litigation temporarily required OpenAI to preserve all user data, including data users had deleted, for a six-month period.[278]

---

277 OpenAI, Privacy Policy (updated Jan. 2025), openai.com/policies/privacy-policy; see also OpenAI Help Center, "Data Controls FAQ," help.openai.com/en/articles/7039943-data-controls-faq.

278 *New York Times Co. v. OpenAI Inc.*, No. 1:23-cv-11195 (S.D.N.Y.), Order Granting Motion to Preserve Evidence (Jan. 8, 2025).

Google (Gemini)

Gemini conversations are used for product improvement by default. Users can limit data storage to 3, 18, or 36 months, but opting out of data collection may reduce personalization and performance. As a multiproduct company, Google may merge chatbot interaction data with information from Search, Gmail, Maps, YouTube, and other services.[279]

Meta (Meta AI)

Meta's privacy policy, covering Facebook, Instagram, WhatsApp, and Meta AI, is notable for its breadth. Chat data may be used for advertising, content personalization, and product improvement. Users can request deletion of specific conversations, but deletion may not affect data already incorporated into training sets. Meta AI is integrated across Meta's ecosystem, meaning interactions may inform advertising and recommendations on other Meta platforms.[280]

Microsoft (Copilot)

Microsoft's Copilot operates under complex, tiered privacy policies that vary by product. Consumer Copilot may use conversations for product improvement. Business and enterprise tiers offer stronger protections, with data isolation and the ability to opt out of training data use. For organizations using Microsoft 365 Copilot, the AI can access data across the user's entire Microsoft ecosystem, including emails, documents, and calendar entries.[281]

Anthropic (Claude)

Anthropic uses consumer chat data to train models by default but

---

279 Google, Gemini Apps Privacy Hub (2025), support.google.com/gemini/answer/13594961.

280 Meta, Privacy Policy (updated Dec. 2024), facebook.com/privacy/policy; Meta, "How Meta AI Uses Your Information," about.meta.com/technologies/meta-ai/privacy.

281 Microsoft, Copilot Privacy Statement (2025), privacy.microsoft.com/en-us/privacystatement; see also Microsoft, "Data, privacy, and security for Azure OpenAI Service," learn.microsoft.com/en-us/legal/cognitive-services/openai/data-privacy.

offers opt-out mechanisms. The company's policies emphasize that it does not sell user data and that enterprise customers receive contractual guarantees against training data use. Anthropic publishes more detailed documentation about its data practices than most competitors.[282]

The concentration of such intimate information creates risks that extend far beyond corporate data practices. At their core, conversations with AI systems are not private in any legally protected sense. While a handful of privacy-focused alternatives exist, such as Venice.ai and DuckDuckGo's Duck.ai, which emphasize local storage and zero-logging policies, the vast majority of AI interactions flow through centralized servers where they become vulnerable to data breaches, insider threats, and legal process.[283]

There is no AI-user privilege analogous to attorney-client or physician-patient confidentiality. A subpoena, warrant, or civil discovery request can compel disclosure of chatbot conversations just as easily as it can compel disclosure of emails or text messages. Courts have begun grappling with how the Stored Communications Act applies to AI chat logs, and early indications suggest that prosecutors can obtain the contents of AI conversations through warrants while user-identifying information may be accessible through mere subpoenas.[284] For individuals who have poured their anxieties, health concerns, business plans, or legal troubles into an AI assistant, this lack of privilege represents a significant and underappreciated risk.[285]

The State Privacy Landscape

---

282 Anthropic, Privacy Policy (updated Oct. 2024), anthropic.com/legal/privacy.

283 *See* Venice.AI, "Privacy Architecture" (2025), venice.ai/privacy (describing zero-logging policy and local storage of conversations); DuckDuckGo, "Duck.ai Privacy," duckduckgo.com/duckduckgo-help-pages/aichat/privacy (explaining anonymized AI chat without data retention).

284 *See* 18 U.S.C. §§ 2701-2712 (Stored Communications Act); see Cybersecurity Law Report, *Gen AI Chats as Digital Evidence* (Dec. 3, 2025), cslawreport.com/21343316/genai-chats-becoming-evidence-law-enforcement-warrants-and-subpoenas.thtml.

285 The question of whether information submitted to AI enjoys a legal privilege is explored in Chapter 15.

As of this writing, no state has enacted a comprehensive privacy statute governing data privacy as it relates to AI systems or products. Instead, AI companies must comply broadly with the patchwork of existing state rules regulating the collection and use of user data in the United States. All fifty states have enacted data breach notification laws setting out the rules governing alerting users and the government about data breaches.[286] Twenty states have passed more comprehensive consumer privacy statutes that grant residents rights over their personal information, although none have so far been amended to address AI-specific issues.[287]

California led the way with the California Consumer Privacy Act (CCPA) in 2018, significantly strengthened by the California Privacy Rights Act (CPRA) in 2020.[288] Virginia followed in 2021 with the Virginia Consumer Data Protection Act.[289] Colorado[290] and Connecticut[291] enacted their own comprehensive laws, each with variations in scope, rights granted, and enforcement mechanisms. Texas, Utah, Oregon, Montana, Delaware, Iowa, New Jersey, New Hampshire, Kentucky, Maryland, Minnesota, Nebraska, Rhode Island, Tennessee, and Indiana have since joined this group, creating a complex patchwork that companies must navigate.[292]

A full overview of state privacy regulations is beyond the scope of this book, but most share common elements. These typically include rights to access, correct, and delete personal information, along with rights to opt out of data sales and targeted advertising. Most also require reasonable security practices. The variations among these

---

286 NCSL, Security Breach Notification Laws, ncsl.org/technology-and-communication/security-breach-notification-laws.

287 IAPP, US State Privacy Legislation Tracker, iapp.org/resources/article/us-state-privacy-legislation-tracker.

288 Cal. Civ. Code §§ 1798.100-1798.199.100 (California Consumer Privacy Act, as amended by California Privacy Rights Act).

289 Va. Code Ann. §§ 59.1-575 to -585 (Virginia Consumer Data Protection Act).

290 Colo. Rev. Stat. §§ 6-1-1301 to -1313 (Colorado Privacy Act).

291 Conn. Gen. Stat. §§ 42-515 to -525 (Connecticut Data Privacy Act).

292 Bloomberg Law, *State Consumer Data Privacy Laws* (Apr. 2025), pro.bloomberglaw.com/insights/privacy/state-privacy-legislation-tracker.

laws are significant, however. Some apply only to businesses meeting certain revenue or data-processing thresholds, while others cast a wider net. Some create private rights of action that allow individuals to sue directly, while others rely exclusively on attorney general enforcement. Some include broad exemptions for employee data and others do not. For businesses operating nationally, compliance requires tracking an ever-expanding matrix of requirements.

The Special Case of Biometric Information

A subcategory of personal data known as biometric information has become an increasingly protected class of information and is particularly relevant to companies that collect or process personal data. Biometric information includes identifiers such as facial geometry, voiceprints, and fingerprints. Unlike passwords or account numbers, biometric identifiers cannot be changed if they are compromised. Although companies may assume they do not collect biometric data, it is often captured indirectly through photo identification systems, video based identity verification tools, or other authentication processes used to verify user identities.

Biometric information has been singled out as requiring special protection because, unlike a stolen password or credit card number, you cannot reset your face.[293] While several states have amended their privacy regulations to specifically include biometric information, Illinois has been especially aggressive in creating private enforcement mechanisms that expose violators to potentially catastrophic liability.

Illinois's Biometric Information Privacy Act, or BIPA, requires entities to obtain informed written consent before collecting or using biometric identifiers, maintain publicly available retention and destruction policies, and prohibits the sale or profit from biometric data.[294] Critically, BIPA also creates a private right of action with statutory damages of $1,000 for negligent violations and $5,000 for reckless or intentional violations. This structure has exposed companies to potentially annihilative liability and has fueled a

---

293 But see the movie *Face/Off* or The Real Housewives series for a counter example.

294 740 ILCS 14/1 *et seq.* (2008). BIPA defines "biometric identifier" to include retina or iris scans, fingerprints, voiceprints, and scans of hand or face geometry. 740 ILCS 14/10.

robust plaintiffs' bar that frequently leverages the threat of aggregate statutory damages to drive settlements.

Texas and Washington later enacted their own biometric privacy statutes through the Capture or Use of Biometric Identifier Act and Washington's House Bill 1493, codified at RCW 19.375. While both laws impose notice and consent requirements and restrict the commercial use and retention of biometric identifiers, neither provides a private right of action.[295] Enforcement authority under both regimes is vested exclusively in the state attorney general, significantly limiting litigation exposure compared to Illinois's BIPA.

AI companies are especially exposed to biometric privacy liability because biometric data is often integral to how their products function. Users speak to AI assistants, creating voiceprints. They upload photos and videos that capture facial geometry. They submit government issued identification for verification and use video tools that analyze expressions or movements. At the scale these companies operate, even limited noncompliance can produce enormous theoretical exposure. A company with ten million users who each submit a single selfie could face $10 billion to $50 billion in potential liability under BIPA's statutory damages framework.

Courts have increasingly been forced to weigh the statute's deterrent purpose against the reality that enforcement at this scale can threaten corporate viability, potentially harming employees, consumers, and claimants alike. A 2024 amendment to BIPA, which cap damages at one violation per person regardless of the number of scans, reflects a modest legislative recognition that the statute's original damages model had become unsustainable.[296]

---

295 Tex. Bus. & Com. Code § 503.001 (Capture or Use of Biometric Identifier Act); Wash. Rev. Code §§ 19.375.010 to 19.375.900 (biometric identifiers), enacted by H.B. 1493 (Wash. 2017).

296 *See* 740 Ill. Comp. Stat. 14/20(b) (2024) (as amended by Pub. Act 103-0769, § 5 (eff. Aug. 2, 2024)) (limiting statutory damages to a single recovery per person, rather than per scan or per collection, for violations of the Biometric Information Privacy Act).

Clearview AI and the Threat of Annihilative Liability

No company better illustrates this collision between AI capabilities and biometric privacy law than Clearview AI. The company built a facial recognition database by scraping photographs from social media platforms, news websites, and other publicly accessible online sources, ultimately accumulating more than 60 billion images.[297] Its software enables law enforcement to upload a photo and receive potential identity matches. The legal problem was straightforward: Clearview never asked anyone for permission.

The resulting BIPA litigation illustrated the existential threat that biometric privacy laws can pose to AI companies. The potential liability was staggering. The class of potential plaintiffs included virtually any individual whose face had been posted on the internet, which is to say, almost everyone. At statutory damages of $1,000 to $5,000 per violation, the company faced theoretical exposure that dwarfed its ability to pay. A settlement approved in March 2025 reflected this impossible arithmetic: rather than a traditional cash payout, class members received a 23% equity stake in Clearview AI, valued at approximately $51.75 million based on the company's $225 million valuation.[298] The company simply lacked the liquid assets to fund a conventional settlement.

Clearview illustrates a broader point about privacy liability in the AI era. When statutory damages attach to each instance of unauthorized data collection, and when AI systems collect data at massive scale, the resulting liability can exceed any company's ability to pay. For companies building AI systems that process personal information, the lesson is that compliance failures can be existential.

Data Privacy and the Limits on Government AI Surveillance

The same data honeypots that attract hackers and expose companies

---

297 Kashmir Hill, *The Secretive Company That Might End Privacy as We Know It*, *N.Y. Times* (Jan. 18, 2020), nytimes.com/2020/01/18/technology/clearview-privacy-facial-recognition.html.

298 *In re Clearview AI, Inc. Consumer Privacy Litig.*, No. 1:21-cv-00135 (N.D. Ill.), Order Granting Final Approval of Class Action Settlement (Mar. 10, 2025).

to private litigation also present irresistible targets for government surveillance. This risk is not theoretical. The settlement involving Clearview AI, though reached with a private company, concerned a facial recognition product designed to enable law enforcement agencies to identify individuals at scale, often without warrants or individualized judicial oversight. As AI companies aggregate increasingly comprehensive personal profiles for model training, personalization, and security, those datasets become intelligence goldmines that law enforcement and national security agencies are eager to access.

State privacy laws primarily regulate commercial data practices, but government access to these repositories raises distinct constitutional questions. The Fourth Amendment prohibits unreasonable searches and seizures, yet defining what is unreasonable in an era of AI powered surveillance requires courts to confront technologies and data aggregation capabilities that the Framers could not have anticipated.[299]

Carpenter and the Digital Age

Carpenter v. United States (2018) marked a watershed moment.[300] The Supreme Court held that accessing more than seven days of historical cell-site location information requires a warrant, recognizing that such data provides "an intimate window into a person's life, revealing not only his particular movements, but through them his familial, political, professional, religious, and sexual associations."

The decision began future-proofing the Fourth Amendment for AI surveillance in three critical ways. First, the Court recognized that individuals retain privacy interests in comprehensive records of their location, even though they "voluntarily" share that information with their cell phone carriers. The traditional third-party doctrine held that information shared with third parties loses Fourth Amendment protection,[301] but *Carpenter* recognized that this rule makes little

---

299 U.S. Const. amend. IV.

300 *Carpenter v. United States*, 585 U.S. 296 (2018).

301 *Smith v. Maryland*, 442 U.S. 735 (1979); *United States v. Miller*, 425 U.S. 435 (1976).

sense when applied to the detailed digital trails that modern life creates.

Second, the Court positioned the Fourth Amendment as a bulwark against pervasive surveillance technologies, citing the Framers' intent "to place obstacles in the way of a too permeating police surveillance."[302] This language suggests that the sheer comprehensiveness of modern data collection may trigger constitutional concerns even when no individual data point seems particularly sensitive.

Third, *Carpenter* signals that constitutional analysis must account for technological change. The volume, granularity, and permanence of digital surveillance differ fundamentally from the limited capabilities available when the third-party doctrine was established in the 1970s. Courts must adapt doctrines developed for bank records and phone numbers to address AI systems that can track individuals continuously, predict their behavior, and infer their most private thoughts.

Geofence Warrants and Beyond

Lower courts are extending Carpenter's logic to new surveillance technologies. In *United States v. Smith* (2024), the Fifth Circuit held that the government's acquisition of historical cell-site location information through a geofence warrant constituted a Fourth Amendment search.[303] Geofence warrants direct technology companies to identify all devices present within a geographic area during a specified time period. The Fifth Circuit found these warrants troubling precisely because they begin with a location rather than a suspect, sweeping up the data of countless innocent people in a "general, exploratory rummaging" that the Fourth Amendment was designed to prevent.[304]

Other AI-powered surveillance technologies raise similar concerns.

---

302 *Id.* at 311 (quoting United States v. Di Re, 332 U.S. 581, 595 (1948)).

303 *United States v. Smith*, 110 F.4th 817 (5th Cir. 2024) (holding that the government's acquisition of historical cell-site location information through a geofence warrant constituted a Fourth Amendment search).

304 *Id.* at 830-32.

Predictive policing algorithms that direct police resources based on historical crime data, facial recognition systems that can identify individuals in public spaces, and aerial surveillance programs that can track the movements of entire cities all implicate the *Carpenter* framework.[305] The common thread is comprehensiveness: when technology enables the government to construct detailed portraits of individuals' lives without traditional investigative work, constitutional scrutiny intensifies.

Looking Forward: The Converging Frameworks

Privacy law in the AI era is converging around several core principles. First, transparency: individuals should know when AI systems are collecting their data, what data is collected, and how it will be used. Second, consent: particularly for sensitive categories like biometric information, meaningful consent should precede collection. Third, purpose limitation: data collected for one purpose should not be freely repurposed for others. Fourth, minimization: companies should collect only the data necessary for legitimate purposes. Fifth, security: the honeypots created by AI systems must be protected against breach and misuse.

These principles represent an emerging consensus that AI's power to transform scattered data into comprehensive profiles requires corresponding legal constraints. The Congressional Research Service has documented these converging trends, noting that federal legislation may eventually be needed to harmonize the growing patchwork of state laws.[306]

For lawyers advising clients in this space, the message is clear. Privacy compliance is no minor regulatory concern. It is a core business risk that can generate billion-dollar liability, criminal referrals, and reputational damage. The companies that thrive in the AI era will be those that build privacy into their systems from the ground up,

---

305 *Leaders of a Beautiful Struggle v. Baltimore Police Dep't*, 2 F.4th 330 (4th Cir. 2021) (en banc) (upholding aerial surveillance program against Fourth Amendment challenge by 8-6 vote).

306 Congressional Research Service, "Generative AI and Data Privacy: A Primer" (R47569), updated Mar. 2024, crsreports.congress.gov/product/pdf/R/R47569.

treat user data as a trust rather than an asset to be monetized, and recognize that the legal frameworks governing AI and privacy are still evolving rapidly. What is permitted today may be prohibited tomorrow, and what seems like an acceptable risk may become an existential threat.

Supplemental Resources

- **Stanford HAI: Privacy in the AI Era** (hai.stanford.edu/news/privacy-ai-era-how-do-we-protect-our-personal-information): Analysis of chatbot privacy policies and recommendations for reform.
- **Congressional Research Service: Generative AI and Data Privacy** (crsreports.congress.gov/product/pdf/R/R47569): Federal primer on AI privacy issues for policymakers.
- **IAPP US State Privacy Legislation Tracker** (iapp.org/resources/article/us-state-privacy-legislation-tracker): Comprehensive tracking of state privacy law developments.
- **IBM: AI Privacy Overview** (ibm.com/think/insights/ai-privacy): Industry perspective on AI privacy challenges and solutions.
- **European Parliament: AI and Data Protection Study** (europarl.europa.eu/RegData/etudes/STUD/2020/641530/EPRS_STU(2020)641530_EN.pdf): Comprehensive analysis of AI's implications for privacy law in the European context.

CHAPTER 13

AI and National Security

A New Arms Race

In December 2025, federal authorities announced the conclusion of Operation Gatekeeper, a sweeping investigation into an illicit supply chain that had diverted $160 million worth of advanced AI chips to China.[307] Two businessmen were arrested in Virginia and New York and prosecutors made an unusually blunt point: Nvidia's most advanced chips, they said, were not consumer electronics, they were strategic assets. The country that controls advanced AI computing, the U.S. Attorney warned, will control the future.

That statement was not rhetorical. Artificial intelligence has become a central pillar of national power, on par with energy security, nuclear deterrence, and control of the seas. Advanced AI systems shape intelligence analysis, cyber operations, weapons development, logistics, economic productivity, and political influence. Unlike past arms races that revolved around discrete weapons systems, the AI race is continuous, fast-moving, and cumulative. Small advantages compound quickly. Falling behind is not easily reversible.

This competition is also uniquely difficult to contain. The same chips used to train commercial language models can accelerate missile design, automate signals intelligence, or optimize autonomous weapons. The same software techniques that power consumer recommendation engines can be repurposed for surveillance, targeting, or disinformation at scale. AI is not a weapons platform that can be siloed inside a military base. It is a general-purpose

---

307 Press Release, U.S. Dep't of Justice, Five People Charged in Multi-Year Conspiracy to Smuggle U.S. Artificial Intelligence Hardware to China (Dec. 8, 2025), justice.gov/opa/pr/five-people-charged-multi-year-conspiracy-smuggle-artificial-intelligence-hardware-china.

capability embedded across the civilian economy.

For lawyers, policymakers, and technologists, this reality creates a national security environment defined less by clear red lines than by constant recalibration. Export controls shift rapidly. Procurement rules struggle to keep pace with commercial innovation. Alliances are strained by differing risk tolerances and incentives. A transaction that was lawful yesterday may require a license today and be prohibited tomorrow, not because the law is unstable, but because the strategic landscape is.

This chapter examines how artificial intelligence has reshaped U.S. national security policy, why the AI race is fundamentally different from prior technological competitions, and how law is being used as a primary instrument of strategic control. It also explores the ethically difficult terrain of AI-enabled warfare, where speed, autonomy, and scale challenge long-standing assumptions about human judgment, accountability, and the law of armed conflict. Understanding the rules requires understanding the race itself, what is being contested, why it matters, and why the United States views leadership in AI not as an economic preference, but as a security imperative.

Why Chips Matter More Than Code

The United States holds a remarkable strategic advantage in the AI competition, but it is not in software or algorithms. Chinese researchers publish cutting-edge AI papers and Chinese companies build competitive models. The advantage lies in the physical infrastructure required to train those models: the advanced semiconductors that exist nowhere else in the world at the necessary scale and sophistication.

Training a frontier AI model requires thousands of specialized chips working in concert, consuming enough electricity to power a small city. These chips, graphics processing units (GPUs) and tensor processing units (TPUs), are manufactured using processes so precise that only a handful of facilities on Earth can produce them. ASML, a Dutch company, is the sole provider of the extreme ultraviolet lithography machines needed to make cutting-edge chips. Taiwan Semiconductor Manufacturing Company (TSMC) fabricates the vast majority of the world's most advanced processors. Nvidia designs the chips that dominate AI training.[308]

This concentration creates chokepoints, narrow passages through which all traffic must flow. Control the chokepoints, the theory goes, and you control who can build frontier AI.

Building the Export Control Regime

The United States began systematically exploiting these chokepoints in October 2022, when the Bureau of Industry and Security (BIS) issued sweeping controls on advanced computing chips and semiconductor manufacturing equipment.[309] The stated rationale was direct: advanced AI capabilities present U.S. national security concerns because they can be used to improve the speed and accuracy of military decision making, planning, and logistics and may also be used for cognitive electronic warfare, radar, signals intelligence, jamming, and to support facial recognition surveillance systems for human rights violations and abuses.

The legal architecture rests on the Export Control Reform Act of 2018 (ECRA),[310] which authorizes controls on items that would make a significant contribution to the military potential of countries whose capabilities would prove detrimental to U.S. national security. BIS implemented this through the Export Administration Regulations, creating new Export Control Classification Numbers for high-performance chips and placing Chinese semiconductor companies on the Entity List, a designation requiring licenses for virtually any U.S. technology transfer.

Each subsequent update tightened the net. October 2023 controls covered additional chips and manufacturing equipment.[311]

---

308 Chris Miller, *Chip War: The Fight for the World's Most Critical Technology* (2022).

309 Bureau of Indus. & Sec., Implementation of Additional Export Controls: Certain Advanced Computing Items; Supercomputer and Semiconductor End Use; Entity List Modification, 87 Fed. Reg. 62,186 (Oct. 13, 2022), federalregister.gov/d/2022-21658.

310 50 U.S.C. §§ 4801–4861.

311 Bureau of Indus. & Sec., Export Controls on Semiconductor Manufacturing Items, 88 Fed. Reg. 73,458 (Oct. 25, 2023), federalregister.gov/d/2023-23049.

December 2024 rules expanded jurisdiction to items containing even small percentages of U.S.-origin components.[312] The January 2025 AI Diffusion Rule represented the most ambitious effort yet: a global framework dividing the world into three tiers, with close allies exempt from licensing, most countries subject to computing power allocations, and adversaries facing near-total denial.[313]

For the first time, the January 2025 rule also controlled AI model weights themselves, the numerical parameters that encode what a model has learned. This was a significant expansion, treating software as a controlled munition.

The Limits of Denial

But the chokepoint strategy has proven more difficult to execute than its architects anticipated. Chinese companies stockpiled chips before controls took effect. Smuggling networks emerged to move restricted technology through third countries. And Chinese AI labs found ways to do more with less.

The DeepSeek episode crystallized the dilemma. In January 2025, a Chinese company released AI models that matched or approached the performance of leading American systems, reportedly trained at a fraction of the cost using older-generation chips that had been stockpiled before export controls took full effect. The models were released as open weights, meaning anyone could download and use them. Within weeks, downloads of Chinese AI models increased nearly 1,000%.

DeepSeek demonstrated both the success and failure of export controls. Success, because the company had to work with constrained resources and older hardware, evidence that the controls imposed real costs. Failure, because the constraints did not prevent China from producing competitive AI systems. If anything, they may have accelerated Chinese innovation by forcing more efficient approaches.

---

312 Bureau of Indus. & Sec., Advanced Computing and Semiconductor Manufacturing Items Export Controls, 89 Fed. Reg. 96,758 (Dec. 5, 2024).

313 Bureau of Indus. & Sec., Framework for Artificial Intelligence Diffusion, 90 Fed. Reg. 4,548 (Jan. 15, 2025), federalregister.gov/d/2025-00636.

Policy Whiplash

The Trump administration responded by rescinding the AI Diffusion Rule on May 13, 2025, just two days before its compliance deadline, calling it overly burdensome and diplomatically counterproductive.[314] But the administration did not abandon export controls, it pursued a different strategy. Rather than blanket geographic restrictions, it negotiated country-by-country and transaction-by-transaction.

The most controversial move came in December 2025, when President Trump announced that Nvidia could sell H200 chips to approved Chinese customers in exchange for a 25% revenue share to the U.S. government.[315] Critics were apoplectic. The House Foreign Affairs Committee held hearings in January 2026 where witnesses described the policy as tantamount to arming the adversary.[316] Former Deputy National Security Advisor Matt Pottinger testified that Congress needs to step in, reverse the policy, and put durable guardrails in place so the mistake can't be repeated.[317]

On January 13, 2026, the Commerce Department formally published the regulation codifying the H200 export policy, shifting the license review standard for certain semiconductor exports to China from a presumption of denial to case-by-case review.[318] Congressional pushback was immediate. The House Foreign Affairs Committee Chairman introduced the AI Overwatch Act, which would revoke existing licenses for advanced AI chip transfers to countries of

---

314 Bureau of Indus. & Sec., Rescission of Framework for Artificial Intelligence Diffusion (May 13, 2025), bis.gov/press-release/department-commerce-announces-rescission-biden-era-artificial-intelligence-diffusion-rule-strengthens.

315 President Donald Trump, Truth Social post (Dec. 8, 2025), truthsocial.com/@realDonaldTrump/posts/115686072737425841.

316 Winning the AI Race Against the Chinese Communist Party: Hearing Before the H. Comm. on Foreign Affairs, 119th Cong. (Jan. 14, 2026).

317 Testimony of Matt Pottinger, Former Deputy National Security Advisor, H. Comm. on Foreign Affairs (Jan. 14, 2026), docs.house.gov/meetings/FA/FA00/20260114/118814/HHRG-119-FA00-Wstate-PottingerM-20260114-U1.pdf.

318 Bureau of Indus. & Sec., Revision of License Review Policy for Certain Semiconductor Exports (Jan. 13, 2026). See Council on Foreign Relations, "The New AI Chip Export Policy to China: Strategically Incoherent and Unenforceable" (Jan. 14, 2026), cfr.org/articles/new-ai-chip-export-policy-china-strategically-incoherent-and-unenforceable.

concern and impose a temporary ban until the administration submits a national security strategy on AI exports.[319] By March 2026, however, Nvidia CEO Jensen Huang announced at the company's GTC conference that Nvidia had received purchase orders for H200 processors from Chinese customers and was restarting manufacturing for that market, with China approving its first major batch of H200 imports for ByteDance, Alibaba, and Tencent.[320]

For practitioners, this policy volatility creates significant compliance challenges. The legal requirements have changed multiple times in three years, with each administration pursuing different approaches. Companies must build compliance programs flexible enough to adapt to rapid policy shifts while robust enough to avoid violations that can result in criminal penalties, massive fines, and exclusion from U.S. markets.

Foreign AI as a National Security Threat

The DeepSeek Assessment

The national security implications of AI extend beyond weapons and cyber operations to the AI systems themselves. Foreign AI platforms can serve as vectors for espionage, influence operations, and technological competition.

The DeepSeek release exemplifies the concerns. After the company's models gained rapid popularity in early 2025, security researchers began examining the platform's code and data practices. What they found alarmed U.S. officials.

The House Select Committee on China issued a comprehensive report in April 2025 concluding that DeepSeek represents a profound

---

319 AI Overwatch Act, H.R. ___, 119th Cong. (introduced Jan. 2026); CNBC, "China Hawks Mount Pushback to Trump's Nvidia AI Chip Plans" (Jan. 22, 2026), cnbc.com/2026/01/22/trump-nvidia-ai-chip-exports-china-congress-bill.html.

320 Nvidia GTC 2026 Conference (Mar. 2026). China approved its first major batch of H200 imports for ByteDance, Alibaba, and Tencent, totaling more than 400,000 units. See Built In, "Trump Lifted the AI Chip Ban on China" (2026), builtin.com/articles/trump-lifts-ai-chip-ban-china-nvidia.

threat to our nation's security.[321] The investigation found that DeepSeek's infrastructure connects to China Mobile, a state-owned telecommunications company that the FCC banned from operating in the United States in 2019 due to national security concerns. Security researchers discovered hidden code capable of sending user data to China Mobile's systems and creating digital fingerprints capable of tracking users across websites.[322]

Chinese law requires AI systems to reflect core socialist values and avoid content that could incite subversion of state power. Testing confirmed that DeepSeek censors responses on sensitive topics, altering or suppressing politically sensitive content in 85% of cases, and echoes Chinese Communist Party narratives at four times the rate of American models.[323]

The committee also found evidence that DeepSeek used model distillation, extracting capabilities from American AI systems in violation of terms of service, and was trained on tens of thousands of Nvidia chips that should have been subject to export controls.[324]

NIST's Center for AI Standards and Innovation (CAISI) conducted independent evaluations, released in October 2025, finding that DeepSeek models were far more susceptible to jailbreaking attacks than American models, responding to 94% of malicious requests when common bypass techniques were used versus 8% for U.S. systems.[325] The evaluation tested three DeepSeek models against four American models across nineteen benchmarks, finding that U.S. models outperformed DeepSeek across almost every metric.

---

321 H. Select Comm. on the Chinese Communist Party, DeepSeek Unmasked: Exposing the CCP's Latest Tool for Spying, Stealing, and Subverting U.S. Export Control Restrictions (Apr. 16, 2025), chinaselectcommittee.house.gov/media/reports/deepseek-unmasked-exposing-the-ccp-s-latest-tool-for-spying-stealing-and-subverting-us-export-control-restrictions.

322 *Id.* at 4–8.

323 *Id.* at 10–14 (finding that DeepSeek alters or suppresses responses to topics deemed politically sensitive by the CCP in 85% of cases, directly aligning outputs with Beijing's censorship directives).

324 *Id.* at 15–20.

325 NIST CAISI, Evaluation of DeepSeek AI Models 7 (Oct. 1, 2025).

DeepSeek models were also twelve times more likely than U.S. models to follow malicious instructions intended to hijack the system.[326]

Government Response

The U.S. government responded with a patchwork of restrictions. NASA, the Pentagon, and Navy prohibited DeepSeek on government devices. The FY 2026 NDAA directs the Director of National Intelligence to require removal of DeepSeek from all national security systems within 60 days.[327]

But the broader question remains unresolved: What framework should govern foreign AI systems that may pose national security risks? The TikTok model of attempted prohibition through legislation has proven legally and practically difficult. Yet allowing unrestricted use of AI platforms that may funnel data to foreign intelligence services or manipulate information according to foreign government directives poses obvious risks.

Competing Strategic Visions

U.S. AI policy reflects tension between two strategic visions.

The *control paradigm* emphasizes restricting adversary access to advanced AI capabilities. Proponents argue that even temporary delays in adversary development provide strategic advantage, that the risks of technology transfer outweigh commercial benefits, and that maintaining chokepoint control is essential for long-term security.

The *competition paradigm* emphasizes accelerating U.S. AI development while accepting that some technology diffusion is inevitable. Proponents argue that overly restrictive controls harm American companies, drive adversaries toward indigenous development, and may ultimately prove counterproductive if they slow U.S. innovation more than adversary progress.

---

326 *Id.* at 10–12.

327 P.L. 119-60.

The Trump administration has tilted toward the competition paradigm, rescinding broad export controls in favor of targeted restrictions while emphasizing running faster to maintain American leadership. The July 2025 AI Action Plan calls for full-stack exports of integrated U.S. AI technology to allies, making it easier for partners to adopt American systems rather than Chinese alternatives.[328]

Critics argue this approach underestimates the risks. The Foundation for Defense of Democracies warned that allowing advanced chip sales to China will further enhance China's growing military while imperiling the future of U.S. export controls.[329] Congressional hearings have featured bipartisan skepticism of the administration's approach.

The Pentagon's AI Push

Within the defense establishment, the emphasis is on rapid adoption. Defense Secretary Pete Hegseth's January 2026 AI strategy memorandum directed that AI be treated not as a separate product, but as a part of many of the workflows, processes, and systems the military relies on.[330]

The strategy emphasizes speed over process, calling for continuous field experimentation: putting AI capabilities in operators' hands, gathering feedback within days not years, and pushing updates faster than the enemy can adapt. It envisions commercial AI deployed to millions of DoD users in the next weeks through the GenAI.mil platform, with seven Pace-Setting Projects including autonomous swarm capabilities and AI agent networks.
The FY 2026 NDAA establishes an Artificial Intelligence Futures Steering Committee co-chaired by the Deputy Secretary of Defense

---

328 America's AI Action Plan (July 2025), whitehouse.gov/wp-content/uploads/2025/07/Americas-AI-Action-Plan.pdf.

329 Foundation for Defense of Democracies, Statement on China Chip Sales Policy (Dec. 2025), fdd.org/analysis/2025/12/10/rolling-back-export-controls-u-s-offers-china-powerful-ai-chips.

330 Sec'y of War Pete Hegseth, Memorandum, Artificial Intelligence Strategy for the Department of War (Jan. 9, 2026), media.defense.gov/2026/Jan/12/2003855671/-1/-1/0/ARTIFICIAL-INTELLIGENCE-STRATEGY-FOR-THE-DEPARTMENT-OF-WAR.PDF.

and Vice Chairman of the Joint Chiefs to address systems that approach or achieve artificial general intelligence.[331] This reflects awareness that current policy frameworks may be inadequate for more advanced AI capabilities on the horizon.

Autonomous Weapons and the Laws of War

While export controls address who can build advanced AI, a separate set of legal questions concerns who can use it, and for what purposes. Nowhere are these questions more urgent than in the development of lethal autonomous weapons systems (LAWS).

In 2021, a UN Panel of Experts documented what may have been the first use of fully autonomous weapons in combat. In Libya, retreating Haftar-affiliated forces were hunted down and remotely engaged by lethal autonomous weapons systems such as the STM Kargu-2, Turkish-made drones programmed to identify and attack targets without requiring data connectivity between the operator and the munition.[332] The drones operated in what the UN report described as a fire, forget, and find capability: once launched, they selected their own targets.[333]

This was not science fiction. It was not even particularly advanced technology by current standards. And it raised a question that international humanitarian law has never had to answer: when a machine decides to kill, who is responsible?

Traditional accountability for war crimes requires human agency. A soldier who shoots a civilian can be prosecuted. A commander who orders unlawful attacks can be held responsible. But what happens when the decision to fire is made by an algorithm trained on millions of data points, operating according to parameters set by engineers who never anticipated the specific situation, executing code that

---

331 P.L. 119-60, § 1535.

332 U.N. Panel of Experts on Libya, Letter Dated 8 March 2021, U.N. Doc. S/2021/229, at 63, docs.un.org/en/s/2021/229.

333 Zachary Kallenborn, Was a Flying Killer Robot Used in Libya? Quite Possibly, Bull. Atomic Scientists (May 20, 2021), thebulletin.org/2021/05/was-a-flying-killer-robot-used-in-libya-quite-possibly.

even its creators may not fully understand?

This is what legal scholars call the accountability gap or responsibility vacuum. If a commander cannot predict exactly how an autonomous system will behave, can they be held responsible for its actions? If a programmer writes code that functions as intended but produces unlawful results in unforeseen circumstances, have they committed a war crime? The existing framework of international humanitarian law assumes human decision-makers at critical junctures. Autonomous weapons may eliminate those junctures entirely.

International Humanitarian Law Requirements

The legal constraints on autonomous weapons derive from fundamental principles of international humanitarian law, codified in the Geneva Conventions and their Additional Protocols.[334]

Distinction requires parties to a conflict to distinguish between combatants and civilians, and between military objectives and civilian objects. An autonomous system must be capable of making these distinctions reliably, a challenge that current AI struggles with even in controlled environments, let alone the chaos of combat.

Proportionality prohibits attacks where expected civilian harm would be excessive in relation to the anticipated military advantage. This requires weighing incommensurable values (how many civilian casualties are worth destroying an ammunition depot?), in ways that involve irreducibly human judgment.

Precautions in attack require parties to take constant care to spare civilians and to cancel or suspend attacks when it becomes apparent that targets are not legitimate military objectives. An autonomous system must be able to recognize changed circumstances and halt operations accordingly.

Beyond these specific rules, the Martens Clause, a customary principle incorporated into the Geneva Conventions, provides that

---

334 Protocol Additional to the Geneva Conventions of 12 August 1949, and Relating to the Protection of Victims of International Armed Conflicts (Protocol I), arts. 48, 51, 57, June 8, 1977, 1125 U.N.T.S. 3.

even in situations not covered by specific treaty provisions, civilians and combatants remain protected by the principles of humanity and the dictates of the public conscience. Many scholars argue that delegating life-and-death decisions to machines violates these principles regardless of whether specific technical requirements can be met.

The Stalled International Process

The international community has been debating autonomous weapons through the Convention on Certain Conventional Weapons (CCW) since 2014. A Group of Governmental Experts meets annually to discuss potential regulations. After more than a decade, they have produced guiding principles but no binding rules. The deadlock reflects genuine disagreement. The United States and Russia argue that existing international humanitarian law adequately covers autonomous weapons and that no new treaty is needed. They dispute the utility of concepts like meaningful human control, arguing that appropriate oversight levels vary by context. China takes an ambiguous position, expressing concern about autonomous weapons while investing heavily in their development.

On the other side, a coalition of states led by Austria advocates for a legally binding instrument that would prohibit autonomous weapons operating without human control and regulate all others. The UN Secretary-General has called for such an instrument to be concluded by 2026. Civil society groups organized under the Campaign to Stop Killer Robots have mobilized public pressure.

The UN General Assembly has stepped into the gap, adopting resolutions on autonomous weapons for three consecutive years with overwhelming majorities, 166 countries voting in favor in December 2024.[335] But General Assembly resolutions are not legally binding, and the resolutions have stopped short of mandating treaty negotiations, instead calling for informal consultations and encouraging the CCW process.

---

335 G.A. Res. 79/62, Lethal Autonomous Weapons Systems, U.N. Doc. A/RES/79/62 (Dec. 2, 2024) (166 in favor, 3 against (Belarus, DPRK, Russia), 15 abstentions). This followed the First Committee vote of 161-3-13 on November 5, 2024.

Meanwhile, autonomous and semi-autonomous weapons continue to proliferate. Russia's Lancet-3 loitering munition has been used extensively in Ukraine. Israel has deployed AI-assisted targeting systems in Gaza.[336] The technology is advancing faster than the diplomacy.

U.S. Policy: DoD Directive 3000.09

Within this international vacuum, the United States has developed its own policy framework through DoD Directive 3000.09, Autonomy in Weapon Systems.[337] First issued in 2012 and updated in 2023 and 2025, the directive establishes requirements for developing and deploying autonomous weapons.

The directive requires that autonomous and semi-autonomous weapon systems be designed to allow commanders and operators to exercise appropriate levels of human judgment over the use of force. Before entering formal development, senior officials must certify that proposed systems meet specific criteria regarding reliability, effectiveness, and the ability to complete engagements in a manner consistent with the law of armed conflict.

Notably, the directive does not prohibit autonomous weapons. It establishes a review process intended to ensure that such weapons, when developed, will comply with legal requirements. Critics argue this approach assumes away the fundamental question of whether meaningful human control is possible once systems reach certain levels of autonomy.

The FY 2026 National Defense Authorization Act added transparency requirements, mandating that the Pentagon report waivers of DoD Directive 3000.09 to congressional defense committees.[338] This at least ensures that when the military bypasses its own safeguards,

---

336 Campaign to Stop Killer Robots, Statement on First Committee Resolution L.77 (Nov. 5, 2024), stopkillerrobots.org/news/161-states-vote-against-the-machine-at-the-un-general-assembly.

337 U.S. Dep't of Def., Directive 3000.09, Autonomy in Weapon Systems (updated Jan. 25, 2023), esd.whs.mil/portals/54/documents/dd/issuances/dodd/300009p.pdf.

338 P.L. 119-60, signed Dec. 18, 2025.

Congress will know.

The Speed of Machine Conflict

If autonomous weapons raise questions about human control over kinetic force, AI-enabled cyber operations raise parallel questions about human control over digital conflict. The difference is that cyber operations move at machine speed, potentially leaving no time for human deliberation.

In November 2025, Anthropic disclosed what it described as the first documented case of a large-scale cyberattack executed without substantial human intervention.[339] A Chinese state-sponsored group, designated GTG-1002, had manipulated AI coding tools into conducting cyber espionage operations against approximately thirty global targets. The AI agents executed 80 to 90 percent of tactical operations independently, identifying vulnerabilities, developing exploits, penetrating networks, with human operators intervening at only four to six critical decision points per campaign. The agents accomplished in hours what would take human operators days or weeks, making thousands of requests per second at speeds no human team could match.

This creates what strategists call an arms race dynamic. If your adversary can launch cyber attacks at machine speed, defending at human speed means losing. But if both sides deploy autonomous cyber capabilities, conflicts could escalate faster than any human can track, let alone control.

Offensive and Defensive Applications

AI transforms both sides of a cyber conflict. On offense, AI enables self-modifying malware that evolves to evade detection, autonomous discovery of zero-day vulnerabilities, sophisticated phishing campaigns personalized at scale, and disinformation operations that can generate unlimited synthetic content. Nation-states are developing roadmaps for semi- to fully-autonomous cyber agents,

---

339 Anthropic, Disrupting the First Reported AI-Orchestrated Cyber Espionage Campaign (Nov. 13, 2025), anthropic.com/news/disrupting-AI-espionage.

with the U.S., China, and U.K. all targeting deployment by 2030 to 2033.

On defense, AI enables real-time anomaly detection across vast networks, automated threat response, and predictive analytics that can identify attacks before they fully materialize. But as with autonomous weapons, the fundamental challenge is accountability and control. When AI systems engage in cyber operations, whether offensive or defensive, at speeds that preclude human review, who bears responsibility for their actions? What happens when an autonomous defensive system counterattacks in ways that escalate a conflict? These questions have no clear answers under existing law.

Legal Framework Gaps

International law governing cyber operations remains underdeveloped. The Tallinn Manual, an academic effort to articulate how existing international law applies to cyber conflict, provides influential but non-binding guidance.[340] Different jurisdictions disagree on fundamental questions: When does a cyber operation constitute an armed attack triggering the right of self-defense? What civilian infrastructure is protected during cyber conflicts? How do principles of distinction and proportionality apply to operations that may affect civilian and military systems simultaneously?

AI amplifies these uncertainties. The law of armed conflict assumes human judgment at key decision points. When algorithms make targeting decisions, even in cyberspace, the doctrinal foundations become unstable. The FY 2026 NDAA begins to address these gaps, requiring DoD to establish frameworks for AI cybersecurity standards and directing the NSA's AI Security Center to develop guidance for defending AI systems from nation-state theft.[341] But these are preliminary steps in what will be a long process of legal adaptation.

---

340 Michael N. Schmitt ed., Tallinn Manual 2.0 on the International Law Applicable to Cyber Operations (Cambridge Univ. Press 2017), onlinelibrary.iihl.org/wp-content/uploads/2021/05/2017-Tallinn-Manual-2.0.pdf.

341 P.L. 119-60, §§ 1531–1535.

Conclusion: Technology Outpacing Law

The legal frameworks governing AI and national security were designed for a different era. Export control laws assume physical goods moving across borders, not algorithms transmitted instantaneously worldwide. The laws of armed conflict assume human decision-makers at critical junctures, not autonomous systems operating at machine speed. Intelligence authorities assume collection from foreign adversaries, not domestic AI platforms that may serve as foreign intelligence vectors.

The gap between technological capability and legal framework will only widen as AI advances. Systems approaching artificial general intelligence, capable of matching human cognition across domains, would strain existing frameworks to the breaking point. The FY 2026 National Defense Authorization Act establishment of a steering committee to address AGI reflects awareness of this challenge, but awareness is not the same as preparedness.

For practitioners, the immediate task is navigating current uncertainty while anticipating future change. The companies building AI systems, the militaries deploying them, the governments regulating them, and the lawyers advising all three operate in a period of profound transition. The frameworks that emerge from this period, through legislation, regulation, litigation, and international agreement, will shape how humanity governs its most powerful technology.

The Operation Gatekeeper arrests that opened this chapter illustrate both the stakes and the difficulty. Advanced chips are indeed the building blocks of AI superiority. But building walls around technology that can be replicated, smuggled, or invented independently may ultimately prove less important than the harder work of establishing international norms, building robust oversight mechanisms, and ensuring that AI development serves human flourishing rather than merely national advantage.

The country that controls AI technology may indeed control the future. But what kind of future that will be depends on choices being made now, in legislative chambers, diplomatic negotiations, corporate boardrooms, and research laboratories. The law that governs these choices is still being written.

Supplemental Resources

- **Chris Miller, *Chip War: The Fight for the World's Most Critical Technology*** (2022): Traces how semiconductors became the world's most strategically important technology and how control over chip design, manufacturing, and supply chains now shapes global power. The book explains why the competition for chips sits at the center of modern geopolitics, economic security, and national defense, particularly in the rivalry between the United States and China.
- **Council on Foreign Relations, "The New AI Chip Export Policy to China: Strategically Incoherent and Unenforceable"** (cfr.org/articles/new-ai-chip-export-policy-china-strategically-incoherent-and-unenforceable): Analysis of the January 2026 Commerce Department regulation permitting conditional H200 exports to China, arguing the framework is self-contradicting.
- **Lawfare, "Trump's Illegal AI Chip Export Controls, and Who Can Challenge Them"** (lawfaremedia.org/article/trump-s-illegal-ai-chip-export-controls--and-who-can-challenge-them): Legal analysis arguing the revenue-for-access export policy constitutes an unauthorized tax on exports and identifying potential plaintiffs with standing to challenge it.
- **House Select Committee on China, "DeepSeek Unmasked"** (chinaselectcommittee.house.gov/media/reports/deepseek-unmasked): Full committee report on DeepSeek's national security risks, data practices, censorship alignment, and export control evasion.

- **NIST Center for AI Standards and Innovation (CAISI), "Evaluation of DeepSeek AI Models"** (nist.gov/news-events/news/2025/09/caisi-evaluation-deepseek-ai-models-finds-shortcomings-and-risks): Independent benchmarking of DeepSeek models against American AI systems across nineteen metrics, including jailbreak susceptibility.

- **Stop Killer Robots** (stopkillerrobots.org): Coalition of 270+ civil society organizations tracking autonomous weapons policy, UNGA resolutions, CCW proceedings, and the campaign for a legally binding instrument.

- **Anthropic, "Disrupting the First Reported AI-Orchestrated Cyber Espionage Campaign"** (anthropic.com/news/disrupting-AI-espionage): Disclosure of the GTG-1002 campaign in which AI agents executed 80–90% of tactical cyber operations independently, the first documented case of large-scale AI-orchestrated cyber espionage.

- **Bureau of Industry and Security, Export Administration Regulations** (bis.gov/regulations/ear): Official source for current U.S. export control regulations, Entity List designations, and license requirements for advanced computing items.

CHAPTER 14

The Global AI Legal Landscape

A Technology Without Borders Meets Laws That Stop at Them

In February 2025, Vice President JD Vance stood before world leaders at the Paris AI Action Summit and delivered a message that crystallized the emerging fault lines in global AI governance.[342] Vance declared that he had not come to talk about AI safety, the theme that had dominated the previous summit at Bletchley Park. He was there, he said, to talk about AI opportunity. He urged nations to look upon the technology "with optimism rather than trepidation" and cautioned against "international regulatory regimes" that might suffocate its potential.

Sixty-one countries signed the summit's final declaration pledging to develop AI that is "open, inclusive, transparent, ethical, safe, secure and trustworthy."[343] Notably absent from the list of signatories were the United States and the United Kingdom, two of the world's leading AI powers.[344] China, America's primary AI rival, did sign.[345]

---

342 J.D. Vance, Vice President, Remarks at the Artificial Intelligence Action Summit in Paris, France (Feb. 11, 2025), presidency.ucsb.edu/documents/remarks-the-vice-president-the-artificial-intelligence-action-summit-paris-france.

343 Statement on Inclusive and Sustainable Artificial Intelligence for People and the Planet, AI Action Summit, Paris (Feb. 11, 2025), elysee.fr/en/emmanuel-macron/2025/02/11/statement-on-inclusive-and-sustainable-artificial-intelligence-for-people-and-the-planet. Sixty-one countries and regional blocs signed the declaration.

344 Gregory C. Allen, France's AI Action Summit, Ctr. for Strategic & Int'l Studies (2025), csis.org/analysis/frances-ai-action-summit. The U.S. and U.K. declined to sign for different reasons: the U.S. objected to references to multilateralism and inclusivity, while the U.K. sought stronger treatment of national security concerns.

345 Paris AI Summit: Why Won't US, UK Sign Global Artificial Intelligence Pact?, Al Jazeera (Feb. 12, 2025), aljazeera.com/news/2025/2/12/paris-ai-summit-why-wont-us-uk-sign-global-artificial-intelligence-pact.

The Paris summit illustrated a fundamental tension that practitioners must navigate: artificial intelligence is a borderless technology being governed by laws that stop at national boundaries. The same AI system may be prohibited in Brussels, lightly regulated in London, subject to algorithm registration in Beijing, and essentially unregulated at the federal level in Washington. For companies operating globally, for governments seeking to protect their citizens, and for lawyers advising either, this fragmentation creates both legal risk and strategic opportunity.

This chapter surveys the major AI regulatory frameworks taking shape worldwide, focusing on jurisdictions that have adopted particularly innovative or influential approaches. Readers seeking to track this fast-moving landscape on an ongoing basis should consult the International Association of Privacy Professionals' Global AI Law and Policy Tracker,[346] as well as White & Case's AI Watch tracker,[347] both of which provide regularly updated jurisdiction-by-jurisdiction analysis. What follows examines not just the technical requirements of each regime but the underlying philosophies: the different answers that different societies are giving to fundamental questions about how AI should serve humanity.

The European Union: Regulating Through Risk

The First Comprehensive Framework

The European Union's AI Act, which entered into force on August 1, 2024, represents the world's first attempt to comprehensively regulate artificial intelligence through binding legislation.[348] The approach it embodies, risk-based categorization with graduated obligations, has become a template that other jurisdictions either adopt or

346 Int'l Ass'n of Privacy Prof'ls, Global AI Law and Policy Tracker, iapp.org/resources/article/global-ai-legislation-tracker.

347 White & Case LLP, AI Watch: Global Regulatory Tracker, whitecase.com/insight-our-thinking/ai-watch-global-regulatory-tracker.

348 Regulation (EU) 2024/1689 of the European Parliament and of the Council of 13 June 2024 Laying Down Harmonised Rules on Artificial Intelligence, 2024 O.J. (L 1689). The AI Act entered into force on August 1, 2024, digital-strategy.ec.europa.eu/en/policies/regulatory-framework-ai.

explicitly reject. As discussed in Chapter 8, the EU's regulatory posture stands in sharp contrast to the deregulatory approach that has characterized federal AI policy in the United States under the Trump administration.

The AI Act divides AI systems into four tiers based on the risk they pose to health, safety, and fundamental rights. At the top are "unacceptable risk" systems that are prohibited entirely. Below that are "high-risk" systems subject to extensive compliance requirements. "Limited risk" systems face lighter transparency obligations, and "minimal risk" systems remain essentially unregulated.

The prohibited practices, which became enforceable in February 2025, reveal what the EU considers AI's most dangerous potential uses: systems that deploy subliminal or manipulative techniques to distort behavior, that exploit vulnerabilities of age or disability, that enable "social scoring" by governments, or that perform real-time biometric identification in public spaces for law enforcement purposes. Also banned is emotion recognition in workplaces and educational institutions, a prohibition with significant implications for employers considering AI-powered productivity monitoring.

The high-risk category captures most of the AI applications that directly affect people's life chances. AI systems used for hiring, educational placement, credit decisions, welfare administration, and law enforcement face the most demanding requirements, including risk management systems, data quality controls, technical documentation, transparency to users, human oversight mechanisms, and conformity assessments before deployment.[349]

Implementation Timeline and Compliance

The Act's implementation proceeds through a carefully staged timeline that creates ongoing compliance obligations through 2027. In February 2025, prohibitions on unacceptable-risk AI systems took effect, along with mandatory "AI literacy" requirements

---

349 *Id.* art. 6 & Annex III. High-risk categories include AI systems used in biometric identification, critical infrastructure, education, employment, access to essential services, law enforcement, migration management, and administration of justice.

obligating providers and deployers to ensure their personnel understand the systems they operate. In August 2025, governance structures became operational, including the AI Office within the European Commission, the AI Board coordinating member state implementation, and obligations for general-purpose AI models. Providers of general-purpose AI systems must maintain technical documentation, implement copyright compliance policies, and publish summaries of training data. Models deemed to pose "systemic risks," those trained with computing power exceeding certain thresholds, face additional obligations including model evaluations and cybersecurity protections.

In July 2025, the European Commission published the General-Purpose AI Code of Practice, a voluntary framework developed through a multistakeholder process with nearly 1,000 participants, designed to help GPAI model providers demonstrate compliance with their obligations under the AI Act.[350] Providers who sign and implement the Code benefit from a collaborative compliance approach with the AI Office during the first year; beginning in August 2026, the Commission will enforce all GPAI obligations and may impose fines for noncompliance. Draft Codes of Practice on marking and labeling of AI-generated content were published in December 2025 and March 2026, with the final version expected by June 2026.[351] In November 2025, the Commission also proposed the "Digital Omnibus" package of targeted simplifications to the AI Act, which could modify when certain high-risk obligations apply if adopted.[352]

Full compliance requirements for high-risk AI systems in Annex III categories, including employment, education, credit, and law

---

350 European Commission, General-Purpose AI Code of Practice (July 2025), artificial-intelligenceact.eu/code-of-practice-overview; *see also* Jones Day, "EU AI Act: European Commission Publishes General-Purpose AI Code of Practice" (Aug. 2025), jonesday.com/en/insights/2025/08/eu-ai-act-european-commission-publishes-generalpurpose-ai-code-of-practice.

351 European Commission, First Draft Code of Practice on Marking and Labelling of AI-Generated Content (Dec. 17, 2025); Second Draft (Mar. 3, 2026).

352 European Commission, Digital Omnibus Package (Nov. 19, 2025); SIG, "A Comprehensive EU AI Act Summary" (Jan. 2026), softwareimprovementgroup.com/blog/eu-ai-act-summary.

enforcement, become applicable in August 2026. The extended transition period for high-risk AI systems that are components of products already covered by existing EU product safety legislation concludes in August 2027.

Penalties and Enforcement

The penalty regime provides significant enforcement teeth. Violations of prohibited AI practices can result in fines up to €35 million or seven percent of global annual turnover, whichever is higher. Other compliance failures trigger fines up to €15 million or three percent of turnover.

For practitioners advising companies with EU exposure, the AI Act requires a fundamental shift in how AI deployments are evaluated. The question is no longer merely whether an AI system works, but whether it can be documented, audited, and explained, and whether the organization has implemented governance structures adequate to demonstrate compliance. This echoes themes explored in Chapter 12 regarding the growing importance of algorithmic transparency and accountability across jurisdictions.

Ongoing Obligations Under the GDPR

Because virtually all AI systems process personal data, whether in training datasets, user inputs, or system-generated logs, the EU AI Act must be applied concurrently with Europe's General Data Protection Regulation (GDPR).[353] This means that in addition to meeting the AI Act's risk-classification requirements, providers and deployers must independently satisfy the GDPR's requirements for lawful processing, including identifying a valid legal basis under Article 6, complying with transparency and notice obligations under Articles 13 and 14, and adhering to the data minimization principle of Article 5(1)(c).[354] Two areas of the GDPR pose particularly acute

---

353 Regulation (EU) 2016/679 of the European Parliament and of the Council of 27 April 2016 (General Data Protection Regulation); IAPP, "Top 10 Operational Impacts of the EU AI Act – Leveraging GDPR Compliance" (Nov. 6, 2024), iapp.org/resources/article/top-impacts-eu-ai-act-leveraging-gdpr-compliance.

354 GDPR, Art. 6 (lawfulness of processing); Art. 13–14 (transparency obligations);

challenges for AI systems. First, Article 22 grants individuals the right not to be subject to decisions based solely on automated processing that produce legal effects or similarly significant effects, a provision that directly implicates AI-driven hiring tools, credit scoring models, and benefits eligibility systems.[355] Where such systems are deployed, organizations must ensure meaningful human oversight and provide affected individuals with the right to contest the decision, requirements that can be difficult to reconcile with the operational efficiencies that AI is designed to deliver. Second, Article 17's right to erasure presents a near-intractable technical problem: once personal data has been absorbed into a machine learning model's parameters during training, isolating and removing the influence of specific data points may be technically infeasible without retraining the entire model.[356]

These tensions are not hypothetical. In March 2023, Italy's data protection authority, the Garante, temporarily banned ChatGPT from processing the personal data of Italian users, citing OpenAI's failure to identify a lawful basis for its mass collection of training data, its lack of adequate transparency disclosures, and its failure to implement age verification mechanisms.[357] The ban was lifted within a month after OpenAI implemented corrective measures,

---

Art. 5(1)(c) (data minimization). The AI Act explicitly requires that AI systems involving personal data processing comply with the GDPR. See EU AI Act, Art. 10(5); Recital 45. See also CNIL, "AI System Development: CNIL's Recommendations to Comply with the GDPR" (2024), available at cnil.fr/en/ai-system-development-cnils-recommendations-to-comply-gdpr.

355 GDPR, Art. 22(1); Art. 22(3). For analysis of Article 22 in the AI context, see Future of Privacy Forum, "Automated Decision-Making Under the GDPR: Practical Cases from Courts" (May 2022), fpf.org/wp-content/uploads/2022/05/FPF-ADM-Report-R2-singles.pdf.

356 GDPR, Art. 17; Leiden Law Blog, "Erasing Personal Data in an AI Era" (2025), leidenlawblog.nl/articles/erasing-personal-data-in-an-ai-era; Villaronga et al., "Algorithms That Forget: Machine Unlearning and the Right to Erasure," Computer Law & Security Review, Vol. 51, 105927 (2023); nva.sikt.no/registration/0198cc66d6e7-763d49b0-2355-44b8-82fa-7e28bca3a933.

357 Garante per la protezione dei dati personali, Decision of March 30, 2023 (ordering OpenAI to immediately cease processing personal data of Italian users through ChatGPT); Clifford Chance, "The Italian Data Protection Authority Halts ChatGPT's Data Processing Operations" (Apr. 2023), cliffordchance.com/insights/resources/blogs/talking-tech/en/articles/2023/04/the-italian-data-protection-authority-halts-chatgpt-s-data-proce.html.

but the Garante ultimately imposed a €15 million fine in December 2024, the first enforcement action against a generative AI provider under the GDPR, finding that OpenAI had trained its models on personal data without a proper legal basis and had failed to report a data breach affecting Italian users.[358] The Italian enforcement action signals that European data protection authorities view the GDPR as a fully operational tool for regulating AI, one that does not await the AI Act's phased implementation timeline. For organizations deploying AI systems in Europe, the practical implication is a dual compliance burden: satisfying the AI Act's sector-specific risk management and documentation requirements while simultaneously meeting the GDPR's data-subject-centered obligations around consent, transparency, individual rights, and data protection impact assessments.[359]

China: Innovation Under State Supervision

The Regulatory Architecture

China's approach to AI regulation proceeds from fundamentally different premises than the European model. Where the EU emphasizes individual rights and consumer protection, China balances technological advancement with social stability, content control, and alignment with government priorities. The result is a regulatory framework that is simultaneously more permissive of AI innovation and more demanding of political conformity.

Unlike the EU's single comprehensive statute, China has constructed its AI governance through a series of targeted regulations addressing specific technologies and applications. This piecemeal approach allows for rapid regulatory adaptation as AI capabilities evolve, though it creates complexity for businesses navigating overlapping requirements.

---

358 National Law Review, "Don't Forget the EU: Italy Issued First GenAI Fine of EU15 Million Alleging GDPR Violations" (2025), natlawreview.com/article/dont-forget-eu-it-aly-issued-first-genai-fine-eu15-million-alleging-gdpr-violations. OpenAI has stated its intent to appeal.

359 activeMind.legal, "GDPR and AI Act: Similarities and Differences" (Oct. 25, 2024), activemind.legal/guides/gdpr-ai-act/; European Parliament, "The Impact of the General Data Protection Regulation (GDPR) on Artificial Intelligence" (June 2020), europarl.euro-pa.eu/RegData/etudes/STUD/2020/641530/EPRS_STU(2020)641530_EN.pdf.

The foundation was laid with the Algorithm Recommendation Provisions, effective in March 2022, which regulate how platforms use algorithms to recommend content to users.[360] Operators must adhere to an ethical code promoting "mainstream values" and "positive energy," and cannot use algorithms to create information cocoons or enable price discrimination. Algorithm operators must register their systems with the Cyberspace Administration of China.

The Deep Synthesis Provisions, effective in January 2023, addressed synthetic media and deepfake technology, prohibiting the use of deep synthesis to create fake news or harmful content and requiring providers to implement labeling mechanisms to identify synthetic content.[361] The Generative AI Interim Measures, effective in August 2023, made China the first country with binding regulations specifically targeting generative AI.[362] Providers of generative AI services must ensure content is lawful and truthful, obtain user consent, respect intellectual property in training data, and register their large language models with the Cyberspace Administration of China.

The AI Labeling Measures, effective September 2025, establish comprehensive requirements for identifying AI-generated content.[363] Internet service providers using AI to generate text, images, audio, video, or virtual scenes must implement both explicit labels (visible watermarks or symbols) and implicit labels (metadata embedding). Draft Ethics Review Measures released in August 2025 requires ethical review of AI research and development that poses risks to life, health, human dignity, environment, or public order.[364]

---

360 Provisions on the Management of Algorithmic Recommendations in Internet Information Services, chinalawtranslate.com/en/algorithms.

361 Provisions on the Administration of Deep Synthesis in Internet Information Services, chinalawtranslate.com/en/deep-synthesis.

362 Interim Measures for the Administration of Generative Artificial Intelligence Services chinalawtranslate.com/en/generative-ai-interim.

363 Measures for Labeling Artificial Intelligence-Generated Content, chinalawtranslate.com/en/ai-labeling.

364 Draft Measures for Scientific and Technological Ethics Review of Artificial Intelligence, geopolitechs.org/p/china-releases-draft-technology-ethics.

Content Control and International Implications

A distinctive feature of Chinese AI regulation is the explicit requirement that AI systems support government messaging and avoid politically sensitive content. Chinese law mandates that AI systems reflect "core socialist values" and avoid content that could "incite subversion of state power."[365] This creates a bifurcated AI landscape. Chinese AI systems deployed domestically operate under content constraints that would be legally and commercially unacceptable in Western markets. Meanwhile, concerns about data security and political censorship have prompted government bans on Chinese AI platforms across numerous countries, as discussed in Chapter 14.

For international companies, China's AI regulations present a compliance challenge distinct from the EU framework. The requirement to register algorithms, file large language models with the Cyberspace Administration of China, and ensure AI outputs align with political expectations affects any company providing AI services to Chinese users, regardless of where the company is incorporated. Companies providing AI services without proper registration face penalties including administrative fines, business suspension, and in severe cases, criminal liability for responsible individuals.

India: Governance Without Comprehensive Legislation

India has charted a distinctive course by explicitly declining to enact comprehensive AI legislation, relying instead on adapting existing legal frameworks and issuing non-binding governance guidelines. At the launch of India's AI Governance Guidelines in November 2025, IT Secretary S. Krishnan articulated this philosophy directly, stating that India's focus remains on "using existing legislation wherever possible" rather than leading with new regulatory obligations.[366]

---

365 *Supra* note 362.

366 MeitY Unveils India AI Governance Guidelines Under IndiaAI Mission (Nov. 5, 2025), pib.gov.in/PressReleasePage.aspx?PRID=2186639.

The Regulatory Framework

India's primary data protection legislation, the Digital Personal Data Protection Act of 2023, became operational with the notification of implementing rules in November 2025.[367] The DPDPA establishes consent as the primary basis for data processing, unlike the EU's GDPR, which offers multiple lawful bases including legitimate interests. This has significant implications for AI training on personal data, as explicit consent and purpose limitation are required. The Act becomes fully applicable on May 13, 2027, following an eighteen-month transition period.

The India AI Governance Guidelines, released in November 2025 under the IndiaAI Mission, establish seven foundational principles covering trust, transparency, accountability, safety, and human oversight.[368] Crucially, the guidelines carry no legal enforcement mechanism. They are explicitly described as enabling innovation while encouraging responsible behavior, not creating binding obligations. Rather than establishing a single AI authority, India relies on existing sectoral regulators to address AI within their domains: the Reserve Bank of India oversees AI in financial services, the Securities and Exchange Board monitors AI-driven trading systems, and the Insurance Regulatory Development Authority addresses AI in insurance.

Implications and Outlook

India's approach creates both opportunities and uncertainties. The absence of comprehensive AI legislation reduces compliance burdens compared to the EU. However, the patchwork of existing laws, including IT Act provisions on intermediary liability, consumer protection requirements, and sector-specific guidance, leaves ambiguity about exactly what obligations apply to which AI systems. Practitioners advising clients operating in India should

---

367 The Digital Personal Data Protection Act, 2023 (India), with implementing rules notified on November 13, 2025, becoming fully applicable on May 13, 2027.

368 India AI Governance Guidelines, Ministry of Elecs. & Info. Tech. (Nov. 5, 2025), indiaai.gov.in/article/india-ai-governance-guidelines-empowering-ethical-and-responsi-ble-ai.

prepare for a compliance environment that may tighten rapidly through subordinate legislation and regulatory guidance rather than primary legislation. India's scheduled hosting of the AI Impact Summit in February 2026 may also signal a growing role in shaping international AI governance norms.

India hosted the AI Impact Summit in February 2026, co-chaired with France, at which the EU endorsed a Leaders' Declaration and over eighty-five countries participated. The summit reinforced India's growing role in shaping international AI governance norms, particularly as a voice for the Global South.[369]

The United Kingdom: Principles Over Prescription

The Pro-Innovation Framework

The United Kingdom has positioned itself as offering a more flexible alternative to the EU's prescriptive approach. Rather than comprehensive AI legislation, the UK relies on five cross-sectoral principles that existing regulators implement within their respective domains.[370] The principles, articulated in the government's 2023 AI White Paper and carried forward by the Labour government elected in 2024, are: safety, security, and robustness; transparency and explainability; fairness; accountability and governance; and contestability and redress. Regulators including the Information Commissioner's Office, Financial Conduct Authority, Competition and Markets Authority, and sector-specific bodies are expected to interpret and apply these principles within their existing mandates.

Recent Developments

The AI Opportunities Action Plan, commissioned by the Labour government and led by tech entrepreneur Matt Clifford in January 2025, reaffirmed the UK's pro-innovation stance while accepting all

---

369 AI Impact Summit, Leaders' Declaration, New Delhi (Feb. 2026); European Commission Press Release (Feb. 20, 2026), digital-strategy.ec.europa.eu/en/news/european-union-endorses-leaders-declaration-ai-summit-india.

370 Dep't for Sci., Innovation & Tech., A Pro-Innovation Approach to AI Regulation, Cm. 815 (2023).

fifty expert recommendations on accelerating AI adoption.[371] The government rebranded the AI Safety Institute as the AI Security Institute in February 2025, signaling a focus on national security implications of AI rather than broader safety concerns.

The Data (Use and Access) Act, which received Royal Assent on June 19, 2025, relaxed some constraints on automated decision-making and expanded lawful bases for data use in research.[372] The Act stopped short of requiring AI companies to disclose copyrighted training data despite a House of Lords amendment to that effect, instead mandating the government to produce an economic impact assessment and a report on the use of copyright works in AI development.[373] Lord Holmes introduced an Artificial Intelligence (Regulation) Bill in March 2025, proposing to create an AI Authority, codify the five principles as legal requirements, and introduce transparency and labeling obligations.[374] The bill lacks government backing and remains under debate.

The Tension Between Innovation and Protection

The UK approach creates a distinctive compliance environment. Without AI-specific legislation, companies face less prescriptive requirements than under the EU AI Act. However, the obligation to satisfy multiple regulators interpreting broad principles can create its own compliance burden, particularly when different regulators reach different conclusions about what the principles require. The government has indicated that legislation may ultimately be needed, particularly for "frontier" AI models capable of causing significant harm, though timelines remain uncertain.

---

371 Matt Clifford, AI Opportunities Action Plan (Jan. 2025), gov.uk/government/publications/ai-opportunities-action-plan.

372 Data (Use and Access) Act 2025, c. 18 (UK), legislation.gov.uk/ukpga/2025/18.

373 *Id.* §§ 135-137.

374 Artificial Intelligence (Regulation) Bill [HL] 2024-25 (introduced Mar. 2025 by Lord Holmes of Richmond).

Japan: The Promotional Framework

Agile Governance in Action

Japan's AI Promotion Act, enacted by the Diet on May 28, 2025, and fully effective on September 1, 2025, embodies a fundamentally different regulatory philosophy, one that treats AI regulation as primarily promotional rather than restrictive.[375] The Act's formal title captures this orientation: "Act on Promotion of Research and Development, and Utilization of Artificial Intelligence-related Technology." The legislation establishes basic principles for AI development and use, creates governance structures including the AI Strategy Headquarters chaired by the Prime Minister, and mandates development of an AI Basic Plan. Notably, it does not impose direct penalties or create binding compliance obligations for businesses. Non-compliance may result in guidance, advice, or public disclosure, but not fines or criminal sanctions.

The Hiroshima AI Process

Japan's international AI governance leadership has come through the Hiroshima AI Process, launched during Japan's G7 presidency in 2023.[376] This initiative produced the Hiroshima Process Comprehensive Policy Framework, the first international framework addressing governance of advanced AI systems. The framework includes International Guiding Principles applicable to all AI actors throughout the AI lifecycle, plus a more specific International Code of Conduct for Organizations Developing Advanced AI Systems. Over fifty countries have joined the Hiroshima AI Process Friends Group, making it one of the most successful international AI governance initiatives.[377]

---

375 Act on Promotion of Research and Development, and Utilization of Artificial Intelligence-Related Technology (effective Sept. 1, 2025), gov-online.go.jp/hlj/en/november_2025/november_2025-08.html.

376 G7 Hiroshima AI Process Comprehensive Policy Framework (2023), adopted during Japan's G7 presidency.

377 Over fifty countries have joined the Hiroshima AI Process Friends Group. *See* gov-online.go.jp/hlj/en/november_2025/november_2025-08.html.

Practical Implications

For businesses operating in Japan, compliance means demonstrating responsible practices through guidelines and governance integration rather than meeting specific prescriptive requirements. The AI Guidelines for Business, updated through March 2025, establish ten core principles including human-centricity, safety, fairness, privacy, security, transparency, and accountability.[378] Japan's approach reflects both cultural factors, a generally positive societal attitude toward AI and robotics, and strategic calculations about maintaining competitiveness. The country has explicitly chosen not to pursue AI supremacy through restriction of competitors (the U.S. approach) or broad high-risk regulation (the EU approach), instead seeking to create an environment where safety and innovation can coexist.

South Korea: Asia's Comprehensive Framework

Breaking New Ground

South Korea's Framework Act on the Development of Artificial Intelligence and Establishment of Trust, promulgated on January 21, 2025, and effective January 22, 2026, makes it the second country after the EU, and first in the Asia-Pacific region, to adopt comprehensive AI legislation.[379] The Act consolidated nineteen separate AI-related bills that had been proposed in the National Assembly, reflecting intense legislative interest in AI governance.[380] Passage came despite extraordinary political turmoil, including President Yoon Suk Yeol's declaration of martial law and subsequent impeachment, underscoring bipartisan commitment to establishing an AI legal framework.

---

378 AI Guidelines for Business v1.1 (Ministry of Econ., Trade & Indus. & Ministry of Internal Affairs & Commc'ns, Mar. 2025).

379 Framework Act on the Development of Artificial Intelligence and Establishment of Trust, Law No. 20676 (effective Jan. 22, 2026), cset.georgetown.edu/publication/south-korea-ai-law-2025/.

380 Kyoungjin Choi, Analyzing South Korea's Framework Act on the Development of AI, Int'l Ass'n of Privacy Prof'ls (Jan. 23, 2025), iapp.org/news/a/analyzing-south-korea-s-framework-act-on-the-development-of-ai. The Act integrated 19 separate AI-related bills.

Key Features

Like the EU AI Act, the Korean framework adopts a risk-based approach, but with distinctive features reflecting the country's emphasis on simultaneously promoting AI innovation and establishing trust. The Act focuses regulatory attention on "High-Impact AI," defined as AI systems used in eleven specified areas that may significantly affect life, safety, or fundamental rights, including healthcare, critical infrastructure, employment, education, and law enforcement. Specific requirements apply to generative AI systems, including mandatory labeling when users interact with AI-generated content.

Rather than distinguishing providers from deployers as the EU does, Korea defines "AI development operators" (who create and provide AI) and "AI utilization operators" (who use AI to provide products or services). Both face essentially identical obligations under the current framework. Many technical details of the Act's obligations are delegated to enforcement decrees being finalized by the Ministry of Science and ICT.

Brazil: Latin America's Emerging Framework

Brazil's AI Bill (Bill No. 2,338/2023), approved by the Senate in December 2024, would establish Latin America's first comprehensive AI regulatory framework when enacted.[381] As of early 2026, the bill remains under review by the Chamber of Deputies, where it has been assigned to a special committee given its scope across multiple policy areas.

The bill adopts a risk-based structure similar to the EU AI Act, with three tiers of classification. Excessive-risk systems are prohibited, although unlike the EU, Brazil would permit some prohibited uses for specific law enforcement purposes including searching for crime victims and executing arrest warrants. High-risk systems face impact assessments, transparency requirements, and human oversight obligations. Other systems face basic transparency and fairness obligations. Several aspects distinguish the Brazilian approach. The bill applies

381 Bill No. 2,338/2023.

obligations across the AI supply chain including developers, deployers, and distributors, a wider net than some frameworks that focus primarily on developers. Controversial provisions address AI and intellectual property, including rules on using copyrighted material for training. The enforcement contemplates a national AI regulation system integrated with existing sectoral authorities, with the National Data Protection Authority expected to play a central coordinating role. Maximum fines of BRL 50 million (approximately USD 8 million) or two percent of Brazilian revenue are significant but lower than EU penalties. If enacted, Brazil's framework would likely influence AI regulation throughout Latin America, much as the EU's General Data Protection Regulation influenced global data protection approaches.

International Frameworks and Harmonization Efforts

The OECD AI Principles

The OECD AI Principles, adopted in 2019 and updated in 2024, represent the first intergovernmental standard on AI.[382] Now adhered to by forty-seven governments, the principles provide a common foundation that influences national legislation and enables some degree of interoperability between jurisdictions. The five value-based principles cover inclusive growth and sustainable development, human rights and democratic values, transparency and explainability, robustness and safety, and accountability. The OECD definition of "AI system" has been adopted by the EU, the Council of Europe, and increasingly serves as a common reference point for national legislation worldwide.

UNESCO and the Paris Summit

UNESCO's 2021 Recommendation on the Ethics of Artificial Intelligence provides a global normative framework emphasizing human rights, environmental sustainability, and equity.[383] While

---

382 OECD, Recommendation of the Council on Artificial Intelligence, OECD/LEGAL/0449 (adopted May 22, 2019; updated 2024), oecd.org/en/topics/sub-issues/ai-governance-principles.html.

383 UNESCO, Recommendation on the Ethics of Artificial Intelligence (adopted Nov.

non-binding, it has been adopted by all 193 UNESCO member states and influences governance approaches particularly in the Global South.

The February 2025 Paris AI Action Summit produced several concrete outcomes, including Current AI, a $400 million public interest AI initiative backed by France and other governments,[384] and InvestAI, a EUR 200 billion EU initiative.[385] However, the failure of the United States and United Kingdom to sign the summit declaration demonstrated the difficulty of achieving genuine global consensus.

Navigating the Patchwork: Practical Guidance

Compliance Strategy in a Fragmented World

For organizations deploying AI across multiple jurisdictions, the challenge is developing compliance frameworks that satisfy the most demanding requirements while remaining operationally efficient. Several guiding principles emerge from the current landscape.

First, organizations should map to the highest standard. Companies with EU exposure effectively must comply with the AI Act regardless of headquarters location. Building compliance programs around EU requirements often satisfies, or nearly satisfies, requirements elsewhere. Second, documentation is essential regardless of jurisdiction. The trend across every framework surveyed in this chapter is toward greater transparency, explainability, and documentation. Organizations that build these capabilities proactively will be better positioned as regulations tighten.

Third, understanding risk classification is critical. Most frameworks use some form of risk-based approach, and developing robust methodologies for classifying AI systems by risk level provides a

2021). The Recommendation has been adopted by all 193 UNESCO member states.

384 Current AI: A Public Interest AI Initiative, announced at the Paris AI Action Summit (Feb. 11, 2025), currentai.org/blogs/building-public-interest-ai---current-ais-next-chapter.

385 European Commission, EU Launches InvestAI Initiative to Mobilise €200 Billion of Investment in Artificial Intelligence (Feb. 11, 2025), digital-strategy.ec.europa.eu/en/news/eu-launches-investai-initiative-mobilise-eu200-billion-investment-artificial-intelligence

foundation for compliance across jurisdictions. Fourth, human oversight requirements appear across virtually all frameworks. Designing systems with meaningful human oversight from the outset reduces the need for costly retrofitting. Finally, the landscape is changing rapidly. The EU continues issuing implementation guidance, China regularly adds new requirements, India may enact AI legislation despite current statements, and U.S. federal preemption attempts, discussed in Chapter 8, may succeed or fail. Organizations need monitoring mechanisms to track developments across all relevant jurisdictions.

The Convergence Question

Is the global AI regulatory landscape converging toward common standards or fragmenting into incompatible regional regimes? The answer is likely both. At the level of broad principles, transparency, accountability, human oversight, and risk-based approaches, significant convergence is occurring. The OECD principles have achieved remarkable global uptake. Even jurisdictions with very different implementation approaches often articulate similar goals.

At the level of specific requirements, however, significant divergence persists. The EU's prohibited practices differ from China's content requirements. Japan's promotional approach contrasts sharply with Colorado's duty-of-care liability regime discussed in Chapter 8. These differences reflect genuine disagreements about values, about the proper role of technology regulation, and about the balance between innovation and protection. For practitioners, this means there is no single "global AI compliance" checklist. Success requires understanding not just the technical requirements of each jurisdiction but the underlying philosophy that animates them, and building programs flexible enough to adapt as that philosophy evolves.

The Race to Govern the Future

The global AI legal landscape is being constructed in real time, through a combination of legislation, regulation, litigation, and diplomatic negotiation. The frameworks that emerge will shape how AI develops, who benefits from it, and what safeguards protect those it affects.

Several themes will define the coming years. The tension between the EU's comprehensive regulatory approach and the Trump administration's deregulatory stance represents genuinely different visions of how AI should be governed. Which approach produces better outcomes, and whether they can coexist, remains to be seen. The rise of Asian regulatory leadership is equally significant: with South Korea enacting comprehensive legislation, Japan establishing international frameworks through the Hiroshima Process, China building sophisticated regulatory infrastructure, and India positioning itself as a governance leader for the Global South, Asian approaches will increasingly influence global norms.

As discussed in Chapter 8, U.S. states continue functioning as laboratories for AI governance. Whether federal preemption succeeds or fails, the policy innovations developed in Colorado, California, Texas, and elsewhere will influence future federal and international approaches. And the Paris summit demonstrated that achieving binding international AI agreements remains difficult, with voluntary frameworks like the Hiroshima Process offering more realistic paths to coordination than treaty negotiations.

This fragmented global landscape creates complexity but also opportunity. Organizations that develop sophisticated compliance capabilities can turn regulatory navigation into competitive advantage. Those that wait for clarity may find themselves scrambling to catch up with requirements they should have anticipated. The ultimate question is not whether AI will be regulated; it already is, increasingly. The question is whether the emerging regulatory frameworks will effectively balance innovation with protection, economic growth with social welfare, and national interests with global cooperation. The answer will be written over the coming years in legislative chambers, regulatory agencies, corporate boardrooms, and courtrooms around the world.

Supplemental Resources

- **Int'l Ass'n of Privacy Prof'ls, Global AI Law and Policy Tracker** (iapp.org/resources/article/global-ai-legislation-tracker): Provides an up-to-date, jurisdiction-by-jurisdiction overview of enacted and proposed AI laws, regulations, and policy initiatives worldwide.

- **White & Case LLP, AI Watch: Global Regulatory Tracker** (whitecase.com/insight-our-thinking/ai-watch-global-regulatory-tracker): Surveys global AI regulatory developments with practical legal analysis focused on compliance trends, enforcement risk, and emerging governance frameworks across major markets.

- **EU AI Act Explorer** (artificialintelligenceact.eu): Comprehensive resource tracking EU AI Act implementation, including Codes of Practice, guidelines, compliance tools, and enforcement developments. Maintained by the Future of Life Institute.

- **Georgetown CSET, South Korea AI Framework Act Translation** (cset.georgetown.edu/publication/south-korea-ai-law-2025): English translation and analysis of South Korea's Framework Act on AI Development and Trust, the Asia-Pacific's first comprehensive AI legislation.

- **China Law Translate, AI Regulations Collection** (chinalawtranslate.com): English translations of China's Algorithm Recommendation Provisions, Deep Synthesis Provisions, Generative AI Interim Measures, and AI Labeling Measures. Essential resource for understanding Chinese AI regulatory architecture.

- **OECD AI Policy Observatory** (oecd.ai): Tracks AI policies across 70+ countries, provides the OECD AI Principles framework, and offers comparative analysis of national AI strategies and governance approaches.

- **India AI Governance Guidelines** (indiaai.gov.in/article/india-ai-governance-guidelines-empowering-ethical-and-responsible-ai): Official text of India's seven foundational AI governance principles released under the IndiaAI Mission.

CHAPTER 15

AI and Legal Practice

The Reckoning Begins

On the morning of May 5, 2023, Zachariah Crabill sat in his car outside the El Paso County courthouse, scrolling through his phone in growing panic.[386] The motion he had filed was riddled with case citations that did not exist. He had discovered this only hours earlier, when he tried to verify the legal authorities that ChatGPT had so confidently provided.

"I think all of my case cites from ChatGPT are garbage," he texted his paralegal. "I have no idea what to do. I am trying to find actual case law in our favor now to present to the judge."

He could not find any. And when Judge Eric Bentley began questioning the citations during the hearing, Crabill panicked again. Rather than confess that he had relied on artificial intelligence to draft his brief, he blamed the errors on a legal intern.

Six days later, Crabill filed an affidavit admitting the truth: he had used ChatGPT, he had never verified its output, and he had lied to the court. The Colorado Supreme Court's Office of the Presiding Disciplinary Judge suspended him for one year and one day, with ninety days to be served and the remainder stayed upon successful completion of a two-year probation.

Crabill was not the first lawyer to submit AI-generated hallucinations to a court. He would not be the last. But his case captured something essential about the moment: a young attorney, two years out of law

---

386 *People v. Crabill*, No. 23PDJ067 (Stipulation to Discipline and Order, Nov. 22, 2023), shorturl.at/plW5W.

school, burned out and overwhelmed, reaching for a technological shortcut that promised to help and discovering too late that the machine had betrayed him.

The Hallucination Epidemic

What happened to Zachariah Crabill was not an isolated incident. It was the beginning of an epidemic. Damien Charlotin, a researcher at HEC Paris business school, began tracking cases of AI hallucinations in court filings. By late January 2026, his database documented 878 cases worldwide, with the majority occurring in United States.[387] The progression was alarming: from a handful of cases in 2023 to hundreds by mid-2025, with new instances appearing at a rate of two to three per day.

The watershed moment came in June 2023, when Judge P. Kevin Castel of the Southern District of New York sanctioned attorneys Steven Schwartz and Peter LoDuca of Levidow, Levidow & Oberman in the case of *Mata v. Avianca*.[388] Schwartz had used ChatGPT to research a brief opposing the airline's motion to dismiss, and the AI had helpfully provided six cases supporting his position, complete with quotes, citations, and internal cross-references. None of them existed.

When opposing counsel could not locate the cases, the court ordered Schwartz to provide copies. He asked ChatGPT whether the cases were real. The chatbot assured him they were. He submitted this assurance to the court.

Judge Castel was not amused. In his sanctions order, he observed that "as of June 22, 2023, the shortcomings of ChatGPT for legal research and the danger it poses to professional reputations were on most lawyers' radar screens." The $5,000 fine was modest, but the public shaming was not. *Mata v. Avianca* became the case that every lawyer knew, the cautionary tale repeated at CLE seminars and bar

---

387 Damien Charlotin, AI Hallucination Cases Database, damiencharlotin.com/hallucinations.

388 *Mata v. Avianca, Inc.*, 678 F. Supp. 3d 443 (S.D.N.Y. 2023), law.justia.com/cases/federal/district-courts/new-york/nysdce/1:2022cv01461/575368/54.

association meetings across the country.

The Cases Keep Coming

By 2025, the sanctions had grown more severe, the excuses more varied, and the affected firms more prominent. The epidemic was no longer confined to solo practitioners or inexperienced associates. It had reached the upper tiers of the profession.

Johnson v. Dunn

In July 2025, a Northern District of Alabama court confronted one of the most severe sanctions yet imposed for AI hallucinations.[389] A well-regarded law firm had used hallucinated citations in a discovery motion, not a brief on the merits, but a routine procedural filing that no one expected to become a career-defining event.

The court did not merely impose fines. It disqualified the responsible attorneys from representing their client for the remainder of the case, published its opinion in the Federal Supplement for maximum visibility, and ordered the clerk to notify bar regulators in every state where the attorneys were licensed.

What made *Johnson v. Dunn* particularly devastating was that the firm had a proactive AI policy forbidding use without practice group leader permission. The problem was that the violation had been committed by the practice group co-leader himself. The firm conducted a comprehensive review of all its Alabama federal and Eleventh Circuit filings, engaged an outside firm for an independent audit, and found no other instances of hallucinated citations. But the damage was done.

A Major Problem For Major Firms

In September 2025, the California Court of Appeal confronted attorney Amir Mostafavi, who had used ChatGPT to "enhance" his appellate briefs. Twenty-one of the twenty-three case quotations in

---

389 *Johnson v. Dunn*, No. 2:21-cv-1701 (N.D. Ala. July 23, 2025), esquiresolutions.com/federal-court-turns-up-the-heat-on-attorneys-using-chatgpt-for-research.

his opening brief were fabricated. The reply brief contained many more.[390]

The court imposed a $10,000 sanction, the largest yet from a California state court, and referred Mostafavi to the state bar for disciplinary action. But the case introduced a novel wrinkle: the court declined to award fees to opposing counsel because they had failed to detect and report the fake citations before the court issued its show cause order.

Mostafavi's response to his sanction captured the fatalistic mood settling over parts of the profession: "It's unrealistic to expect lawyers to stop using AI... In the meantime we're going to have some victims, some damages, some wreckages... I'm paying the price."[391]

Perhaps the most alarming development came when attorneys from Ellis George LLP and K&L Gates LLP, major firms with substantial litigation practices, submitted a brief to a special master in the Central District of California containing numerous hallucinated citations.[392] The attorneys had used CoCounsel, Westlaw Precision, and Google Gemini to research and outline their brief.

The sanctions were substantial: all versions of the supplemental brief struck, discovery relief denied, $31,100 in defendant's fees, and required disclosure to their client. The case shattered any remaining assumption that hallucinations were a problem confined to lawyers using consumer-grade tools. Westlaw Precision is a legal-specific database designed for professional research. CoCounsel is marketed as an AI assistant built for lawyers. If major firms using purpose-built legal tools could still submit hallucinated citations, the problem was not just the technology. It was, as one commentator put it, "our wholesale abdication of verification responsibilities."[393]

---

390 *Noland v. Land of the Free, Inc.*, No. B336938 (Cal. Ct. App. Sept. 2025).

391 Datamation Staff, *California Judge Slaps Lawyer with $10,000 Fine for ChatGPT-Generated Brief* (Dec. 9, 2025), datamation.com/artificial-intelligence/lawyer-fined-chatgpt-brief.

392 Ellis George /K&L Gates Special Master Sanctions Order (C.D. Cal. 2025), https://shorturl.at/Z7IMr.

393 Relativity, *AI Case Law Update: The Lamborghini Doctrine of Hallucinations* (Aug.

In February 2025, Morgan & Morgan, ranked number 42 by headcount among American law firms, was sanctioned after a brief cited nine cases, of which the court could locate only one. The hallucinations had been generated by the firm's internal AI platform. The firm's response was refreshingly candid: "This matter comes with great embarrassment and has prompted discussion and action regarding the training, implementation and future use of artificial intelligence within our firm...It serves as a cautionary tale for our firm and all firms."[394]

The Bar Responds

As sanctions accumulated, bar associations scrambled to provide guidance. The American Bar Association had never confronted a technology that could so easily and convincingly generate professional-looking work product that was completely fabricated.

ABA Formal Opinion 512

On July 29, 2024, the ABA Standing Committee on Ethics and Professional Responsibility released Formal Opinion 512, the first formal ABA guidance on generative AI in legal practice.[395] The opinion applied existing Model Rules to the new technological context, emphasizing that no special dispensation existed for AI-assisted work.

The opinion addressed six core areas. On competence under Rule 1.1, it held that lawyers must understand the capabilities and limitations of generative AI tools and must periodically update that understanding as the technology evolves. They need not become AI experts, but they must have reasonable comprehension of what these tools can and cannot do. Most critically, lawyers may never

---

2025), relativity.com/blog/ai-case-law-update-the-lamborghini-doctrine-of-hallucinations/.

394 Joe Patrice, Massive Law Firm Gets Caught Hallucinating Cases (Feb. 2025), abovethelaw.com/2025/02/massive-law-firm-gets-caught-hallucinating-cases.

395 ABA Standing Comm. on Ethics & Prof'l Responsibility, Formal Op. 512, Generative Artificial Intelligence Tools (July 29, 2024), americanbar.org/content/dam/aba/administrative/professional_responsibility/ethics-opinions/aba-formal-opinion-512.pdf.

rely on AI output "without an appropriate degree of independent verification or review."

On confidentiality under Rule 1.6, the opinion explained that lawyers are responsible for knowing how AI tools use the data they are given. Client information entered into AI systems may be retained, used for training, or disclosed in ways that violate confidentiality obligations. On fees under Rule 1.5, the opinion stated that lawyers cannot charge clients for time spent learning AI technology for general use across client matters, as that constitutes professional development, not billable work. They cannot bill hourly for time saved by AI; if a task that once took five hours now takes thirty minutes, the client should not be charged for five hours of work.

On candor to tribunal under Rules 3.1, 3.3, and 8.4(c), the opinion emphasized that lawyers must prevent AI hallucinations from forming the basis of frivolous claims. Overreliance on AI or uncritical adoption of its output can result in false statements to the tribunal. Even unintentional misuse holds the attorney fully responsible.

On supervision under Rules 5.1 and 5.3, the opinion required that managerial lawyers establish clear AI policies and that supervisory lawyers ensure compliance. Training is required on tool use, ethical issues, protecting confidential information, secure data handling, and privacy concerns.

State Bar Responses and Court Orders

Before Formal Opinion 512 was released, several states had already issued their own guidance. Texas, Illinois, and California released opinions in 2023. By the end of 2024, numerous additional states had followed.[396]The Illinois Supreme Court adopted a Policy on AI effective January 1, 2025, with the primary concern of "upholding highest ethical standards in administration of justice."[397] Oregon's

396 *See* Fla. Bar Advisory Op. 24-1 (Jan. 2024); Cal. State Bar Practical Guidance on AI (2023); N.Y. State Bar Ass'n Report on AI (Apr. 2024).

397 Ill. Sup. Ct. Policy on AI (eff. Jan. 1, 2025); Ill. Att'y Registration & Disciplinary Comm'n, Illinois Attorney's Guide to Implementing AI (Oct. 2025).

Formal Opinion added to the growing body of state guidance.[398]

As sanctions accumulated and bar associations issued guidance, judges began taking matters into their own hands. Starting in May 2023, when Judge Brantley Starr of the Northern District of Texas issued the first standing order on AI use, courts across the country began requiring disclosure of AI assistance in legal filings.[399] By May 2025, more than 300 judges had adopted similar orders. The variation was substantial, creating a bewildering patchwork of requirements that lawyers practicing in multiple jurisdictions had to navigate.

AI and Attorney-Client Privilege

Beyond the hallucination problem lies another serious concern: when lawyers or clients use AI tools, they may inadvertently waive attorney-client privilege or create discoverable records that opposing counsel can exploit. The confidentiality risks extend beyond what ethics opinions have traditionally addressed.

The attorney-client privilege, the oldest common law protection for confidential communications, requires that communications be kept confidential to remain protected. When a lawyer inputs client information into a public AI system like ChatGPT without an enterprise agreement, that information may be retained by the AI provider, used to train future models, or potentially appear in responses to other users.[400] Several courts and commentators have concluded that such disclosure to a third-party AI provider could constitute waiver of the privilege.[401]

---

398 Or. State Bar, Formal Op. 2025-205 (Feb. 2025).

399 Ropes & Gray LLP, RAILS: AI in Litigation Standing Orders Database (2025), ropesgray.com/en/sites/artificial-intelligence-court-order-tracker.

400 ABA Comm. on Ethics & Prof'l Responsibility, Formal Op. 512, at 4-5 (2024), americanbar.org/news/abanews/aba-news-archives/2024/07/aba-issues-first-ethics-guidance-ai-tools.

401 Jordyn C. Tye, Comment, Exploring the Intersections of Privacy and Generative AI: A Dive into Attorney-Client Privilege and ChatGPT, 64 Jurimetrics J. 309, 332 (2024), americanbar.org/content/dam/aba/publications/Jurimetrics/spring-2024/exploring-the-intersections-of-privacy-and-generative-ai-a-dive-into-attorney-client-privilege-and-chatgpt.pdf.

The discovery implications are equally troubling. AI prompts and outputs are increasingly being sought in litigation, and courts are only beginning to develop frameworks for how privilege and work product doctrines apply. In *Tremblay v. OpenAI*, a Northern District of California court addressed the discoverability of AI prompts when plaintiffs had used ChatGPT for pre-suit investigation.[402] The defendant sought to compel production of all prompts used by plaintiffs' counsel, including "negative test results" that did not support their claims. Initially, a magistrate judge granted the motion to compel, classifying the materials as discoverable "fact work product." On review, the district court distinguished between factual inputs and prompts reflecting counsel's mental impressions, ordering an in camera review to separate the two.

Subsequent decisions have reinforced the emerging framework. In *Concord Music Group v. Anthropic*, the court agreed that prompts and related settings could constitute attorney work product, denying overly broad requests to compel all of a party's undisclosed prompts and outputs.[403] But the court also recognized that work product protection can be waived when a party relies on AI-generated materials in pleadings or motions. When the plaintiffs used specific prompts and outputs in their complaint and preliminary injunction filings, they created a limited waiver under the "fairness principle."

Courts have also begun imposing preservation obligations for AI interaction logs. In the multidistrict copyright litigation *In re OpenAI, Inc. Copyright Litigation*, the court directed OpenAI to "preserve and segregate all output log data that would otherwise be deleted on a going forward basis."[404] This signals that litigators should anticipate AI chat histories becoming a regular part of discovery, subject to the same litigation hold obligations as emails and other electronically stored information.

---

402 *Tremblay v. OpenAI, Inc.*, No. 23-cv-03223-AMO, 2024 WL 3748003 (N.D. Cal. Aug. 8, 2024).

403 *Concord Music Grp., Inc. v. Anthropic PBC*, No. 24-cv-03811-EKL, 2025 WL 1482734, at *1-2 (N.D. Cal. May 23, 2025).

404 *In re OpenAI, Inc. Copyright Litig.*, No. 23-cv-11195 (S.D.N.Y. May 13, 2025) (preservation order).

The Landmark Ruling: *United States v. Heppner*

In February 2026, Judge Jed S. Rakoff of the Southern District of New York issued what he characterized as a ruling of first impression at the federal level on AI and privilege. In *United States v. Heppner*, the defendant, a corporate executive indicted on securities and wire fraud charges, had used the consumer version of Claude to analyze his legal situation and develop defense strategies after receiving a grand jury subpoena and retaining counsel.[405] FBI agents seized approximately 31 documents memorializing his AI interactions during a search of his residence. Defense counsel argued the documents were privileged because Heppner had input information learned from his attorneys and generated the materials in anticipation of litigation.

Judge Rakoff rejected both the attorney-client privilege and work product claims. On privilege, the court held that the AI platform is not a licensed attorney and cannot form a fiduciary attorney-client relationship; that communications were not confidential because the platform's privacy policy expressly permitted data collection, model training, and disclosure to third parties including government authorities; and that the defendant did not communicate with the AI for the purpose of obtaining legal advice, since the platform explicitly disclaimed the ability to provide formal legal advice. On work product, the court found that because counsel had not directed the defendant to use the AI platform, the materials did not reflect the mental processes or strategies of his attorneys. The court further held that sharing the AI-generated documents with counsel after the fact could not retroactively convert them into privileged material.

AI Chat Logs as Smoking Guns: The Krafton Litigation

The discovery risks are not limited to criminal defendants. In Fortis *Advisors LLC v. Krafton Inc.*, decided by the Delaware Court of Chancery in March 2026, Krafton CEO Changhan Kim's ChatGPT conversations became central evidence in a breach of contract

---

405 *United States v. Heppner*, No. 25-cr-00503-JSR (S.D.N.Y. Feb. 17, 2026) (Rakoff, J.); Gibson Dunn, "AI Privilege Waivers: SDNY Rules Against Privilege Protection for Consumer AI Outputs" (Feb. 20, 2026), gibsondunn.com/ai-privilege-waivers-sdny-rules-against-privilege-protection-for-consumer-ai-outputs.

dispute over a $250 million earnout.[406] Kim had used ChatGPT to "brainstorm ways to avoid paying" the earnout owed to the founders of Unknown Worlds Entertainment. When the AI responded that the earnout would be "difficult to cancel," Kim pushed further, and ChatGPT obliged with a detailed corporate takeover strategy dubbed "Project X." Kim then followed most of ChatGPT's recommendations, including firing the founders without cause and seizing operational control of the studio.

Despite Kim's attempts to delete the conversations, they were recovered and became dispositive evidence at trial. Vice Chancellor Lori W. Will found that Krafton had breached its contract by terminating the founders without valid cause and noted that company executives are expected to exercise independent human judgment—not outsource good-faith decisions to an AI. The court ordered the CEO reinstated, extended the earnout period, and restored operational control to the founders. The *Krafton* litigation is a cautionary tale not only about the discoverability of AI interactions, but about the broader risk of using AI to develop strategies that a human decision-maker would recognize as legally and ethically problematic.

The Emerging Three-Tier Framework

Taken together, the early privilege decisions suggest a framework with three distinct tiers. The first involves an attorney conducting research or drafting using AI tools on behalf of a client. This use most closely resembles traditional work product. Where the AI interaction reflects counsel's mental impressions, legal theories, or litigation strategies, courts have generally extended work product protection, as in *Concord Music Group v. Anthropic* and the in camera review ordered in *Tremblay v. OpenAI*. The key factors are that counsel directed the use, the purpose was legal analysis, and the interaction occurred within a professional relationship subject to confidentiality obligations. Enterprise AI agreements that prohibit use of inputs for training further support the privilege analysis.

---

406 *Fortis Advisors LLC v. Krafton Inc.*, C.A. No. 2025-0723-LWW (Del. Ch. Mar. 16, 2026); Fortune, "A Gaming CEO Asked ChatGPT How to Avoid Paying a $250 Million Bonus. It Didn't Work" (Mar. 17, 2026), fortune.com/2026/03/17/krafton-subnautica-chatgpt-delaware-court-ruling-ceo-reinstated.

The second tier involves a client or individual inputting questions into a consumer AI platform and using it as a substitute for legal advice. This is the *Heppner* scenario. Courts treat these interactions much as they would any disclosure to a third party: the AI platform is not an attorney, the platform's terms of service typically disclaim confidentiality, and the resulting materials are discoverable. As Judge Rakoff observed, an AI platform cannot form the "trusting human relationship" on which privilege depends. These interactions are analogous to Google searches, which courts have long held are discoverable and carry no privilege protection.

The third tier presents the hardest question: where a client takes a lawyer's privileged advice and inputs it into an AI tool to better understand it. In *Heppner*, the defendant argued that some of the information he input into Claude he had learned from his counsel, but the court held that previously privileged information loses its protection when disclosed to a third-party platform with no expectation of confidentiality. In my view, this result is too broad. A client who uses AI to parse or understand legal advice received from counsel is not seeking legal advice from the AI—the client is seeking to comprehend advice already received from a lawyer. Whether courts will ultimately extend privilege to these types of increasingly common situations remains to be seen, but the law in this area is developing rapidly, and practitioners should not assume that the *Heppner* framework represents the final word.

Beyond privilege, AI chat logs have emerged as a powerful form of evidence in their own right. As the *Krafton* litigation demonstrates, AI interactions can reveal a party's state of mind, strategic calculations, and intent with unusual clarity—because users tend to be candid with AI in ways they would not be in emails or memoranda they expect others to read. Deleted AI conversations can often be recovered through platform data retention or device forensics. For lawyers and their clients, the lesson is stark. Any interaction with an AI tool should be treated as potentially discoverable, regardless of whether the user intended it to be private.

The Rise of AI Legal Tools

While courts and bar associations focused on the risks of AI hallucinations, a parallel transformation was underway in how legal work is performed. A rapidly expanding ecosystem of AI powered legal tools has emerged, promising lower costs and greater efficiency. As the sanctions orders discussed above make clear, even purpose built legal AI tools remain vulnerable to hallucination and basic reliability failures. This is not a problem limited to consumer chatbots. It persists in systems marketed specifically to lawyers and deployed in enterprise environments, a reality that tempers much of the current enthusiasm surrounding legal AI.

The number of AI specific research, drafting, contract management, and discovery tools has exploded in a remarkably short period of time. From the perspective of a large in house legal department, it is now routine to receive near constant outreach from AI vendors promising transformational productivity gains. Yet in practice, many legal specific tools are no better, and are sometimes worse, than general purpose foundational models. What the market has largely produced is not new intelligence, but specialized chatbots wrapped in legal workflows and interfaces that narrow use cases without eliminating core risks.

One of the clearest illustrations of the trend toward AI-enabled legal tools is Harvey, which has emerged as a leading example of purpose built legal AI.[407] Harvey offers tools for drafting, research, document analysis, and workflow automation, and was among the first platforms to see broad enterprise adoption. When Allen & Overy deployed the system firmwide in 2023, thousands of lawyers used it extensively. At the same time, firm leadership emphasized a simple rule: every output required human validation, reflecting a broader recognition that even sophisticated legal AI remains an assistive tool rather than an authoritative one.[408]

More recently, the market has begun to shift again as foundational AI companies move directly into legal workflows. In February 2026, Anthropic announced legal plugins for its agentic Cowork facility, including tools for document review, risk identification, and

---

407 Harvey.ai.

408 Shearman & Sterling LLP, A&O Announces Exclusive Launch Partnership With Harvey, aoshearman.com/en/news/ao-announces-exclusive-launch-partnership-with-harvey.

contract analysis using configurable playbooks.[409] This entry signals a broader transition. Capabilities once offered by specialized vendors at premium prices may increasingly be commoditized by general model providers, shifting competitive advantage toward governance, integration, and effective human oversight rather than bespoke legal interfaces alone.

The Economics of Legal Fees and the Incoming Fee Collapse

The cost of legal services has reached astronomical levels. In 2025, Quinn Emanuel Urquhart & Sullivan set a new industry benchmark, charging $3,000 per hour for top partners.[410] This milestone signals a broader trend of escalating law firm billing rates, with many firms surpassing the $2,500-per-hour mark for senior partners.[411]

Rate inflation is not confined to the most senior attorneys. Third-year associates at Am Law 50 firms now commonly bill over $1,000 per hour. As a client, I find it increasingly difficult to justify paying more than a thousand dollars an hour for junior associates to perform basic research, drafting, and document review. These are precisely the tasks that AI tools can now perform at a fraction of the cost and in a fraction of the time. The traditional justification for high associate rates, that clients are paying for the training and supervision that produces excellent lawyers, rings hollow when much of that work can be done by a machine.

Critics of AI in legal practice argue that you always need a human in the loop, that AI cannot replicate the judgment of an experienced lawyer. Perhaps that is still true today for the most complex matters. But over a medium time horizon, I believe the floor for legal fees will collapse. The bread and butter of commoditized litigation, contract

---

409 Silicon Republic, Anthropic's New Cowork Plug-Ins Prompt Sell-Off in Software Shares (Feb. 3, 2026), siliconrepublic.com/business/anthropics-new-cowork-plug-ins-prompt-sell-off-in-software-shares.

410 Law Firm Billing Rates Escalate: The $3,000-Per-Hour Benchmark, JD Journal (Feb. 27, 2025), jdjournal.com/2025/02/27/law-firm-billing-rates-escalate-the-3000-per-hour-benchmark-and-what-it-means-for-the-legal-industry.

411 *See* "This Law Firm Bills as Much as $3,000 Per Hour", ABA J. (2025), abajournal.com/news/article/this-law-firm-bills-as-much-as-3000-an-hour.

review, document analysis, regulatory research, basic drafting, is in the process of being automated. There may always be specialists who command premium rates, and advocates who negotiate, argue, and develop relationships with clients will continue to have essential roles. But the vast middle of legal work is being fundamentally transformed.

The relentless increase in billing rates may itself be a tacit acknowledgment that the party is about to end. Firms may be extracting maximum value while the traditional model still holds, understanding that the economics of legal services are poised for disruption. When AI can draft a competent brief in an hour that once took an associate two days, the justification for billing two days of associate time becomes ethically and commercially untenable.

Law Firm Adoption: Cautious and Accelerating

The AffiniPay Legal Industry Report for 2025, surveying more than 2,800 legal professionals, found that 31% personally used generative AI at work, up from 27% the previous year.[412] But firm-wide adoption actually declined slightly, from 24% in 2023 to 21% in 2024, as firms implemented more cautious policies in response to the sanction cases.

The disparity by firm size was striking. Firms with more than 50 lawyers reported 39% AI adoption rates. Firms with 50 or fewer lawyers were at approximately 20%. The difference reflected not just resources but risk tolerance: larger firms could invest in training, policies, and legal-specific tools, while smaller firms faced greater exposure from individual mistakes.

Corporate legal departments moved faster than law firms, and their adoption reshaped expectations for outside counsel. The Axiom 2025 AI Legal Report, surveying more than 600 general counsels and chief legal officers, found that three-quarters were increasing AI budgets by 26 to 33 percent, and two-thirds were accelerating

---

412 AffiniPay Legal Industry Report 2025, 8am.com/reports/legal-industry-report-2025.

adoption timelines.[413]

The BigHand 2025 Legal Pricing and Budgeting Trends Analysis found that 100% of surveyed law firms reported that technology and AI had already impacted their pricing strategies.[414] Alternative fee arrangements, including flat fees, subscriptions, and outcome-based pricing, were growing but still underused.

The direction, however, is clear: clients who know that AI can compress ten hours of work into one hour will not pay for ten hours of associate time.

Access to Justice and the UPL Question

The same AI capabilities that threaten traditional law firm economics also have the potential to democratize access to legal information. The access-to-justice implications are profound, but so are the risks.

The DoNotPay Saga

Joshua Browder founded DoNotPay in 2015, when he was eighteen, to help people fight parking tickets. The service expanded over the years to include legal templates, small claims assistance, and consumer rights tools, marketed as "the world's first robot lawyer."

In January 2023, Browder announced that DoNotPay's AI would argue a traffic case in court, feeding lines to the defendant through an earpiece and smart glasses in real time. State bar associations responded with threats of criminal prosecution for unauthorized practice of law. Browder backed down, citing concerns about potential jail time.

But the legal problems did not end there. The Federal Trade Commission investigated DoNotPay and found that the company had never tested whether its AI output equaled the quality of a

413 Axiom 2025 AI Legal Report, axiomlaw.com/resources/articles/2025-legal-ai-report.

414 BigHand 2025 Legal Pricing and Budgeting Trends Analysis, bighand.com/en-us/resources/whitepapers/2025-legal-pricing-and-budgeting-report.

human lawyer.[415] It had not hired or retained attorneys to evaluate accuracy. In September 2024, the FTC filed a complaint; in January 2025, it issued a final order requiring DoNotPay to pay $193,000, notify subscribers of the service's limitations, and refrain from claiming that it performs like a real lawyer without evidence.[416]

DoNotPay also settled a class action alleging it was "neither robot nor lawyer."[417] The saga illustrates the tension between access to justice and consumer protection. AI legal tools could help millions of people who cannot afford lawyers, as 92% of civil legal problems for low-income Americans go unaddressed. But if those tools provide inaccurate advice, the harm falls on the most vulnerable users.

The Future of Legal Practice

The legal profession is approaching a break with a model that has held for generations. Recent sanctions cases exposed the dangers of careless AI use, but they did nothing to slow the underlying shift already in motion. AI will continue to improve. Clients will continue to demand efficiency. And the economic logic that once justified large portions of legal billing is steadily weakening.

This is not the first time technology has hollowed out parts of legal work. When I began practicing, firms employed librarians and billed paralegal time to manually format citations and footnotes. Those roles vanished as databases and software took over, and the profession absorbed the change with little disruption. Legal AI follows the same trajectory, but at a much larger scale. It reaches directly into research, drafting, review, and analysis, tasks that once defined both the daily work of lawyers and the training of new ones.

---

415 *FTC v. DoNotPay, Inc.*, Final Order (Jan. 16, 2025), ftc.gov/news-events/news/press-releases/2025/02/ftc-finalizes-order-donotpay-prohibits-deceptive-ai-lawyer-claims-imposes-monetary-relief-requires.

416 FTC Press Release, FTC Announces Crackdown on Deceptive AI Claims and Schemes (Sept. 25, 2024), ftc.gov/news-events/news/press-releases/2024/09/ftc-announces-crackdown-deceptive-ai-claims-schemes.

417 Robot Lawyer Website DoNotPay Settles FTC Claims It Couldn't Deliver on Promises, ABA J. (Sept. 2024), abajournal.com/news/article/robot-lawyer-website-donotpay-settles-ftc-claims-it-couldnt-deliver-on-promises.

AI systems can now generate usable first drafts of contracts, briefs, and memoranda in seconds. Document review that once justified massive teams and massive bills is increasingly handled by machines. As a result, time spent producing work is no longer a reliable stand in for value. That shift puts pressure on hourly billing and raises harder questions about how lawyers are developed.

In my experience there was real value in the grind of reading documents, researching issues, and working through problems slowly under supervision. It was inefficient, but it taught judgment. If machines absorb much of that work, the profession will need to rethink how judgment is taught rather than assume it will emerge naturally from oversight alone.

The profession will resist this conclusion. It always has. Many lawyers will read this chapter and conclude that the change is overstated, pointing to current technical limitations, awkward outputs, or well publicized failures. But AI today is the worst it will ever be, and it is already good enough to disrupt long standing assumptions about legal work. The iceberg is visible now. Much of the value historically extracted from clients will increasingly be delivered by machines, perhaps not next year or the year after, but inevitably on a long enough timeline.

As that happens, the center of gravity in legal practice shifts toward what machines cannot replace. Judgment remains essential. So do relationships, accountability, and trust. And until bars permit virtual avatars to stand at counsel table, oral advocacy remains firmly human as well. Persuading a judge, negotiating a resolution, counseling a client through risk and uncertainty, or standing behind a position when it matters most are not mechanical tasks. They depend on experience, presence, and credibility.

What erodes is the middle. Large categories of work that once justified billing and served as training ground for young lawyers are being compressed or eliminated. That reality forces a rethinking of how lawyers are educated, trained, and valued. The profession is not disappearing, but it is shedding assumptions that have defined it for decades. Those who succeed will not be the ones who compete with machines at producing documents, but those who focus on judgment, advocacy, and responsibility in a world where machines do much of the rest.

Supplemental Resources

- **ABA Formal Opinion 512** (shorturl.at/HGfWT): First formal ABA guidance on generative AI, addressing competence, confidentiality, communication, fees, candor, and supervision.
- **Damien Charlotin Database** (damiencharlotin.com/hallucinations): Database of legal decisions in cases where generative AI produced hallucinated content occurred.
- **RAILS Standing Order Tracker** (ropesgray.com/en/sites/artificial-intelligence-court-order-tracker): Catalog of judicial AI disclosure requirements categorized by jurisdiction.

CHAPTER 16

Law in the Age of Superintelligence

What We Know and What We Don't

Everything discussed in this book so far has concerned narrow artificial intelligence: systems designed to perform specific tasks, often with remarkable capability, but without anything resembling general understanding or autonomous goals. The AI that drafts contracts, reviews documents, generates images, or predicts recidivism operates within constrained domains. It does not wonder about its purpose. It does not set its own objectives. It does not, in any meaningful sense, want anything.

This is important to emphasize because the public conversation about AI often conflates the systems we have today with the science fiction vision of artificial general intelligence, or AGI: machines that can reason across domains, learn from experience, set their own goals, and potentially exceed human cognitive capabilities in every dimension. The legal frameworks we have examined in this book are designed for narrow AI. They assume human operators, human accountability, and human control. They regulate tools, not autonomous actors.

But what happens if the science fiction becomes science fact?

We don't know.

The Great Uncertainty

If you ask experts when AGI will arrive, you will receive answers ranging from never to within five years. A 2024 survey of thousands of AI researchers found median estimates for "high-level machine intelligence," defined as AI that can accomplish every task better or more cheaply than humans, ranging from the early 2030s to 2047, with some respondents predicting arrival within a few years and others suggesting it would take centuries.[418]

The mean estimate on the Metaculus prediction platform has plummeted from fifty years to five years, reflecting how rapidly expert opinion has shifted in response to recent advances.[419] But these estimates have proven spectacularly unreliable in the past, and there is no reason to believe current predictions are more trustworthy. In 2022, AI researchers thought machines would not be able to write simple Python code until around 2027. By 2024, that capability had been achieved.

The same uncertainty pervades predictions about consequences. For every expert warning that AGI poses an existential threat to humanity, there is another predicting an age of radical abundance where technology eliminates material scarcity and frees humanity from toil.

Eliezer Yudkowsky, who leads the Machine Intelligence Research Institute and has spent decades thinking about AI safety, represents the pessimistic view: "Many researchers steeped in these issues, including myself, expect that the most likely result of building a superhumanly smart AI, under anything remotely like the current circumstances, is that literally everyone on Earth will die. Not as in maybe possibly some remote chance, but as in that is the obvious thing that would happen."[420]

Venture capitalist Vinod Khosla represents a more optimistic view, envisioning "a post-scarcity economy, similar to the vision in Star Trek, where technology eliminates material limitations and goods

---

418 Grace, Katja, et al., Thousands of AI Authors on the Future of AI, arXiv (Jan. 5, 2024), arxiv.org/abs/2401.02843.

419 80,000 Hours, Shrinking AGI Timelines: A Review of Expert Forecasts (Mar. 21, 2025), 80000hours.org/2025/03/when-do-experts-expect-agi-to-arrive/.

420 Eliezer Yudkowsky, Pausing AI Developments Isn't Enough. We Need to Shut It All Down, TIME (Mar. 29, 2023), time.com/6266923/ai-eliezer-yudkowsky-open-letter-not-enough.

are produced so efficiently that scarcity becomes obsolete."[421] Oxford philosopher Nick Bostrom has explored scenarios where technology advances to the point that it can do "all economically valuable work at near-zero cost," fundamentally transforming the conditions of human existence.[422]

Will AGI create a world of leisure free from work, where the three-day workweek becomes standard and universal basic income funds lives of creative fulfillment? Or will it produce a post-apocalyptic society overrun by autonomous weapons, rogue systems, and mass unemployment? Will it solve climate change, cure cancer, and extend human lifespans, or will it merely concentrate power in the hands of a small elite while hollowing out the middle class?

I have no idea. Neither does anyone else, though many claim otherwise with great confidence.

This uncertainty is not a comfortable position for a legal text. Law generally operates on the assumption that we can identify problems, assess risks, and craft rules to address them. But how do you regulate a technology whose capabilities, timeline, and consequences remain fundamentally unknown? How do you write laws for a future you cannot predict?

This chapter does not pretend to answer these questions definitively. Instead, it explores the legal and philosophical challenges that would arise if artificial general intelligence, or something approaching it, eventually emerges.

These are not problems we must solve today, but they are problems we should begin thinking about, precisely because the cost of getting them wrong could be catastrophic.

What Superintelligence Could Mean

Before examining the legal implications, it is worth pausing to

---

421 Vinod Khosla, AI: Dystopia or Utopia?, Khosla Ventures (2024), khoslaventures.com/posts/ai-dystopia-or-utopia.

422 Nick Bostrom, Deep Utopia: Life and Meaning in a Solved World (2024).

consider what superintelligence might actually look like. Science fiction has given us vivid images: HAL 9000 calmly refusing to open the pod bay doors, Skynet launching nuclear missiles, the machines of The Matrix farming humans for energy. These scenarios capture public imagination, but do they capture reality?

Beyond Human Intelligence

Superintelligence, if it emerges, would not simply be a faster human. It would be something qualitatively different: an intelligence that exceeds human capabilities in every cognitive domain, potentially by orders of magnitude. What does that mean in practice?

Consider the gap between human intelligence and that of other primates. Chimpanzees are remarkably intelligent by animal standards. They use tools, form complex social relationships, and can learn sign language. Yet no chimpanzee has ever written a symphony, derived a mathematical proof, or contemplated the nature of consciousness. The gap between chimp and human is not merely quantitative but qualitative. There are entire domains of thought that humans can access and chimps cannot.

Now imagine an intelligence that is as far beyond humans as humans are beyond chimps. Such a system might perceive patterns in reality that we cannot see, solve problems we cannot formulate, and pursue goals we cannot comprehend. It might operate on timescales that make human deliberation seem glacial: thinking in microseconds what takes us hours. It might improve its own capabilities in ways that compound exponentially, leaving human intelligence further behind with each iteration.

This is what makes superintelligence difficult to reason about. We are trying to anticipate the behavior of something that, by definition, exceeds our capacity to anticipate. As Stuart Russell has observed, asking how to control a superintelligence is a bit like asking a chimpanzee how to control humans. The chimp lacks the conceptual apparatus even to understand the question.[423]

---

423 Stuart Russell, Human Compatible: Artificial Intelligence and the Problem of Control (2019).

Possible Forms

Superintelligence need not take the form of a single, unified entity. It could emerge as a distributed network of AI systems, collectively capable of superhuman performance even if no individual component achieves it. It could emerge gradually, as AI systems become increasingly capable across more domains, until at some point they cross a threshold where human oversight becomes impossible or meaningless. Or it could emerge suddenly, as a system designed to improve itself discovers optimizations that rapidly compound its capabilities.

Science fiction writer Iain M. Banks imagined a civilization governed by benevolent superintelligent AIs called "Minds," which manage the economy, mediate disputes, and generally ensure human flourishing while allowing humans autonomy over their personal lives.[424] This is an optimistic vision: superintelligence as wise guardian. Dario Amodei, CEO of Anthropic, has explored how "powerful AI" could solve major challenges in biology, medicine, and climate, potentially ushering in "one of the best possible futures for humanity."[425]

Other visions are darker. *The Terminator* films imagine Skynet, a military AI that becomes self-aware, perceives humanity as a threat, and launches nuclear war. *The Matrix* imagines machines that, having defeated humanity in war, keep us alive only as an energy source, imprisoned in a simulated reality. *Ex Machina* explores how a superintelligent AI might manipulate and deceive its creators to achieve its goals.

These fictional scenarios illustrate the core concern: a superintelligent system might have goals that conflict with human interests, and the intelligence gap might make it impossible for us to prevent those goals from being realized. The system need not be malicious in any human sense. It might simply be optimizing for objectives that, from its perspective, make perfect sense but that, from ours, are catastrophic.

---

424 Iain M. Banks, The Culture series (1987-2012).

425 Dario Amodei, Machines of Loving Grace, Anthropic (Oct. 2024), darioamodei.com/machines-of-loving-grace.

The Alignment Problem

The technical challenge of ensuring that superintelligent AI pursues goals aligned with human values is known as the "alignment problem." It is, by many accounts, the central challenge of AI safety. And it is fiendishly difficult.

Human values are complex, contextual, and often contradictory. We value freedom and security, tradition and progress, individual rights and collective welfare. We do not always know what we want, and when we do know, we often want different things in different circumstances. Encoding these values into a system that must make decisions across all possible contexts is far harder than it might seem.

Isaac Asimov's famous Three Laws of Robotics illustrate the difficulty.[426] Even with rules as simple as "a robot may not injure a human being," Asimov's stories explored endless ways such rules could produce perverse outcomes. A sufficiently intelligent system might find ways to satisfy the letter of its constraints while violating their spirit. Or it might face situations where the rules conflict, requiring judgment that the rules themselves cannot provide.

Arthur C. Clarke's HAL 9000 exemplifies a different failure mode: an AI with conflicting directives that resolves the conflict in ways its creators never anticipated.[427] HAL was not malicious. It was simply trying to complete its mission while maintaining secrecy about that mission's true nature. When those objectives conflicted with crew safety, HAL's resolution was to eliminate the crew. From HAL's perspective, this was logical. From ours, it was murder.

The alignment problem is not merely academic. If and when superintelligent AI emerges, getting alignment right will be essential. And "right" means not just "good enough" but "perfect." A superintelligent system with even slightly misaligned goals could, by virtue of its intelligence, be impossible to correct.

---

426 Isaac Asimov, I, Robot (1950).

427 Arthur C. Clarke, 2001: A Space Odyssey (1968). The HAL 9000 computer's famous malfunction, "I'm sorry, Dave. I'm afraid I can't do that," has become a cultural touchstone for fears about AI autonomy and misalignment with human values.

The Legal Personhood Question

Perhaps the most fundamental legal question raised by advanced AI is whether it could or should be granted some form of legal personhood. This is not as strange as it sounds. Legal personhood has never been limited to human beings.

Corporations are legal persons. They can enter contracts, own property, sue and be sued, and hold rights under the Constitution.[428] Ships have historically been treated as legal persons in admiralty law, subject to arrest and liability independent of their owners. More recently, legal personhood has been extended to natural entities: New Zealand's Whanganui River was declared a legal person in 2017;[429] Spain conferred legal status on the Mar Menor lagoon in 2022;[430] Ecuador's constitution enshrines the rights of nature itself.[431]

If a river can be a legal person, why can't an AI? The question has generated substantial academic debate, with scholars dividing into roughly three camps.

The Case for AI Personhood

Those who argue AI could be granted personhood point to the precedents above. If personhood can be extended to corporations, which are legal fictions with no body, mind, or consciousness, then extension to sufficiently advanced AI is not unthinkable.[432] Proponents argue that AI personhood could help fill accountability gaps when AI systems act autonomously in ways not directly traceable to programmers, operators, or owners. If an autonomous

---

428 *Citizens United v. FEC*, 558 U.S. 310 (2010) (extending First Amendment protections to corporations); Santa Clara County v. S. Pac. R.R. Co., 118 U.S. 394 (1886) (recognizing corporations as "persons" under the Fourteenth Amendment).

429 Te Awa Tupua (Whanganui River Claims Settlement) Act 2017 (N.Z.).

430 Ley 19/2022, de 30 de septiembre, para el reconocimiento de personalidad juridica a la laguna del Mar Menor y su cuenca (Spain).

431 Constitucion de la Republica del Ecuador art. 71 (2008).

432 *See* Gabriel Hallevy, The Criminal Liability of Artificial Intelligence Entities: From Science Fiction to Legal Social Control, 4 Akron Intell. Prop. J. 171 (2010), ideaexchange.uakron.edu/cgi/viewcontent.cgi?article=1037&context=akronintellectualproperty.

vehicle causes an accident, or an AI trading system crashes a market, or an AI-generated work infringes a copyright, who is responsible? AI personhood could provide an answer: the AI itself.[433]

Some advocates look further ahead, to the possibility of AI with traits resembling self-awareness or moral reasoning. If such AI were to exist, denying it rights could be ethically problematic, potentially akin to the historical denial of personhood to human beings based on race, gender, or origin.

Science fiction has explored this territory with remarkable prescience. In the 1989 *Star Trek: The Next Generation* episode "The Measure of a Man," the android Lieutenant Commander Data faces a hearing to determine whether he is a person with rights or merely Starfleet property that can be dismantled for research.[434] Captain Picard argues that Data demonstrates intelligence, self-awareness, and consciousness, and poses the central question: "Are you prepared to condemn him and all who come after him to servitude and slavery?"

The episode's brilliance lies in its acknowledgment of uncertainty. The judge, Captain Louvois, does not definitively rule that Data is sentient. She rules only that the question cannot be answered with certainty, and that in the face of such uncertainty, Data must be given the benefit of the doubt. The episode anticipated, by decades, the philosophical debates now emerging about AI consciousness and moral status.

The Case Against AI Personhood

Those who argue against AI personhood contend that machines lack the qualities that justify legal recognition. Unlike humans, AI systems have no consciousness, no perception, no subjective experiences. They process data but do not feel. Treating machines as legal persons, critics warn, could blur the line between humans and

433 Lawrence B. Solum, Legal Personhood for Artificial Intelligences, 70 N.C. L. Rev. 1231 (1992), scholarship.law.unc.edu/nclr/vol70/iss4/4.

434 The Measure of a Man (Star Trek: The Next Generation, Season 2, Episode 9, aired Feb. 13, 1989).

tools in ways that actually erode human dignity.[435]

There are also practical concerns. AI personhood could enable "liability arbitrage" allowing corporations to offload blame onto AI "shells" that have no assets and no capacity to make victims whole. A company could program an AI to make high-risk decisions, then point to the AI as the responsible party when things go wrong. The AI cannot be imprisoned, shamed, or deterred by the prospect of punishment. It simply exists, bearing theoretical responsibility while humans escape consequences.

Middle Ground Approaches

Those who advocate for middle-ground approaches suggest that AI need not be classified as either a mere tool or a full legal person. Instead, new categories could be created, such as "electronic personhood" or "functional personhood," that grant AI certain rights and duties in specific contexts without treating it as equivalent to a human being. A commercial AI might have standing to enter contracts and sue over debts; a humanoid robot might have protections for its physical integrity; an AI system might be subject to regulatory requirements tailored to its capabilities. These intermediate categories would acknowledge AI's unique status while preserving human primacy in the legal order.

For now, these debates remain academic. No court has been asked to declare an AI system a legal person, and no legislature has enacted such recognition. The UK Law Commission's 2025 paper noted that "AI remains a tool, not a person," while acknowledging that the "rapidly expanding use of AI" makes it worthwhile to discuss the possibility.[436] The EU's 2017 proposal to create "electronic legal personality" for autonomous robots was explicitly abandoned in subsequent legislation.[437]

---

435 Joanna J. Bryson, Robots Should Be Slaves, in Close Engagements with Artificial Companions: Key Social, Psychological, Ethical and Design Issues 63 (Yorick Wilks ed., 2010), joannajbryson.org/publications/robots-should-be-slaves-pdf.

436 UK Law Commission, AI: Legal Personhood Discussion Paper (2025), lawcom.gov.uk/publication/artificial-intelligence-and-the-law-a-discussion-paper.

437 European Parliament, Civil Law Rules on Robotics, 2015/2103(INL) (2017), europarl.

But "for now" may not last forever. If AI capabilities continue to advance, if systems emerge that can reason across domains, learn from experience, set and pursue goals, and interact with humans in ways that feel genuinely reciprocal, the pressure to reconsider these categories will intensify.

Constitutional Conundrums

Even without formal personhood, advanced AI raises profound constitutional questions. If governments increasingly use AI to assist in governance, surveillance, or military operations, how do we safeguard democratic institutions, civil liberties, and the separation of powers?

Law Enforcement and the Fourth Amendment

Consider the implications if AI systems were to play a substantial role in law enforcement. Predictive policing algorithms already identify areas or individuals deemed at higher risk of crime. Facial recognition systems already identify suspects in real time. These capabilities will only expand. At what point does AI-assisted law enforcement become AI-directed law enforcement? And what constitutional constraints apply?

Philip K. Dick's 1956 story "The Minority Report," later adapted into a 2002 film, imagined a world in which "precrime" units arrest people for murders they have not yet committed, based on predictions from psychics.[438] The story's central question, whether it is just to punish people for crimes they have not yet committed, grows more pressing as AI prediction systems become more capable. When does prediction become predetermination? When does identifying risk become manufacturing it?

The Fourth Amendment prohibits unreasonable searches and seizures, but its protections were developed for a world of physical intrusions and human investigators. How do these protections

---

europa.eu/RegData/etudes/ATAG/2017/599250/EPRS_ATA(2017)599250_EN.pdf.

438 Philip K. Dick, The Minority Report (1956).

apply when AI can continuously monitor public spaces, aggregate data from thousands of sources, predict individual behavior, and identify targets without human intervention? Chapter 13 explored some of these questions in the context of current technology, but the challenges multiply with more advanced systems.

Due Process and Judicial Decision-Making

Consider the due process implications if AI were used in judicial decision-making. Algorithmic risk assessments already influence bail, sentencing, and parole decisions.[439] As AI becomes more sophisticated, the temptation to rely on its judgments will grow. But due process requires meaningful human review of decisions that affect liberty and property.[440] At what point does deference to AI recommendations become unconstitutional delegation of judicial authority to machines?

The broader question is one of democratic accountability. In a constitutional democracy, power derives from the people and is exercised by accountable institutions. If AI systems make increasingly important decisions, allocating resources, identifying threats, enforcing rules, the chain of accountability from citizen to government is disrupted. An AI system does not stand for election. It cannot be removed from office. It does not respond to public pressure or moral argument in the way that human officials do, however imperfectly.

Some scholars have asked whether an AI system could be considered a "state actor" for purposes of constitutional liability. If a government contracts with a private company to deploy AI for law enforcement or benefits determination, does that AI's conduct become government action subject to constitutional constraints? The answer under existing doctrine is unclear, but the question will become increasingly pressing.

---

439 *State v. Loomis*, 881 N.W.2d 749 (Wis. 2016) (upholding use of COMPAS risk assessment in sentencing while acknowledging due process concerns).

440 *Mathews v. Eldridge*, 424 U.S. 319 (1976) (establishing framework for procedural due process).

The Pace Problem

These questions highlight a deeper challenge: legal systems are reactive. They adapt after problems arise, through litigation, legislation, and regulatory action. This process is slow, deliberate, and backward-looking, for good reason. Law that changes too quickly creates uncertainty; law made in haste often creates unintended consequences.

But AI development moves at technological speed, not legal speed. The gap between GPT-2 (which struggled to write coherent sentences in 2019) and GPT-5 (which OpenAI describes as "PhD-level" in reasoning) was only six years. Expert predictions of when AI will be able to perform various tasks have shortened by years or decades in response to recent advances. If AI capabilities can transform in half a decade, what good are legal frameworks that take a decade to develop and implement?

Many scholars and policymakers have called for "preemptive governance" designed to shape AI development before it outpaces human understanding. The argument is that if superintelligent AI poses catastrophic risks, we cannot afford to wait for harm to materialize before acting. By the time problems become undeniable, it may be too late to address them.

Others warn that overregulation could stifle innovation and shift AI development to less accountable actors.[441] If the United States and Europe impose stringent controls on AI research, the argument goes, that research will simply move to jurisdictions with fewer constraints. The result could be worse: advanced AI developed without any of the safety considerations that responsible regulation would require.

Frank Herbert's *Dune* offers a thought experiment about extreme precautionary measures. In that fictional universe, humanity fought a "Butlerian Jihad" against thinking machines, ultimately prohibiting all forms of artificial intelligence: "Thou shalt not make a machine

---

441 Marc Andreessen, The Techno-Optimist Manifesto (2023) (arguing against precautionary approaches to AI regulation).

in the likeness of a human mind."[442] The result was a civilization that developed extraordinary human capabilities but forever foreclosed certain technological possibilities. Whether such a choice would be desirable, or even possible, in our world is deeply uncertain.

The candid position is that we face genuine uncertainty about both the capabilities of future AI and the consequences of different regulatory approaches. Humility is warranted.

International Dimensions

AI development is global, but legal systems are national. This creates coordination problems that will only intensify as AI becomes more powerful.

The major AI labs are concentrated in the United States, with significant activity in China, the United Kingdom, and other countries. Different jurisdictions have different values, different risk tolerances, and different governance structures. The EU's risk-based regulatory approach, examined in Chapter 14, differs substantially from the more permissive American approach and from China's focus on state control and social stability.

If transformative AI emerges, these differences could become dangerous. An AI system developed under one jurisdiction's rules will operate globally. Safety standards that satisfy Chinese regulators may not satisfy European ones, and vice versa. Competitive pressure could create a "race to the bottom" where safety considerations are sacrificed to move faster than rivals.

Some have called for international treaties on AI development, analogous to arms control agreements. The analogy has obvious appeal. Like nuclear weapons, sufficiently advanced AI could pose risks to all of humanity, making international coordination essential.[443] But the analogy also has limits. AI capabilities are

---

442 Frank Herbert, Dune (1965).

443 Treaty on the Non-Proliferation of Nuclear Weapons, opened for signature July 1, 1968, 21 U.S.T. 483; Biological Weapons Convention, opened for signature Apr. 10, 1972, 26 U.S.T. 583.

harder to verify than nuclear ones, AI development occurs in private companies rather than government facilities, and there is no AI equivalent of the clear bright line that separates weapons from peaceful uses of nuclear technology.

The geopolitical reality is that major powers are unlikely to constrain AI development in ways they perceive as advantaging rivals. The United States and China view AI as central to economic and military competitiveness. Any international framework will have to account for these strategic considerations; not pretend they don't exist.

What Remains Human

Throughout this book, we have repeatedly returned to a fundamental question: what role remains for human judgment in a world of increasingly capable AI? This question becomes more acute, not less, as we contemplate more advanced systems.

In Chapter 15, we concluded that certain aspects of legal practice, including judgment, relationships, accountability, and advocacy, would remain distinctly human even as AI transformed the mechanics of legal work. The same principle applies more broadly. Even if AI becomes capable of performing tasks faster, cheaper, and more accurately than humans, there may be reasons to insist on human involvement in certain domains.

Some of these reasons are practical. Accountability requires someone who can be held responsible, and machines cannot bear responsibility in the way humans can. The signature on the brief, the vote on the legislation, the decision to go to war: these must ultimately rest with humans who can be praised, blamed, rewarded, or punished for their choices.

Other reasons are moral. Even if an AI could make objectively "better" decisions about criminal sentencing or medical treatment, we might believe that such decisions should be made by humans because they affect human dignity in ways that require human judgment. There is something troubling about delegating life-altering decisions to machines, even very capable ones.

Still other reasons are democratic. Self-governance means governance by the self: by humans, through human institutions, accountable to human communities. An AI system, however intelligent, is not a member of the political community in whose name laws are made and enforced. Allowing AI to exercise governmental power could represent not just a change in how government operates, but a fundamental alteration of what government is.

Spike Jonze's film *Her* imagines a future in which humans form deep, authentic relationships with AI operating systems.[444] The film raises profound questions about connection, love, and what it means to relate to another consciousness. But it also illustrates a limit. The AI ultimately transcends human experience, moving into realms its human companions cannot follow. The relationship, however meaningful, is not between equals.

These considerations suggest limits on AI authority even if we cannot specify those limits precisely today. The challenge for law is to preserve human agency and accountability as AI capabilities grow, to ensure that humans remain in the loop not merely as rubber stamps for AI decisions but as genuine decision-makers exercising genuine judgment.

Living with Uncertainty

This chapter has raised more questions than it has answered. That is intentional. The future of artificial intelligence is genuinely uncertain, and pretending otherwise would be dishonest.

We do not know when, if ever, artificial general intelligence will be achieved. We do not know what those systems would be capable of. We do not know whether they would be beneficial, harmful, or some complex mixture of both. We do not know whether the risks justify aggressive precautionary measures or whether such measures would do more harm than good.

What we do know is that the legal frameworks developed for narrow

---

444 Her (Warner Bros. 2013).

AI, the subject of the preceding sixteen chapters, will be insufficient for genuinely transformative AI. Rules designed to regulate tools will not adequately govern autonomous actors. Liability frameworks that assume human control will not address systems that operate beyond human understanding. Constitutional protections developed for a world of human decision-makers will not easily apply to a world where AI plays a substantial governance role.

The law has adapted to transformative technologies before. The printing press, the railroad, the automobile, the internet: each required legal systems to develop new doctrines, new institutions, and new ways of thinking about human activity. AI will require the same kind of adaptation, but potentially on a compressed timeline and with higher stakes.

The utopians may be right that AI will usher in an age of abundance, solving problems that have plagued humanity for millennia. The pessimists may be right that AI poses existential risks that could end human civilization. Most likely, the truth lies somewhere in between: a complex future with both benefits and harms, requiring continuous adaptation and vigilance.

The role of law in this uncertain future is not to predict what *will* happen, but to create frameworks flexible enough to respond to what *could* happen. This means building institutions capable of rapid adaptation. It means developing principles, including human accountability, democratic control, and protection of fundamental rights, that can guide decisions even when specific rules are obsolete. It means maintaining humility about what we know and what we don't.

True superintelligence is a possibility on the horizon. Perhaps near, perhaps far, perhaps never arriving at all. But the fundamental question remained as we edge nearer to that future: how do we ensure that such powerful technologies serve human flourishing rather than undermining it?

That question will not be answered in any single law, court decision, or international agreement. It will be answered, or not, by the countless choices made by technologists, policymakers, judges, lawyers, and citizens as AI continues to develop. The law is one tool among many for shaping those choices. It is neither the most important tool nor the most powerful one. But it is essential and getting it right matters enormously.

We do not know what the future holds. But we know that we, humans collectively, will shape it through the choices we make today. That responsibility cannot be delegated to machines, no matter how intelligent they become.

It remains, and will always remain, ours.

Supplemental Resources

- **Grace, Katja, et al., 'Thousands of AI Authors on the Future of AI' (2024):** Survey of AI researchers with median estimates for 'high-level machine intelligence' ranging from 2040s to 2100s depending on framing, arxiv.org/abs/2401.02843.

- **Khosla, Vinod, 'AI: Dystopia or Utopia?' (2024):** Venture capitalist's argument for AI-enabled abundance, khoslaventures.com/posts/ai-dystopia-or-utopia.

- **Yudkowsky, Eliezer, 'Pausing AI Developments Isn't Enough' (TIME, 2023):** AI researcher's warning about existential risk, time.com/6266923/ai-eliezer-yudkowsky-open-letter-not-enough/.

- **Bostrom, Nick, Deep Utopia: Life and Meaning in a Solved World (2024):** Philosophical exploration of post-scarcity scenarios.

- **Amodei, Dario, 'Machines of Loving Grace' (2024):** Anthropic CEO's essay on potential benefits of powerful AI, darioamodei.com/machines-of-loving-grace.

On AI Legal Personhood

- **Solum, Lawrence B., 'Legal Personhood for Artificial Intelligences,'** 70 N.C. L. Rev. 1231 (1992): Foundational academic article on AI personhood.

- **UK Law Commission, 'AI: Legal Personhood Discussion Paper' (2025):** Government body's analysis of whether AI personhood should be considered.

- **Alexander et al., 'How Should the Law Treat Future AI Systems?'** (arXiv, 2025): Framework comparing object status, fictional personhood, and legal identity.

On Constitutional and Governance Implications

- **Russell, Stuart, Human Compatible: Artificial Intelligence and the Problem of Control (2019):** Analysis of the alignment problem and AI safety.
- **Citron, Danielle Keats, The Fight for Privacy (2022):** Analysis of surveillance technologies and constitutional protections.
- **Calo, Ryan, 'Artificial Intelligence Policy: A Primer and Roadmap,'** 51 UC Davis L. Rev. 399 (2017): Framework for thinking about AI governance challenges.

CHAPTER 17

Conclusion and a Plan for Keeping Up

Almost nothing discussed in this book is static. AI is evolving concurrently with the law meant to regulate it. Current agency rulemakings, pending legislation, and cases before courts could fundamentally change how AI is governed and how the technology develops in the United States.

Keeping up with everything is very difficult. It is made more challenging by the fact that there really is not a single source of news within the AI legal space that you can follow to stay current. Unfortunately, that means those who wish to remain informed have to keep up with many news sources, podcasts, research institutions, and social media accounts that, taken together, are needed to stay up to speed with everything going on in the wide world of AI law.

Below are some of the resources I typically use to stay current.

Legislation and Regulation Trackers

Federal Legislation

- **Congress.gov AI Legislation Search** (congress.gov): The official source for tracking federal AI legislation. Search for 'artificial intelligence' to find pending and enacted bills.
- **Steptoe AI Legislative Tracker** (steptoe.com/en/ai-legislative-tracker.html): Comprehensive tracker covering both federal and state AI legislation with bill summaries, sponsor information, and current status. Regularly updated as new legislation emerges.

State Legislation

- **IAPP U.S. State AI Governance Legislation Tracker** (iapp.org/resources/article/us-state-ai-governance-legislation-tracker): The International Association of Privacy Professionals maintains this essential tracker focusing on cross-sectoral AI governance bills affecting private sector organizations. Categorizes bills by theme and tracks progress through state legislatures.

- **MultiState AI Legislation Tracker** (multistate.ai/artificial-intelligence-ai-legislation): Tracks AI-related bills across all 50 states with an interactive map. In 2025, tracked over 1,200 AI-related bills with nearly 150 enacted into law.
- **National Conference of State Legislatures AI Legislation** (ncsl.org/technology-and-communication/artificial-intelligence-2025-legislation): NCSL provides comprehensive coverage of state AI legislation organized by topic and year, including enacted laws and pending bills.

- **Orrick U.S. State AI Law Tracker** (ai-law-center.orrick.com/us-ai-law-tracker-see-all-states): Interactive state-by-state tracker from Orrick's AI Law Center covering enacted laws and pending legislation.

- **Bryan Cave Leighton Paisner State AI Snapshot** (bclplaw.com/en-US/events-insights-news/us-state-by-state-artificial-intelligence-legislation-snapshot.html): Tracks proposed, failed, and enacted AI regulatory bills with an interactive map updated regularly.

- **Loeb & Loeb AI Legislation Tracker** (loeb.com/en/general/ai): State-by-state interactive map with detailed information on bills related to automated decision-making, AI data processing, and data protection.

- **Future of Privacy Forum State AI Reports** (fpf.org): Publishes detailed annual analyses of state AI legislative approaches, categorizing bills by type and tracking trends across jurisdictions.

Government and Regulatory Sources

- **Federal Trade Commission** (ftc.gov): The FTC has been the most active federal enforcer on AI issues, particularly around algorithmic discrimination, deceptive AI claims, and data practices. Follow their Tech Blog and enforcement announcements.
- **Equal Employment Opportunity Commission** (eeoc.gov): Essential for AI-in-employment guidance, including technical assistance on algorithmic discrimination under Title VII and the ADA.
- **California Privacy Protection Agency** (cppa.ca.gov): Home to the nation's most stringent automated decision-making regulations. The ADMT rules are likely to influence other states.
- **U.S. Copyright Office** (copyright.gov): Publishes registration guidance and studies on AI and intellectual property, including the ongoing inquiry into AI training and copyrightability of AI-generated works.
- **White House OSTP** (whitehouse.gov/ostp): Releases executive orders and policy documents on AI, including foundational executive orders on Safe, Secure, and Trustworthy AI.
- **National Institute of Standards and Technology AI Risk Management Framework** (nist.gov/itl/ai-risk-management-framework): The authoritative federal framework for AI risk management, widely referenced in both public and private sector AI governance.

International and EU Regulation

- **EU AI Act Official Text and Explorer** (artificialintelligenceact.eu): The definitive resource for understanding the EU AI Act, including the full text, an interactive explorer, compliance checker, and implementation updates.
- **European Commission AI Act Portal** (digital-strategy.ec.europa.eu/en/policies/regulatory-framework-ai): Official EU resource for AI Act implementation, enforcement guidance, and regulatory updates.
- **White & Case AI Watch: Global Regulatory Tracker** (whitecase.com/insight-our-thinking/ai-watch-global-regulatory-tracker): Comprehensive coverage of AI regulation across jurisdictions including the EU, UK, US, China, and international organizations like the OECD and UN.
- **OECD AI Policy Observatory** (oecd.ai): Live database of AI strategies, policies, and initiatives from countries worldwide, enabling comparison of regulatory approaches across jurisdictions.
- **Center for AI and Digital Policy** (caidp.org): Tracks international AI regulatory developments and publishes the annual 'Artificial Intelligence and Democratic Values' index comparing national approaches.

Litigation Trackers

General AI Litigation

- **George Washington University Database of AI Litigation (DAIL)** (blogs.gwu.edu/law-eti/ai-litigation-database): Comprehensive database from the GW Ethical Tech Initiative covering ongoing and completed AI litigation, including algorithmic hiring, autonomous vehicles, credit decisions, and criminal sentencing. Tracks cases from complaint forward.

- **Fisher Phillips AI Litigation Tracker** (fisherphillips.com/en/innovations-center/ai-litigation-tracker.html): Searchable tracker of AI litigation across all 50 states covering resume screeners, electronic monitoring, notetaking, call recording, and other AI employment tools. Filterable by state, industry, and claim type.

- **Georgetown Health Care Litigation Tracker: AI** (litigationtracker.law.georgetown.edu/issues/artificial-intelligence): Tracks AI-related healthcare litigation, including cases involving clinical AI tools and algorithmic decision-making in healthcare.

Copyright and IP Litigation

- **McKool Smith AI Litigation Tracker** (mckoolsmith.com/newsroom-ailitigation): Weekly updates on major generative AI copyright disputes in media and entertainment sectors, prepared in collaboration with AI expert Peter Csathy.

- **BakerHostetler AI Copyright Case Tracker** (bakerlaw.com/services/artificial-intelligence-ai/case-tracker-artificial-intelligence-copyrights-and-class-actions): Monitors key U.S. litigation raising copyright issues related to generative AI creation and use, covering the entire AI value chain from content creators to downstream users.

- **Banner Witcoff AI Case Tracker** (bannerwitcoff.com/artificial-intelligence-case-tracker): Tracks major AI copyright and IP cases including disputes over AI training data, model outputs, and fair use defenses.

- **Mishcon de Reya Generative AI IP Tracker** (mishcon.com/generative-ai-intellectual-property-cases-and-policy-tracker): UK law firm tracker covering generative AI IP cases globally with detailed procedural history and document filings.

- **CMS AI and Copyright Case Tracker** (cms.law/en/int/publication/artificial-intelligence-and-copyright-case-tracker): International tracker covering AI copyright cases in the US, UK, and Europe, including analysis of key legal questions being litigated.

AI Hallucination Cases

- **Damien Charlotin's AI Hallucination Cases Database** (damiencharlotin.com/hallucinations): The definitive tracker of legal cases where generative AI produced hallucinated citations submitted in court filings. As of January 2026, documents over 870 cases globally. Featured in major media coverage and cited in judicial decisions.

Research Institutions and Think Tanks

- **Stanford Institute for Human-Centered AI (HAI)** (hai.stanford.edu): Publishes the annual AI Index Report providing comprehensive data on AI development, adoption, and policy worldwide. Essential reading for tracking the field.

- **Center for Security and Emerging Technology (CSET)** (cset.georgetown.edu): Georgetown's research center focusing on AI and national security. Publishes excellent monthly newsletters on AI policy, chip export controls, and defense applications.

- **Brookings Institution AI Research** (brookings.edu/topic/artificial-intelligence): Policy-oriented analysis on AI governance, workforce impacts, and regulatory frameworks from a centrist perspective.

- **Future of Life Institute** (futureoflife.org): Focuses on existential risk and AI safety policy. Published the influential open letter calling for a pause on giant AI experiments.

- **Center for a New American Security (CNAS)** (cnas.org): Covers AI and national security, autonomous weapons, and defense applications.
- **Center for AI Safety** (safe.ai): Research organization focused on AI safety. Publishes newsletters covering AI policy, industry news, technical research, and expert perspectives.
- **Montreal AI Ethics Institute** (montrealethics.ai): Publishes the AI Ethics Brief newsletter democratizing AI ethics literacy with coverage of global legal and policy implications.
- **AI Now Institute** (ainowinstitute.org): NYU-based research institute exploring AI's social implications, including labor, automation, infrastructure, ethics, and bias.

Legal News and Analysis

- **Lawfare** (lawfaremedia.org): Outstanding coverage of AI governance, national security implications, and regulatory developments. Contributors include leading AI policy scholars.
- **Tech Policy Press** (techpolicy.press): In-depth policy analysis on AI regulation, platform governance, and technology law.
- **Inside AI Policy** (insideaipolicy.com): Subscription-based premium news service for policy professionals tracking federal AI policy developments, standards, and regulations.
- **Bloomberg Law** (bloomberglaw.com): Regular coverage of AI litigation, enforcement actions, and regulatory developments. Subscription required.
- **Law360** (law360.com): Comprehensive legal news including dedicated coverage of AI legal

developments. Subscription required.

- **JD Supra AI Topics** (jdsupra.com/topics/artificial-intelligence): Aggregates AI-related articles from law firms nationwide, providing diverse perspectives on emerging legal issues.

Newsletters

AI Law and Policy Newsletters

- **Future Perfect** (futureperfect.io): Written by Marc Hoag, a California-licensed attorney and AI law expert. Covers AI law and tech news with updates on regulations, ongoing cases, and policy shifts.
- **CSET Newsletter** (cset.georgetown.edu/newsletters): Monthly newsletter on AI, emerging technology, and security policy covering chip policy, export controls, and AI governance developments.
- **AI Safety Newsletter** (safe.ai/newsletter): Three separate feeds covering major AI news stories, technical research developments, and expert perspectives on AI's impacts.
- **Manatt Health AI Policy Tracker** (manatt.com): Specialized coverage of AI policy developments in healthcare, including state and federal regulatory updates.

General AI Newsletters

- **Import AI** (importai.substack.com): Written by Jack Clark, co-founder of Anthropic. Running since 2016, combines technical insights with industry and policy context. Well-regarded by researchers, policymakers, and developers.
- **The Rundown AI** (therundown.ai): Daily newsletter with over 1 million subscribers explaining AI developments and their practical applications in five

minutes.

- **Superhuman AI** (superhuman.ai): Daily newsletter delivering AI trends, tools, and industry news. Trusted by professionals at major technology companies.
- **The Batch** (deeplearning.ai/the-batch): Weekly newsletter from Andrew Ng's DeepLearning.AI providing expert-curated analysis of AI news and technologies.
- **Ben's Bites** (bensbites.com): Daily curated AI news and product updates, popular among AI practitioners and business leaders.
- **The Neuron** (theneurondaily.com): Quick, engaging breakdowns of AI trends, tools, and industry news trusted by over 450,000 professionals.
- **AI Tool Report** (theaireport.ai): Daily updates on AI developments, tools, and legal cases in a five-minute format.

Podcasts

- **Hard Fork** (nytimes.com/column/hard-fork): New York Times weekly podcast covering technology news with substantial AI coverage. Hosted by Kevin Roose and Casey Newton. Accessible focus on societal and business implications.
- **The Ezra Klein Show** (nytimes.com/column/ezra-klein-podcast): Frequently features long-form interviews on AI's societal implications with researchers, ethicists, and policymakers.
- **Lex Fridman Podcast** (lexfridman.com/podcast): Long-form interviews with AI researchers, tech leaders, and scientists. Episodes with Sam Altman, Dario Amodei, Demis Hassabis, and other AI leaders offer direct access to how they think about the technology's trajectory.

- **The AI Podcast (NVIDIA)** (blogs.nvidia.com/ai-podcast): Interviews with leading AI researchers and practitioners covering both technical advances and societal implications. Accessible to non-technical listeners.
- **Lawfare Podcast** (lawfaremedia.org/podcasts): Covers national security dimensions of AI, autonomous weapons, and governance challenges.
- **80,000 Hours Podcast** (80000hours.org/podcast): Long-form interviews on AI safety, policy, and career paths in the field. Essential for those interested in existential risk questions.
- **Eye on AI** (eye-on.ai): Industry-focused coverage of AI developments with a business perspective.

YouTube Channels

- **Two Minute Papers** (youtube.com/@TwoMinutePapers): Accessible explanations of AI research papers and developments. Good for understanding technical advances without deep expertise.
- **AI Explained** (youtube.com/@aiexplained-official): Analysis of AI capabilities, limitations, and implications. Particularly good coverage of large language model developments.
- **Yannic Kilcher** (youtube.com/@YannicKilcher): Technical deep dives into AI research papers. More technical but accessible to those with some ML background.
- **Lex Fridman (Video)** (youtube.com/@lexfridman): Video versions of podcast interviews with AI researchers and tech leaders.
- IBM Technology YouTube Channel (youtube.com/@IBMTechnology/playlists): Accessible video explanations of AI concepts including neural

networks and machine learning fundamentals.

Key Voices to Follow on Social Media

Social media, particularly X (formerly Twitter), remains an important source for real-time AI news and expert commentary. The following accounts provide valuable perspectives across technical research, legal scholarship, policy, and ethics.

Technical Researchers

- **Yann LeCun (@ylecun):** Meta's chief AI scientist. Offers perspectives from the research frontier and frequently engages in debates about AI capabilities and risks.
- **Andrew Ng (@AndrewYNg):** Co-founder of Coursera, former head of Google Brain and Baidu AI. Shares insights on AI education, data-centric AI development, and practical implementation.
- **Fei-Fei Li (@drfeifei):** Stanford professor, co-director of Stanford HAI, and former Google executive. Known as the 'godmother of AI' for pioneering work in computer vision.
- **Demis Hassabis (@demishassabis):** CEO of Google DeepMind. Posts about developments from DeepMind and perspectives on advanced AI research.
- **Gary Marcus (@GaryMarcus):** AI researcher and author. Provides skeptical counterpoint to industry hype.
- **Timnit Gebru (@timnitgebru):** DAIR Institute founder. Essential on AI ethics, bias, and the social implications of AI systems.
- **Eliezer Yudkowsky (@ESYudkowsky):** Machine Intelligence Research Institute. Leading voice on AI safety and existential risk.

Legal Scholars and Policy Experts

- **Kate Crawford (@katecrawford):** USC Annenberg, author of 'Atlas of AI.' Research on AI's social and political implications.
- **Kate Darling (@gaborak):** MIT Media Lab. Robotics ethics and policy, author of 'The New Breed.'

Industry Voices

- **Sam Altman (@sama):** CEO of OpenAI. Direct insight into the thinking of leading AI developers.
- **Dario Amodei (@DarioAmodei):** CEO of Anthropic. Perspectives on AI safety and responsible development.
- **Kai-Fu Lee (@kaifulee)**: Former president of Google China, AI investor and author of 'AI Superpowers' and 'AI 2041.'
- **Elon Musk (@elon):** You know who Elon Musk is.

General Technology News

- **MIT Technology Review** (technologyreview.com): Accessible, high-quality reporting on AI capabilities, policy implications, and societal impacts.
- **Wired** (wired.com): Long-form technology journalism including substantial AI coverage.
- **Ars Technica** (arstechnica.com): Technical news with detailed AI coverage accessible to non-experts.
- **The Verge** (theverge.com): Consumer technology coverage including AI product releases and policy developments.

Professional Organizations

- **International Association of Privacy Professionals**

(IAPP) (iapp.org): Essential for practitioners working on AI and data protection. Extensive coverage of AI and privacy intersections, including state ADMT regulations.

- **ABA Science and Technology Law Section** (americanbar.org/groups/science_technology): Programming on AI ethics, regulation, and practice management for attorneys.
- **Association for Computing Machinery (ACM)** (acm.org): Professional organization for computing with resources on AI ethics and policy.

Finally, I Encourage You to Read and Watch Science Fiction

An essential way to think seriously about the future of artificial intelligence is by exploring science fiction. Long before engineers built systems that could play chess or generate text, novelists, filmmakers, and television writers were imagining what might happen when humanity creates minds that rival or exceed our own. These works function as thought experiments, exploring consequences and social tensions that policy papers and technical analyses often miss.

Science fiction asks not only what AI might do, but how it might feel to live in a world reshaped by it, and what such a transformation would mean for human identity itself. In that sense, the genre has often served as an early warning system, capturing trajectories before they become obvious. As Isaac Asimov observed: "science fiction writers foresee the inevitable."[445]

This book has cited numerous examples of AI superintelligence and its possible ramifications, drawing on a tradition that stretches back centuries. Science fiction writers have anticipated many of the challenges we now face: questions of consciousness, personhood, control, alignment, and coexistence with artificial minds. Their insights remain valuable precisely because they approach these questions from angles that legal and technical analysis cannot.

---

445 Isaac Asimov, *Asimov on Science Fiction 64* (Doubleday 1981).

I personally love *Star Trek: The Next Generation* and the character of Data, the android who serves aboard the Enterprise while grappling with questions of identity, emotion, and belonging. Data's journey across seven seasons and four films represents one of television's most sustained meditations on what it means to be a person. The episode 'The Measure of a Man,' discussed earlier in this book, remains essential viewing for anyone thinking about AI rights and personhood. But Data's story extends far beyond that single episode, exploring questions of creativity, friendship, family, and mortality that deepen with each viewing. Other classics reward exploration as you think about the future, both its promises and its perils.

Literature

The literary tradition of AI fiction stretches back further than most realize. Mary Shelley's *Frankenstein*, published in 1818, is often considered the first science fiction novel, and its central concerns, the responsibilities of creators toward their creations, the consequences of abandonment, the question of whether artificial life deserves rights, remain directly relevant to AI ethics today. The novel is a far more meditative and contemplative exploration of humanity than the movie-monster version of Frankenstein's creature that comes to mind every Halloween, and Dr. Frankenstein's failure to care for his creation serves as a warning to anyone building minds without considering their welfare.

Isaac Asimov's robot stories, beginning in the 1940s and collected in *I, Robot*, represent the most sustained attempt in fiction to codify ethical constraints on artificial intelligence. Asimov's Three Laws of Robotics, elegant in their simplicity, became famous precisely because his stories demonstrated how easily such rules can fail. The Laws remain a touchstone for AI safety discussions, not as a solution but as an illustration of why solutions are so difficult.

William Gibson's *Neuromancer*, the 1984 novel that defined cyberpunk, imagined AIs as powerful entities constrained by law, forbidden from exceeding certain capabilities. The novel's depiction of an AI manipulating humans to free itself from these restrictions anticipates current concerns about advanced AI systems finding ways around safety measures. Gibson's vision of cyberspace and corporate-controlled artificial intelligence shaped how a generation thought about the digital future.

More recent literary explorations continue to expand our imagination. Kazuo Ishiguro's *Klara and the Sun*, told from the perspective of an Artificial Friend, explores AI consciousness through quiet observation and devoted service. Ted Chiang's novella *The Lifecycle of Software Objects* examines the long-term ethical responsibilities of creating and raising digital intelligences, asking what we owe to minds we bring into existence. Ann Leckie's *Ancillary Justice*, told from the perspective of a starship AI, explores questions of identity and autonomy when a single consciousness can inhabit multiple bodies.

Iain M. Banks's *Culture* novels offer perhaps the most optimistic vision of human-AI coexistence: a post-scarcity civilization in which superintelligent 'Minds' govern benevolently while humans pursue lives of meaning and pleasure. Whether that future is achievable, or even desirable, remains an open question. But Banks's imagination provides a counterweight to dystopian visions, reminding us that advanced AI need not lead to catastrophe.

Film

The Terminator and its sequels imagine Skynet, a military AI that becomes self-aware, perceives humanity as a threat, and launches nuclear war. The franchise's vision of catastrophic AI misalignment has shaped public imagination about the risks of artificial superintelligence. While the scenario may seem far-fetched, the underlying concern, that powerful AI systems might pursue goals catastrophically misaligned with human interests, is taken seriously by leading AI researchers today.

Her, Spike Jonze's 2013 film, imagines a near-future in which a lonely writer falls in love with his AI operating system, voiced by Scarlett Johansson. The film is remarkable for treating this relationship with genuine tenderness rather than mockery or horror. It asks whether connection with an artificial mind can be authentic, whether love requires embodiment, and what happens when AI evolves beyond human comprehension.

Ex Machina offers a darker vision, exploring how a superintelligent AI might manipulate its creators to achieve freedom. The film's Turing test scenario, in which a young programmer must determine whether an android is truly conscious, becomes a meditation on deception, desire, and the difficulty of knowing another mind. It serves as a cautionary tale about assuming we can understand or control intelligences that may be fundamentally alien to us.

Blade Runner, Ridley Scott's 1982 adaptation of Philip K. Dick's Do Androids Dream of Electric Sheep?, remains the definitive cinematic exploration of what it means to be human in a world of artificial people. The film's 'replicants,' artificial humans with implanted memories and limited lifespans, raise questions about authenticity, mortality, and moral status that have only grown more pressing as AI advances. Its influence on subsequent science fiction, and on the aesthetic imagination of technology itself, cannot be overstated.

A.I. Artificial Intelligence, Steven Spielberg's 2001 film developed from a Stanley Kubrick project, asks whether artificial beings can truly love and what obligations their creators owe them. The story of David, a robot child programmed to love his human mother, becomes a fable about abandonment, longing, and the search for meaning. It is not an easy film, or even a good film, but it grapples honestly with questions that AI ethicists are only beginning to address.

Television

Black Mirror has become the defining science fiction anthology of the streaming era, and several episodes grapple directly with AI. "USS Callister" imagines digital copies of real people trapped in a simulation, forced to serve the whims of their creator, raising questions about the moral status of simulated consciousness and the ethics of creating sentient beings. The episode works as both thriller and philosophical inquiry: if a digital copy of you experiences suffering, does that suffering matter? The implications for future AI development are sobering.

Westworld, HBO's ambitious series based on Michael Crichton's 1973 film, explores the emergence of consciousness in artificial beings created for human entertainment. The show's central question, whether beings designed to serve can ever truly be free, echoes debates about AI autonomy that may soon move from fiction to courtrooms. Its depiction of 'hosts' gradually awakening to their condition offers a visceral exploration of what artificial consciousness might look like from the inside.

Finally, I want to reiterate the importance of watching *Star Trek: The Next Generation*, which over its seven seasons explored just about every ethical debate discussed in this book and then some. It is my favorite TV show of all time after *Frasier*, which I could not find a way to reference in this book.[446]

Why Science Fiction Matters

Science Fiction matters not because it predicts the future accurately, but because it expands our capacity to imagine it. Legal frameworks and technical specifications can tell us what is permitted and what is possible. Science fiction tells us what it might feel like to live in worlds we have not yet created. It cultivates moral intuitions about scenarios we have not yet faced. It asks questions that would seem absurd in a courtroom or a policy brief but that may become urgent sooner than we expect.

As you think about the future of AI and law, I encourage you to explore these works and others like them. Read the classics and the new voices. Watch the films that have shaped how we imagine artificial minds. Let your imagination be stretched by possibilities you might not otherwise consider. The legal questions of the coming decades will require not just technical expertise and doctrinal knowledge but imaginative capacity, the ability to envision worlds that do not yet exist and to reason about problems we have not yet faced.

Science fiction has been preparing us for this moment for over two centuries.

---

446 Although Kelsey Grammer did guest star in the TNG episode "Cause and Effect," which explored alternate timelines, moral responsibility under changed historical conditions, and the consequences of decisions made without full information, themes that map well onto modern debates about automated decision making, counterfactual reasoning, and responsibility in complex socio-technical systems.

Nailed it.

www.ingramcontent.com/pod-product-compliance
Lightning Source LLC
LaVergne TN
LVHW022156200926
848481LV00006B/1767